"Our world desperately needs entrepreneurs—people who turn their passion into projects to create a better world. This wonderful book is written by a mom to help other moms (and dads) nurture *their* children's entrepreneurial potential. Each page is filled with the inspirational stories of parents and their children. For the sake of our children and our world, this is a must-read."

—**Melanne Verveer**, former US Ambassador for Global Women's Issues, and author of *Fast Forward*

"If you're a mom who ever wondered if your children could be entrepreneurs, and, if so, how you can help, you must read Margot's book—a collection of inspiring stories which inspired me to look at ways we can support our children as future entrepreneurs. This is a *must-own* and a *must-read!*"

—**Alissa Circle**, cofounder and CEO of Pollinate Media Group, and author of the blog *Diary of an Addict*

"Entrepreneurs can change the world by innovating key aspects of our lives, such as health, energy, food, and education. Your child could become the next visionary entrepreneur. Margot guides parents on how to foster their entrepreneurial spark."

—**Steve Case**, chairman of Revolution and The Case Foundation, and author of *The Third Wave*

"Raising kids with the courage to follow their dreams is what all parents should strive for. Margot offers moms, dads, and grandparents the perfect textbook for learning that important lesson."

—**Barbara Harrison**, NBC4 News anchor, and founder of NBC's *Wednesday's Child*

"Margot's book resonated deeply with me as a female founder and mother. She maps the steps to help parents raise their children with the skills they'll need to start companies or nonprofits."

—**Danielle Tate**, author of *Elegant Entrepreneur*, and
founder and CEO of www.missnowmrs.com

"*Raising an Entrepreneur* is a must-read for anyone who wants to raise children to have the courage to be passionate self-starters. Her advice and stories from a diverse cross section of thriving entrepreneurs can help parents champion their children's desires for success—and show how these values are later imparted into the entrepreneurs' own organizations."

—**Keith Ferrazzi**, author of the *New York Times* bestsellers
Who's Got Your Back and *Never Eat Alone*, and founder
and CEO of Ferrazzi Greenlight

"It's what all parents are after—raising our children to be caring and concerned, but also fearless and resilient. To learn early how to harness their passions confidently and grow into fulfilled adults. When it happens, it's not luck or genetics, it turns out. Through dozens of insightful interviews with today's top entrepreneurs and change makers, and, critically, their mothers, Margot has uncovered a recipe we can all use."

—**Claire Shipman**, senior national correspondent for
ABC's *Good Morning America*, and coauthor of
Womenomics

"Entrepreneurs don't just spring up as adults; their childhood helps shape them. Margot shows how parents can guide their development."

—**Tony Hsieh**, *New York Times* bestselling author of
Delivering Happiness, and CEO of zappos.com

RAISING *an* ENTREPRENEUR

10 RULES for NURTURING RISK TAKERS, PROBLEM SOLVERS, *and* CHANGE MAKERS

MARGOT MACHOL BISNOW

New Harbinger Publications, Inc.

Publisher's Note

This publication is designed to provide accurate and authoritative information in regard to the subject matter covered. It is sold with the understanding that the publisher is not engaged in rendering psychological, financial, legal, or other professional services. If expert assistance or counseling is needed, the services of a competent professional should be sought.

Distributed in Canada by Raincoast Books

Copyright © 2016 by Margot Machol Bisnow
New Harbinger Publications, Inc.
5674 Shattuck Avenue
Oakland, CA 94609
www.newharbinger.com

Cover design by Amy Shoup

Acquired by Tesilya Hanauer

Edited by Xavier Callahan and Clancy Drake

Library of Congress Cataloging-in-Publication Data

Names: Bisnow, Margot Machol, author.
Title: Raising an entrepreneur : 10 rules for nurturing risk takers, problem solvers, and change makers / Margot Machol Bisnow.
Description: Oakland, CA : New Harbinger Publications, Inc., 2016. | Includes bibliographical references.
Identifiers: LCCN 2016015124 (print) | LCCN 2016024781 (ebook) | ISBN 9781626253902 (pbk. : alk. paper) | ISBN 9781626253919 (pdf e-book) | ISBN 9781626253926 (epub) | ISBN 9781626253919 (PDF e-book) | ISBN 9781626253926 (ePub)
Subjects: LCSH: Success in business--Case studies. | Risk-taking (Psychology) in children. | Problem solving in children. | Creative thinking in children. | Entrepreneurship, | Parenting.
Classification: LCC HF5386 .B467 2016 (print) | LCC HF5386 (ebook) | DDC 338/.04--dc23
LC record available at https://lccn.loc.gov/2016015124

18   17   16

10   9   8   7   6   5   4   3   2   1   First Printing

This book is dedicated to my family: my wonderful husband Mark, our extraordinary sons Elliott and Austin, and my own inspirational parents.

Contents

Foreword

As teenagers, we must have given our parents fits. We wanted to take big risks for big dreams. We embraced being ourselves rather than conforming. One of us wanted to start a company; the other, a band. We were the only people we knew committed to doing either. We wanted a life of adventure and a chance to do things that hadn't been done before.

Our parents could easily have suffocated our aspirations. Instead, they believed in us. The only career rule in our family was to make sure we did what we loved, because that was going to make us the happiest and most successful in the long run. Our parents helped us figure out what we loved by exposing us to as much as they could.

And because they believed in us, we weren't going to let them down.

We're an extremely close family, so even when we moved away, Mom met our new friends, many of whom, like us, wanted to build things out of nothing. She started asking them how they came to be like that.

To her amazement—and ours—they all said basically the same thing: "My mom believed in me." Mom was really moved, and wanted to shout this revelation to the world.

So we told her she had to write a book. Then ensued a bunch of excuses: "I don't know how. I'm too old to start a new career."

Yada yada. But we told her that with this much wisdom and passion, she would figure it out. We said, "You're the one who told us to believe in ourselves. Now it's our turn to tell you: we believe in you and know you can create whatever it is you want if you want it enough."

Being an entrepreneur and starting something from scratch is hard. Believing you will succeed when the entire world tells you it's impossible is a challenge. It feels as if everyone thinks that your dream is a waste of time and that you shouldn't even try.

The only answer is to believe in yourself. But before you believe in yourself, someone else has to believe in you.

And that someone else often appears to be a mom.

We are so proud of our mom for writing this book. And we're excited that she's sharing these incredible lessons with parents and kids around the world.

Thank you, Mom. We love you.

Elliott and Austin Bisnow

Introduction

It's the classic question every kid gets asked by (almost) every adult: "What do you want to be when you grow up?" These days, more young people than ever before answer with some version of "I want to be an entrepreneur."

Entrepreneurs are not only the new doctors and lawyers; they are the new pro athletes and pop stars. Doing your own thing seems both possible and desirable. In survey after survey, those who have entered the workforce during both a deep recession and the golden age of the start-up—and those coming behind them—say something like:

"I want to control my destiny."

"I want to design my own life."

"I want to make the world a better place."

"I want to do what I love."

"I want to have a start-up."

Many of today's bright kids look to the self-made self-starters who shatter the rules and come out on top. They want to be the kind of independent people who don't need to find jobs, because they create their own. And this is their time.

For parents, these ambitions can sound both compelling and unrealistic. Does "I want to do what I love" mean "I'm going to start a niche design company with my friend" or "I'm going to play video games for a living"? (Spoiler alert: it could mean both.) Not everyone can be Mark Zuckerberg, we parents reason. Wouldn't it be better to choose a career with a safe, clear path? To earn a degree that will get you a job in an established company—or even at Facebook, for that matter?

It might be. Not everyone can tolerate—much less thrive on—the risks and uncertainties of an entrepreneurial life. But for some of our kids, it's the ideal path to success, fulfillment, growth, and joy in their lives. This is true whether they are destined to be the next Zuckerberg or to start a small local business, build a sustainable career in the performing arts, or found a nonprofit. All of these are entrepreneurial paths.

You may not know if your child will be drawn to the entrepreneurial life—to the freedom and excitement of starting something all her own. Yet there's plenty you can know and do, right now, to help her develop her qualities and reach her potential. This book will help you get a picture of what your role in raising an entrepreneur might be. What matters? What doesn't?

Though I am the mom of two happy and driven entrepreneurial sons, these are questions I never thought to ask. When our kids were young, my husband and I could not have foreseen the career paths they would follow—we had no clue.

Looking back, I would have loved to have read real-life stories about how entrepreneurs had grown up—not just Bill Gates and Steve Jobs, but people who would have been easier for us and our kids to identify with. People like the ones in this book. It would have given my husband and me an idea of what our boys might be working toward: a lifelong pursuit they find meaningful.

Not knowing how this most of important of all stories—our child's growing up—will turn out can be nerve-wracking for parents. It can fill us with some very understandable doubts and fears. The world is changing so much, and so quickly. How can we make sure they're successful and, ideally, happy, over the long run? The uncertainty, and the high stakes, can make us want to play it safe.

WHAT ABOUT MONEY?

When I talk to others about entrepreneurship, the dreaded M-word often comes up. I found two common misconceptions about entrepreneurs and money.

The first is the fear that if your children spend their life pursuing their passion, they won't make enough money to live.

Parents who witness a child's total immersion in some favorite pursuit—making music, playing video games, taking things apart, building Lego sets, playing a sport—may feel it's their duty to set limits on the activity, for fear that if it takes too much of the child's time and attention, the child will neglect serious pursuits and be unable to make a living as an adult.

Or parents may urge a college-age son or daughter to take certain types of courses, stay enrolled in college until graduation, and maybe study for an advanced degree, even though their reluctant collegian has zero interest in following that advice.

I have nothing against academic and professional degrees—my husband and I both have graduate degrees and it's worked for us. But a degree may represent an expensive waste of your child's time if it has no connection to his interests, and if his only reason for being in school is to get the piece of paper or make the contacts needed to land a high-paying job. And someone who loves something enough and works hard enough at it will find a way to turn it into a living, even without a degree in that field.

More importantly, they'll be happier than if they were plugging away at something they don't enjoy. And I also believe they will never be great at something if they don't work nonstop at it, and they will never work nonstop if they don't love it.

Michael Mulligan, head of the Thacher School in Ojai, California, cites research showing that many Millennials are depressed because they've had to work so hard to succeed in areas of their parents' choosing. "We can do better," he writes. "The truth is that we are all going to have to work hard to succeed in life, and if that is the case, let's…at least try to work hard on things that matter and that we care about."

A second misconception about money is that it's what drives entrepreneurs. I don't buy it. To the contrary, everyone I talked to insists they pour their passions into their business to make a better product or service, or to make a difference in the world. Even if you don't take their word for it, it's hard to imagine anyone sustaining the energy cheerfully to survive eighteen-hour days, nonstop funding worries, and the vagaries of the marketplace if their only motivation is a wildly speculative and (at best) long-delayed pot of gold.

Duke Business School Dean Bill Boulding says tomorrow's leaders should care about making the world a better place, not making money. He says what they are looking for are "people who care about others, who see that the success of others is what makes them successful, and who have a sense of purpose and want to make a difference in the world" (Cunningham 2015).

Spotting a Future Entrepreneur

As I researched, interviewed, and wrote this book, my idea of what an "entrepreneur" is evolved. For the purposes of this book, an entrepreneur is anyone who starts something, who comes up with an idea and makes it real, who translates a passion into a project. This means that entrepreneurs, in my view, are not just founders of for-profit businesses, but also people who start the nonprofit organizations and "profits for purpose" that are changing lives. Entrepreneurs are actors who organize their own production crews. They're musicians who put together a band and find a manager and a music publisher and an agent. They're activists working to create a better world.

How can you tell if your child has an entrepreneurial mindset? There's no sure giveaway, but there are some signs:

- Your son is a terrific student, but none of his classes excites him as much as something he does after school.

- Your daughter would rather tinker on her computer or paint or sing or build Lego villages or sell Girl Scout cookies than do anything else.

- Your child enjoys taking charge and loves organizing things or events or people.

- Your daughter is always questioning why things are done in a certain way, and she's always thinking of new ways to do them.

- Your son would rather spend ten hours doing something he loves than one hour doing something he's not interested in; and even if he has trouble concentrating on his homework, when he's doing what he likes, he works with great focus and intensity.

- Your child loves selling things or starting little businesses.

- Your children are passionate about sports or other forms of competition.

Even if you don't think you have a budding entrepreneur sitting at the breakfast table, you might be surprised. Most of the people profiled in this book weren't obvious future entrepreneurs. And that's another reason it's so important to keep the path open for your child. In most cases, you won't know which way they'll want to go until they're older.

It can be hard not to try to direct your child's professional future, at least in general terms. Won't making sure he succeeds at what he attempts encourage him and build his self-esteem, leading to future success? Actually, the opposite may be more likely (see rule 2). Shouldn't she be pushed to excel in school? Not necessarily (see rule 3).

So do you have *any* influence over what your son or daughter will become? Over the course of my interviews with over sixty thriving entrepreneurs and/or their moms, I found that the answer is a resounding *yes*. You do have that power, just maybe not in the ways you expect.

The Rule of All Rules: Believe In Your Child

As I talked with entrepreneurs and their moms and thought about what they told me, I became aware of a single rule that holds together the ten raising-an-entrepreneur rules I discovered: *Every child is unique in some way, so help your children figure out their gift, and then nurture it and support it.*

That's the secret, and it sounds simple. But it can actually be very difficult to sustain over the course of many years and through many small but pivotal moments. It means believing in your children's strengths and letting them know you have confidence in their ability to succeed at what they love. I believe all parents want their children to grow up to be happy and successful. But many kids are unhappy because they aren't doing what they love; they may not even know yet what they love—there may not be any space and time to discover it. Instead, they're doing what their parents *think* will make them successful and, by extension, happy.

So it's not just about loving your child and desiring their happiness; I believe most every parent does. It's not about wanting to help your child succeed; again, I think parents do want that. It's about believing in your child's strength, and letting him know you have confidence that he can succeed in doing what he loves.

That's the baseline condition for raising an entrepreneurial child: unwavering belief in your child's abilities, and a mind-set of supporting her in developing them. Simple, but not always easy.

Raising a child to be proud of his skills, to be confident, to be fearless, and to have a strong work ethic seems to me like a fine approach with any child. But I've become convinced it's essential to nurture these traits in a future entrepreneur. If they have these traits, your kids may not become entrepreneurs. But if they don't, they definitely won't. Successful entrepreneurs need a level of confidence, drive, resilience, and courage that's different from that needed to be successful in someone else's organization, whether that's a big corporation or a start-up.

In certain ways, the things you do to nurture the entrepreneurial mind-set look similar to the things you do to support any child. But raising an entrepreneur can call for approaches and attitudes toward parenting that may be somewhat different from the ones you're used to. And that's where this book comes in.

THE SECRET OF ALL SECRETS: MOM POWER

In writing this book, I took the point of view of a mom—which is what I am—rather than the perspective a sociologist, an academic, a psychologist, or family therapist might bring. I wanted to find and share the stories of dozens of families, to discover and distill the parenting secrets that launched a group of creative, confident entrepreneurs on their paths.

A young person today can make a career out of almost anything. The world has changed so much over the last twenty years that someone who wants to start an enterprise doesn't need an office, employees, a battery of attorneys and accountants, professional investment advice, or a bank of phones. Today there are only three requirements for becoming an entrepreneur:

1. A great idea

2. A heck of a lot of confidence

3. The ability to work enthusiastically around the clock

Actually, make that four things: you probably also need a mom who provided the kind of support we'll explore in this book.

This book will tell you how dozens of moms in dozens of different situations, whose kids' interests were all over the map, raised super-successful sons and daughters—even if the road they were traveling didn't always look so promising.

Now, don't get me wrong. Dads are critically important. Many entrepreneurs credit their fathers, grandparents, stepparents, and others with having influenced their development. The rules I discovered apply to anyone nurturing a young entrepreneur-to-be.

In my exploration of the subject, though, it's moms, rather than dads or others, who were identified as the secret ingredient in fostering their children's self-confidence and tolerance for risk, two important traits for an entrepreneur.

So how did I zero in on the moms? It was an organic process, and it started before I had any idea that I might write a book on raising an entrepreneur.

It started with my meeting scores of successful young entrepreneurs—mostly through my older son, Elliott, who founded the Summit Series, a conference for young leaders in a wide range of fields. When I met these remarkable young people, I usually asked them the same basic questions:

How did you become the person you are?

What made you so confident and so willing to put everything on the line?

Who had the biggest impact on your life?

They all told me a version of the same thing: "I couldn't have done it without my mom. She believed in me. She supported my passion. She's the reason I turned out this way."

That really struck me. And it moved me. I know that the moms of other teenagers and young adults, some of whom seem to be floundering, must love their kids as much as these entrepreneurs' moms love theirs. So I decided to interview the entrepreneurs' moms, to try to learn what they had done right. I thought I might find something significant.

I cast a wide net: I chose several dozen young men and women with a variety of interests and skills—creators and innovators from different ethnic and socioeconomic backgrounds, geographic settings, religious traditions, and family structures. It was as I interviewed mom after mom that I started to see more and more clearly that, while in some ways each person's upbringing had been different, in a handful of key areas they all had been raised the same.

I was astonished to discover that all of these entrepreneurs' moms—without consciously realizing it, without knowing one another, and without having a common background—had followed most or all of the ten rules you'll find in this book: rules that emerged and became clear to me over the course of my interviews. I had to share what I was finding, and I decided to write this book.

For the purposes of researching the book, I interviewed either the entrepreneur or his or her mom, or both. Half the entrepreneurs profiled are men, half are women; they have vastly different interests and skills and come from different backgrounds. Some grew up well off, some struggled financially. Some came from big families, some from small families, some from blended families. They came from big cities and small towns, from across the U.S. and from other countries. They have many different ethnic backgrounds. They came from many religious backgrounds. Some have parents who are still married; some have parents who were divorced; some were raised by single moms. Some had parents who died.

Here are a few of the people you'll meet:

- Michael Chasen's mom used to hear from friends that she was letting her son waste his life spending so much time playing with his computer. A few years later, he put that computer skill to use and built a company, Blackboard, that he later sold for $1.5 billion.

- Alexis Jones loved storytelling and acting when she was young. That could have been just a childhood diversion. Instead, she got more serious about it, and eventually founded a massive online community called I AM THAT GIRL. Today she's an international thought leader for the women's movement and for her Millennial generation.

- Jon Chu loved watching videos, then making them, while still in high school. He talked his teachers into letting him submit them instead of papers. Today, he's a big-time movie director.

- Benny Blanco's mom got frequent complaints from his kindergarten teacher that her son wouldn't sit in the reading circle. And when he was in high school, her friends scoffed that he was wasting his time entering rap contests. Yes, he marched to a different drummer. But today, he's one of the top songwriters in the U.S., with twenty number-one hits.

- Paige Mycoskie loved art when she was young, and dreamed of one day designing clothes. When her grandparents each gave her one hundred dollars for her birthday, she bought a sewing machine, moved back home, and started sewing clothes. Today, she has five stores for her company, Aviator Nation.

- Robert Stephens loved to fix things when he was young. His parents might have bemoaned what seemed like a bent for vocational rather than professional work. Yet this interest led him to start Geek Squad.

- Kevin Plank's mom used to tell him, "There are no problems; there are only solutions you haven't found yet." When he was playing college football, he was tired of sweating through his cotton T-shirts. He found a better material and started UnderArmour.

Are you noticing a theme?

When I started interviewing entrepreneurs and their moms for this book, I thought I knew what I'd find. But what I learned was completely different. I was astonished to learn what mattered in raising an entrepreneur—and what didn't. Even more than that, I was amazed by how similarly all the entrepreneurs were raised, despite the fact that their backgrounds differed wildly. These unmistakable common threads make up the ten rules you'll learn about—and that you and your child can benefit from.

This book is not about training your children to become entrepreneurs. Getting your kids to follow a path *you've* chosen for them is a sure way to stifle *their* fulfillment—and, as you'll see when you read these stories, personal fulfillment is essential to an entrepreneur's life. What I hope this book will inspire you to do is to keep the road open for your child to choose—whether a broad, straight, clearly marked road or a twisty, surprising, unique one.

If your kids have the entrepreneurial spirit and a taste for the road less traveled, this book will show you how to nurture it. You'll learn how to support them as they pursue their passion and their purpose, and as they make fearless and fulfilling choices. I'm so excited for your journey.

Rule 1

Support a Passion

Almost all the successful entrepreneurs profiled in this book have one experience in common—they had their parents' (especially their moms') support to pursue a passion, generally one they engaged in outside of school. Whether that passion was sports, computers, music, video games, selling things to neighbors, or even protesting, it made them great future entrepreneurs.

Trust Your Child's Passion

Lots of the moms I talked to didn't "get" the activities their kids were into. But they also knew that their own interest or understanding was beside the point. What they went out of their way to support wasn't so much the activities themselves as the spark it brought to their children's eyes.

Your own children's passions may not be the ones you would have chosen for them. Their passions may not even be something you understand. But that's actually a great thing, even if it doesn't always feel that way. It means your kids are exploring their passions in ways that are most meaningful to them, rather than following in your footsteps or trying to please you.

Letting children run with their passions isn't really about helping them fulfill their childhood fantasies. It's not about helping a kid become an astronaut or a billionaire or president of the United States (though all those are possible). The true benefit is that, even if a child's passion doesn't turn into a profession, they learn the joy of diving deeply into a pursuit, discovering all it has to offer, and making connections with others who are also passionate about it. Kids learn that good things happen when they do the things they love. And if they keep exploring, they find ways to improve or add to or expand or reinvent or promote the things they love—and that's how companies and organizations get started.

It doesn't really matter what your child's passion is, as long as your child is passionate about *something*. And the most important thing you can do is nurture that passion. If you do, your child will devote lots of time to it. That's what it takes to become truly accomplished at something.

Michael Chasen: Playing for Keeps

Glenda Chasen has two sons, Michael and Joel, an entrepreneur and an endodontist. Michael graduated from American University and then got an MBA from Georgetown. In 1997, he started Blackboard, an online educational technology company that he later sold for $1.5 billion. He then went on to cofound SocialRadar, a tech start-up that developed a location-based social app.

When I talked with Glenda, she told me that growing up in the 1980s, Michael had a passion for computers, which were just becoming popular, although most people had no idea that they eventually would transform society. When Michael was in fourth grade and wanted to spend lots of time on the computer and playing video games, she nurtured those interests.

Glenda told me that she had been somewhat alone in this—the other moms encouraged their children to engage in academic pursuits "worthy of their intellect," as Glenda put it. Her friends told her that Michael was wasting his time. But she resisted the peer pressure and continued to encourage him as he played video games. He had a passion for gaming, she said, and he loved computers, so she not only let him spend lots of time on video games, she also told him he was wonderful for doing that. By embracing his expressed interests, she helped lead him to success.

Glenda did the most important thing parents can do if they hope their children will become entrepreneurs: nurture their passion. Sports, art, chess, music, drama, fitness, computer games, volunteering, church…it doesn't really matter, as long as they are passionate about something.

Jon Chu: To Hollywood, with No Connections

Jon Chu is a screenwriter and director best known for directing *Step Up 2: The Streets*; *Step Up 3D*; *Justin Bieber: Never Say Never*; *G.I. Joe: Retaliation* with Bruce Willis and Channing Tatum; and *Now You See Me 2* with Daniel Radcliffe, Jesse Eisenberg, and Mark Ruffalo. When I talked to Jon, he told me about his early life and how his parents supported his passion, once they understood how much it meant to him:

I grew up in Silicon Valley in the eighties, surrounded by people creating stuff, where engineers were the heroes.

My mom came from Taiwan, and my dad from China. They were both around twenty when they came to the U.S. They met when my mom was going to the College of San Mateo and a friend introduced her to my dad. They started a little restaurant in Palo Alto, Chef Chu's. It's been there over forty-five years and has become a neighborhood institution.

I was the youngest of five, and the oldest was only six years older than I was, so we were all very close. My second brother, Howard, is autistic, and so my family became okay with going with the flow. If we all went to a play and Howard didn't want to stay, we left. We learned to adapt. Today my oldest brother, Larry, who graduated from UCLA, helps at the restaurant, which he'll take over some day. My older sister Chrissy is in real estate. Howard is at home with the family. And my sister Jennifer is married and raising two kids.

My grandma helped at the restaurant with the accounting, and she used an abacus. Her feet were messed up from having been bound when she was a girl in China. My parents would tell us to look at her to realize how far our family had come in just one generation. They'd always say, "America is the greatest place on earth—if you work hard, you can achieve anything."

My parents never let us work at the restaurant. They would tell us, "We didn't have many opportunities growing up, and we want you to do everything we didn't."

My mom kept us super busy. I took music lessons on almost every instrument—drums, saxophone, guitar, piano, and violin. I also took tap dancing lessons and played tennis.

Every weekend we would go to San Francisco to see a show—musicals, ballet, symphony, theater. My mom thought we were royalty. My brothers and sisters took etiquette classes and ballroom dancing to learn the foxtrot and waltz. She had a pretty clear idea of who she wanted us to be—the Kennedy family!

My brothers and sisters and I were in all the school plays. I had the most encouraging parents. They came to everything we were in and always supported us. At the time, I thought *we were really good, because that's what my mom kept telling us. Looking back, we were actually really bad, but I didn't know it then.*

Somewhere amid all that exposure to the arts, Jon discovered his calling:

I've loved making movies for as long as I can remember. When I was in second grade, my parents gave me the video camera to shoot our family videos while we were on vacation. I had to figure out how to use it. I loved it. I was cutting stuff and editing on the VHS.

I started an illustration company when I was in third grade. When I was in fourth grade, I saw an ad in a Sharper Image catalog for a $200 mixer. Suddenly you could take music from the stereo and put music on your VHS videos! I had to have it.

I called my dad at the restaurant and begged, and I talked them into buying it for me. When I got it, I cut together my vacation video and put music in it and showed my family. My parents started to cry. I knew then that I wanted to do this for my whole life.

I wasn't the best musician, even though I played lots of instruments. I wasn't the best at drawing, even though I loved to illustrate. And I wasn't the best actor, even though I'd been in lots of school plays. Making movies connected all my interests, and from the very first time, I knew it's what I wanted to do forever.

But even when parents are as supportive as Jon's, they can have a hard time seeing the value of a child's favorite activity. It's easy to worry that what a child loves has become an unhealthy obsession, one that will limit, rather than expand, their options:

> *My freshman year in high school, I convinced a lot of my teachers to let me turn in videos instead of writing papers. One night, very late, when I was supposed to be asleep, my mom came into my room and saw me working on a video.*
>
> *Mom said it had to stop.*
>
> *I started crying. "This is what I love," I said. "You can't make me stop!"*
>
> *The next day, when she came to pick me up after school, she gave me a bunch of filmmaking books and said, "If you want to do this, you have to study it and learn everything about it."*
>
> *From then on, my parents supported me. In fact, my whole family has supported me.*

For many parents, the most important part of supporting a child's passion is giving them a chance to figure out what that passion is. And often the hardest part is accepting it, even if it isn't something you would have chosen. While he was still in high school, Jon started a video company, and by then his parents were behind him:

> *I'd shoot people's weddings and bar mitzvahs. Customers from our restaurant would find out that Chef Chu's youngest son wanted to make movies, and they would bring in beta computers to let me try. They weren't interested in keeping the computers and would give them to me because they were nice, and they knew how much I wanted them. It's also an indication of how supportive my parents are that so many of our customers would give me their slightly used computers.*

In *Outliers*, Malcolm Gladwell argues that it takes ten thousand hours to become really accomplished at something. Jon, with all his experience making movies in high school, was a living example of the ten-thousand-hour rule:

By the time I went to USC film school, I was way ahead of the game.

My senior year, I shot a movie. Seventy people worked nonstop for ten days. I didn't have the money to feed them, which you're supposed to do during a film shoot. So my mom, my sister, and my sister-in-law drove to L.A. and cooked for all of us for ten days.

It was only a short film, but it changed my life. It had its public debut at the Tribeca Film Festival, and it got me an agent and a manager.

I invited my family to the premiere. My parents asked me what I'd be serving, and of course I had no idea. So my family got boxes and boxes of food and champagne, and they brought it to the theater, and they served it to everyone.

That's the kind of support I always have from my family. To this day, everything I tell my parents, everyone in the restaurant will know tomorrow. They put posters of all my movies on the walls. And everyone knows if you bring in a movie ticket from one of my films, you'll get a free drink at the bar.

And then Jon told me something I heard many other entrepreneurs say about their parents, in almost the same words:

I never worry about not working, or make a decision based on fear, because I know I have their support. Having that self-assurance means I have no fear, and so I can create what I want.

My parents' whole life was to give to us, and they've had an amazing journey. They came here not speaking a word of English. They thought they could work hard and achieve the American dream, and they did. And their support and sacrifice allowed me to get into Hollywood with no connections.

I also talked with Jon's mom, Ruth. She was one of the more involved moms I spoke with. Ruth had encouraged Jon's passion with everything she had, even though filmmaking wasn't necessarily what she'd had in mind for him:

I have antennae on top of my head. I always know what's going on.

I always supported what Jon wanted to do. He was full of imagination. I have a clear picture of him at four years old, dreaming about something, telling fantasy stories, happy, singing the songs from Aladdin *and* The Lion King.

With school, sports, and music, he was really busy. Anything he wanted to do was okay with me, except when he played the CDs with bad words. That's where I drew the line.

He never tried to do things the regular way, and I never tried to stop him. When he was eleven, he wanted to be in the Palo Alto Little Theatre production of Pacific Overtures. *They said, "You have to send in a résumé." He asked what that was, and I explained it was a piece of paper saying who he was. So he took a piece of paper and put his school picture on it and started drawing the Phantom of the Opera because he said that's what he wanted to be when he grew up. Everyone laughed when they saw it at the audition, but he got the part. I went to the show for eleven performances.*

Like most other parents, but especially because they're immigrants, Jon's parents wanted their son to have an even better life than theirs, but they never imagined it would be in film. Other parents might have told their son to put his camera away and focus on his schoolwork. But once Jon's parents realized that film was his passion, they supported him completely. Getting him equipment and, later on, feeding his cast and crew were a big help, but the message Jon took from those efforts was even more important—he always knew his parents believed in him.

Jason Russell: A Balance Between Limits and Freedom

For some moms, the best way to provide support is to say, in effect, "I trust that you know what you're doing, and I believe you can succeed at whatever you put your mind to." In my interviews with entrepreneurs and their moms, I heard over and over that granting a child freedom and trust can be every bit as powerful as directly supporting a passion. That was the case with another USC-trained filmmaker, Jason Russell.

Jason, the second of Paul and Sheryl Russell's four children, was born and raised in San Diego. He's the family's only entrepreneur. His brother and one of his sisters help run the Christian Youth Theatre, founded by their parents, now in forty cities. Another sister is a Hollywood hair stylist.

In 2003, with Bobby Bailey and Laren Poole, Jason visited Africa, and subsequently cofounded Invisible Children, a nonprofit advocacy organization created to stop Joseph Kony and his Lord's Resistance Army (LRA) in Uganda from kidnapping children and forcing them to become soldiers. To this end, Invisible Children produced five hundred videos and twelve documentaries, all directed by Jason, including *Kony 2012*, which was intended to pressure the U.S. government to increase its efforts to capture Kony. With 83 million online views over a period of two weeks, *Kony 2012* became the fastest-growing viral video of all time, and Invisible Children eventually became the largest youth movement in the world, with 3.4 million "likes" on Facebook, second only to the Olympics.

Jason told me he had always wanted to direct movies, but his earliest passion was directing plays:

> *I think because I was the second child, a lot of the pressure was taken off me. I grew up in a very fun atmosphere because*

my parents had started a children's theater, and all our friends came through the theater. Our whole life was at rehearsals. We practically lived at the theater and, to this day, most of my closest friends are people I met there. I met my wife when I was seven and she was six, and we were dance partners.

From the time I was in eighth grade, I knew I wanted to be a movie director, and I knew I wanted to go to USC film school. So from the time I was fifteen, my dad let me help direct shows to gain experience. I did go to USC and majored in filmmaking. Jon Chu was my freshman roommate, and we took all our film classes together.

All the mothers I spoke with had in common their trust that their children would do the right thing. But there was a wide range in terms of how many rules their children were expected to follow. As Jason told me, his parents were stricter than others in some respects, yet in others they gave him an enormous amount of freedom:

When I was growing up, my parents were very traditional, and we had no TV in our home. Later we got one, but we could only watch on weekends. Otherwise, my parents kept it in the closet. This inspired us to make up our own games. We had to let our imaginations lead the way. I think this turned out to be important.

My parents were always very trusting. Their rule was you have to be home by midnight, but if you're going to be home later, you have to call them. So that's what I did. Usually, I was home by twelve o'clock, but sometimes I'd call and say, "I can't be home until three o'clock tonight," and they'd say okay.

I made them a promise when I was thirteen, and I got a promise ring. I promised I wouldn't do drugs, drink, or have sex until I was twenty-one. And because I wanted to keep the promise, I didn't do any of those. They trusted me to keep the promise. They never worried about me drinking at parties.

My parents were also always very strong communicating their values. It was never about grades or how much money you should make. They always told us, "Follow your dream. Find what you're most passionate about. We just want you to do your best and be happy in the life you choose."

I had a lot of freedom. If we wanted to go on a skateboard ramp or climb a tree, they would help. I think I had stitches at the hospital twelve different times. The day I turned sixteen, I got my driver's license, and one week later I wanted to drive to L.A., and they let me. Shortly thereafter, I wanted to drive to Mexico with friends, and they let me. And then I wanted to spend time in New York with a friend, visiting my brother, and they let me. They trusted me, and I trusted them.

We would debate everything in a loving, healthy way. I felt I could tell my parents anything, and there was never any judgment.

Jason told me that the freedom his parents gave him also enabled him to go to Africa, which is how he ended up starting his nonprofit:

In 2000, I visited Africa with a friend and loved it. My mom was always supportive. Even when I told her I wanted to visit a war zone, she said, "You need to go. You need to fly. You need to follow your heart."

After college, I bought a camera on eBay and asked a bunch of my friends to go back to Africa with me. Two said yes—Bobby Bailey and Laren Poole. While we were in Uganda, I met Jacob, one of the young boys who lived in terror that he'd be kidnapped by Joseph Kony's Lord's Resistance Army and forced to become a child soldier. I promised Jacob I'd do everything in my power to stop the war. That's what I did. Kony is on the run. We won't stop until he's been caught.

I also talked to Jason's parents, Sheryl and Paul. Here's what Sheryl told me:

I have four kids, and they all have different personalities. We always told them, "Everyone can do something to make a difference in the world in their own way."

From a young age, Jason had a tender heart for people less fortunate. We'd go to Mexico, and he'd see children on the street selling Chiclets, and he'd want to give them all his money.

When Jason was in fourth grade, he got paid for performing in a play. He took his money and bought a camera and started filming. He's been doing it ever since.

We homeschooled each of our kids for two years, separately, when they were in seventh and eighth grade. That's when their bodies and emotions changed, and we didn't want them to feel peer pressure to take unsafe risks. They all went back to public school for high school. Jason used that opportunity when he was homeschooled to spend a lot of his extra time acting.

Obviously, Sheryl was willing to go to great lengths to keep her kids safe and healthy, which makes it all the more impressive that she continued to support Jason's passion even when it led him to dangerous parts of the world:

When he was at USC film school, he went with a friend on a trip to Africa, and he knew he wanted to go back. So at graduation he said, "I want to do a documentary about the conflict in southern Sudan." Even though it was a war zone,

I felt if he wanted to go, he should. But I told him that first he had to do some groundwork and meet with different people so he would have contacts there. I talked to someone who gave him the name of an African woman who worked in a school in Uganda. So he and his friends went there, and she took them to northern Uganda, and that's where he met Jacob and Invisible Children started.

In my conversations with entrepreneurs' mothers, I discovered one reason why entrepreneurs are not afraid to fail—they don't get punished for experimenting. What Sheryl told me reflected that approach:

When Jason was in sixth grade, he put soap bubbles in his aunt's Jacuzzi. She was hysterical. I told her, "You're going to look back on this someday and see him as a creative film director, not a hoodlum!"

We always say, "If you get an idea, you've got to try it." We had a rule—to say yes as often as possible. Whatever their dreams were, or whatever they wanted to accomplish or wanted to try, as long as they weren't putting themselves in harm's way, we would say yes.

With his parents' support for his passion from the time he was in the fourth grade, Jason was able to combine filmmaking with his wish to make the world a better place, and his efforts were instrumental in getting the U.S. military involved in the hunt for Joseph Kony.

ENCOURAGE EXPLORATION

Entrepreneurs tend to be ardent types, but not every future entrepreneur develops a single all-consuming passion at an early age. Lots of future founders move from one enthusiasm to another as they grow. This kind of restless curiosity is a common trait of people who go on to create their own paths in life. That's why supporting exploration, including the possibility of false starts and detours, can be as valuable as supporting a child who's already found a true calling.

Joel Holland: A Little Red Wagon Hitched to a Dream

I've known Joel since 2008, and he has a special place in my heart. Even though he's the same age as my son Elliott, Joel had started a business much earlier. When Elliott wanted to invite eighteen young entrepreneurs to Utah to ski for a networking weekend, which later became Summit Series, he cold-called Joel, who was the first person to sign on. Joel's also one of the nicest people I know. He sold half of his company, VideoBlocks, which sells stock video clips, for $10 million in 2012. His sister, who's two years younger, is also an entrepreneur, with her own fashion business.

Joel was among a few entrepreneurs I spoke with who had a passion for selling things, as opposed to the thing itself. He was running little businesses from the time he was a toddler.

"I was three years old when I started selling gravel," Joel said. "I would walk to people's homes, take their gravel from their driveway, knock on their door, and try to sell it to them. People started calling me the Rock Man. It was crazy, but my folks were so supportive. They never said it was stupid. I loved selling things. My dad was probably standing behind me, passing my customers a dollar bill."

His dad, Kent, is a lawyer; his mom, Judi, a contractor. When Joel was five, the family moved from the D.C. suburbs to southern Virginia. Every year for the next seven years, they would build a new house, move in, sell it, and then start building a new one. Joel acquired a strong work ethic at an early age; he and his sister were given the job of sweeping.

"We weren't allowed to cut corners," he said. "The floor had to be clean enough to eat off of. It taught me the value of hard work."

Joel went on to tell me about the ventures that followed his stint as a door-to-door gravel vendor:

> My next project was selling the little knickknacks I collected from our house. My dad went with me to the local community store and convinced them to let me sit out front and sell them.
>
> By the time I was eight, we lived near a golf course, and I knew where all the old golf balls would be at the end of the day. I would collect them, clean them up, put them in egg cartons, go to the parking lot where the golfers parked, and try to sell them.
>
> Then I decided it wasn't scalable, and I wanted to be able to sell even when I wasn't there. So I took my little red wagon and made a sign that said JOEL'S GOLF BALLS. Then I made another sign that said HONOR SYSTEM: 3 BALLS FOR $2 and set out a Pringles can for the money. The can got stolen, so that's how I learned to protect my assets. I got a mailbox with a lock on it and put the sign on that.
>
> I left the wagon at a spot after the ninth tee. I would go every night and collect my money, usually $20 a day. It was $10 for a sleeve of three new balls at the pro shop, but my used ones were only $2 for a sleeve. People loved it, but the pro shop got upset and took my wagon. My dad was furious. He went over there with me and made them give me back my wagon. After that, I got a big chain and lock and tied my wagon to a tree.
>
> I clearly remember the first time I heard the word "entre-preneur." I was on the tenth tee and heard some guys talking.

One said, "That kid's an entrepreneur." I thought it was a curse word. I ran home and asked my mom, who told me what it meant. I was eleven. I loved that word!

Because Joel had always been encouraged to pursue his interests to the fullest, he was ready to pounce when something new came into his life, and he quickly combined a couple of his passions into a business venture:

When I was twelve—it was in 1997—I got my first computer. It blew my mind! Suddenly I could sell my golf balls to the world, and nobody knew how old I was.

I found eBay. I was big on Hot Wheels cars at the time. I started asking around, and I discovered there was no system to keep track of them. I found a guy who had designed software to manage inventory. I paid him $1,000 to repurpose the software so people could use it to manage hobbies and collections. Before I was thirteen, I was a PowerSeller on eBay, selling thousands of dollars a month of the software.

Nobody knew my age. I realized how powerful it was to be anonymous on the Internet. I had over two thousand transactions with positive ratings. My parents were very supportive. They would drive me to the post office to pick up checks and then drive me to the bank. They never questioned how I was spending my time.

Although Joel stumbled into his next venture, it led to what he does today:

When I was in eighth grade, we took a family trip to Hawaii. I had bought myself a video camera because I thought Hawaii would be so relaxing, and I wanted to share that.

So I took some footage. My ever-supportive parents let me shoot the video, even though it must have seemed ridiculous.

I found a guy who'd made a CD of Hawaiian luau music. I paid him for the rights to the songs. I brought home a couple of trash bags filled with sand and made a Hawaii relaxation video, with scenes of beaches and sunsets, and the luau background music.

I sold the videos on eBay along with little bags of sand. The amazing thing is that it really got me into video, which ended up being my business. I also decided that people would buy anything.

And then Joel told me a story that shows how mastering something often leads to noticing what's missing, a discovery that can be the basis for a company. He was in high school and was interested in technology, video, and sales, but when he sought advice from his guidance counselor about whether to plan for a career in journalism or business, he wasn't able to get satisfactory advice. So he approached Kidz Online, an educational nonprofit, and asked for financial backing to conduct videotaped interviews with top performers in various fields.

Over the next two years, he shot 150 interviews with CEOs and VIPs all over the country, including one in 2003 with Arnold Schwarzenegger, who had just announced that he would be running for governor of California. Joel found the interview interesting, but he realized it was visually boring. He asked himself how the Discovery Channel managed to make such arresting videos; it dawned on him that a captivating video requires more than a talking head:

I decided I needed shots of the Hollywood sign and other interesting visual things. But they were cost-prohibitive. And that was my Aha! moment. I realized if I needed this stock footage, others would need it, too. I took some of my savings and purchased a good video camera. I started shooting footage of Washington, D.C. I put it on eBay. People started buying it. I did this all through high school.

Joel's realization about how to improve his work hadn't come about as a direct result of his shooting Hawaiian relaxation videos—but that's the point. Because his parents encouraged him to pursue his interests even when his activities didn't have a clear reward, they made it possible for him to make the discovery that launched his career.

Some parents resist the idea of following a child's lead. They think it means simply being permissive or letting a kid run wild. But Joel, like a lot of the entrepreneurs I talked with, described a balance between firmly established parental expectations and the freedom to pursue individual interests:

My parents definitely had rules. They made me learn how to type and wouldn't let me hunt and peck. They said I could only watch TV on the weekends. And I couldn't play video games.

My parents also taught me the value of money. I had $2 a week allowance. I wanted a remote-control car, but it cost $20. They told me I'd have to save up for it. Everyone else at school had Rollerblades, and my parents wouldn't buy them for me. They said, "If you want them, you have to save your money." It made me angry at the time, but it really made me appreciate the value of money.

My parents didn't pay for college. I went to Babson on student loans and from the money I was making running my company. And because I paid for college, I never missed a class. I'd calculated the cost of each class at $500. If I was tempted to skip a class, I always thought, There is nothing I could possibly do during this hour that's worth more than $500.

Joel's parents also supported him in his academic choices, even when those choices weren't the ones they would have made for him:

> When I applied to college, I knew I only wanted to go to Babson because I'd read it was the best program for entrepreneurs. Then I decided I wanted to defer my acceptance for a year, to build my business. Again, my parents were supportive, even though it was a big ask. I had never been a normal kid, and they'd always agreed with what I wanted, but I knew they were really excited that I'd been accepted by my first choice and that I was going to college. When I broached taking a year off, they said, "We've always supported what you want, and we're not going to change now." It was very liberating.
>
> So that's how I spent the year. In 2003, right after high school graduation, I took the year off and really launched Footage Firm. I'd go to a city, film it, go home, edit it, put it on eBay, make some money, buy a ticket to the next city, and start again. I did this thirty times.
>
> After that year, I went to Babson to learn more about business. Because of my company, my education was much less abstract—when I studied accounting, marketing, and finance, they were directly applicable to what I was doing with Footage Firm. And after class, I'd go back to my room and work on my business, filling orders and selling film footage.

In 2007, when Joel was twenty-two, the Small Business Administration voted him Young Entrepreneur of the Year in recognition of Footage Firm. In the same year, he was included in *Business Week's* "25 Under 25" list. Also that year, the summer before his senior year, he worked for an investment bank. At the end of that summer, he received an offer for a six-figure job that would begin a year later, after his graduation from Babson:

I had to decide whether to take that offer or move back home with my parents and build my business.

Again, my parents were supportive. They told me, "If you think this is what you want to do, you should do it."

Some of my friends told me I was an idiot to consider turning down that offer. They said, "Only one out of ten businesses succeeds!"

I looked at the worst-case scenario and decided if I could get a job offer once, I could probably get a job offer twice.

A chance encounter with my son Elliott helped him choose.

I was still trying to decide in April 2008, a few months before I graduated, when Elliott Bisnow called to invite me on the first Summit trip. I really appreciated the support my parents had given me. So when Elliott said he was going to put together this group of young entrepreneurs, I didn't think he'd pull it off, but I said yes because I loved his passion. And he did pull it off. So I went to Utah. There were eighteen of us, each under thirty years old. It was the first time I'd spent so much time with other young entrepreneurs like me.

After that, there was no turning back. It really solidified my decision. I was so inspired after meeting the other young entrepreneurs at Summit that I decided to take a year to try to start a multimillion-dollar business. I turned down the investment bank.

My classmates thought I was out of my mind. But I was determined to prove them wrong, and so I worked like crazy.

It turned out Joel made the right decision. In 2013, he was named to *Inc.* magazine's list of "30 Under 30" for disrupting the stock footage industry with a Netflix-like subscription model.

Joel is still working at his company, renamed VideoBlocks, which has more than ninety thousand customers for its stock video clips. He's working to make his business worth even more, and his parents are still supportive.

Paige Mycoskie: Hearts, Rainbows, and a Sewing Machine

Paige Mycoskie is the creator of Aviator Nation, a popular line of vintage-style clothing (we'll meet her brother, TOMS founder Blake Mycoskie, later). When I talked with Paige's mother, Pam, she told me that while growing up in Texas, Paige had always been really creative and loved art of any kind.

"Whenever I took her to the toy store," Pam said, "she always chose art supplies. She drew rainbows and hearts when she was a little girl, and that's where the stripes came from on some of her clothes, especially the kids' line."

In 2006, when Paige was in her mid-twenties, both sets of grandparents gave her $100 apiece for her birthday, and she told Pam that she was going to take that $200, buy a used sewing machine, and fulfill her dream of starting a clothing company. At the time, according to Pam, Paige didn't even know how to sew, but she returned home to Texas from the apartment she'd been renting in California, and she brought her sewing machine with her, saying, "I'm just going to stay home for a couple months to sew."

Paige sewed almost nonstop for three months, "working long hours every day," Pam recalled. "She started making her own patterns, cutting things, sewing things on T-shirts. She made fifty garments."

How many other parents would have been excited to see their twenty-something daughter move back into the family home to teach herself how to sew? But Pam went out of her way to help Paige pursue her dream.

After Paige had sewn enough garments, Pam drove back with her to Los Angeles and helped her find a place to live. When Paige brought her fifty garments to Fred Segal, a high-end store with a fashion-forward clientele, the store's buyer took them all.

Three years later, Paige opened her first store on Abbot Kinney, a trendy street in the Venice area of L.A. She now has five stores selling her surfing-inspired clothes and is negotiating to open several more. Her clothing line is also in Bloomingdale's, and she designed a special line for the Gap. In 2013, GQ magazine named Paige among the year's best new menswear designers.

Kevin Plank: Finding a Better Way

UnderArmour founder Kevin Plank grew up in Kensington, Maryland, a D.C. suburb with a small-town feel. Kevin was the youngest of five boys who spanned thirteen years. His mom, Jayne, worked full time. She was the first woman elected to the Kensington City Council, and later she became the city's first female mayor. After fifteen years with the city, she went to work in the State Department during the Reagan administration, when Kevin was eleven.

Jayne told me that the family's life was often "chaos," but she tried to spend special time alone with each of the boys on a regular basis. She trusted all five of them to choose what they wanted to do, and she supported them in whatever choices they made.

"They all had very different interests," she said, "and they all found their passions."

Because Kevin was the youngest, he traveled with his mom to work-related conferences, and helped her with her inaugurals—and he knew she valued his assistance. As he grew older, since she had already become so busy by the time he came along, Jayne trusted him with even more freedom than she'd given his older brothers.

"We didn't organize our kids' time," she said. "They went over to their friends' homes or hung out at the park across the street. I gave them quarters so they could turn on the lights at the basketball court to keep playing after it got dark. And they'd bike downtown to get their hair cut."

All the boys loved sports:

> *Boys playing sports, working hard, with a coach looking out for them, is the best. But all of my boys pursued different sports. I always let them determine their own goals. One quit school for a while. I said that was fine. I agreed he shouldn't be in college until he figured out what he wanted to do.*

While Kevin was in college, his father died. In five years, Kevin also lost three grandparents. It was a rough period for everyone in the family, but Jayne, with her characteristic ebullience, said her motto became, "Embrace adversity and get over it."

Jayne gave all the boys freedom to choose what they wanted to do, and supported them in whatever choices they made. She told me that Kevin had always figured out how to make his own way in life, and she thought that was great. Today, Bill, the oldest, is a builder who also runs martial arts schools; Stuart is a developer and high school football coach; Scott is a real estate developer; Colin is a movie producer and writer; and Kevin, the baby, runs one of the largest athletic apparel companies in the world.

Kevin was especially passionate about football. At the University of Maryland, he started playing without a football scholarship, but worked hard enough to earn one, becoming special teams captain.

"You know what D.C. is like in August," Jayne said. "You don't perspire. You sweat!"

And Kevin got tired of sweating through his cotton T-shirts during his twice-a-day summer football practices. He'd had a little T-shirt company when he was in high school—he and his friends would tie-dye shirts on the back patio and then sell them at football games and music festivals. So he decided to find a fabric that his skin could breathe through; he drove to all the fabric manufacturers he could find, first in Baltimore and then in New York.

He worked all the time, Jayne told me. He had been driven from the time he was young to make his own way. "His education was an inconvenience on his continuum to success," she said.

Kevin launched UnderArmour from his family's basement. It's now a multibillion-dollar company, one of the largest sellers of sportswear in the U.S., and has transformed what athletes wear.

The outcome of all that trust in Kevin and his brothers, Jayne told me, is that "they got over their humps and bumps on their own and all became successful. Being proud of my children's success is the best reward. I'm very fortunate."

Alexis Jones: "If You Want It, Make It Happen"

Alexis Jones is a thought leader of the women's movement, an expert on Generation Y, and the founder of I AM THAT GIRL, an online empowerment community for young women, with 150 local chapters and over 250,000 members. Alexis has spoken to more than 100,000 young people in person and reached more than five million online. When I talked with her, she told me what her mother, Claudia Mann, helped her learn:

I was taught really young that it's good to make mistakes. Every time I messed up, my mom would say, "That's awesome. What did you learn? It's not real life to think there's one right answer and one wrong answer. It's easy never to step out of your comfort zone, and it's easy to not fail." My mom taught me that if you can learn from your mistakes, you're on a completely different track.

My mom's only rule was "Don't ever lie to me." She told me, "Don't underestimate what I can handle. Talk to me." So there was no need to be rebellious. She trusted me to make good decisions. She told me, "These are your freedoms, as long as you keep up your end of the bargain—getting good grades and getting a scholarship." Mom would say, "I trust you," and that was huge. I didn't want to screw that up. My girlfriends were all lying to their parents. I didn't have to.

Kids will meet expectations. Even when I was twelve, Mom would say, "Let's negotiate. Tell me what you want." I thought it was so cool that I had a say and that I got to participate.

I think things are different for girls. There are a lot of intangibles we need to know, like learning to communicate very directly, and even little things, like shaking hands, looking people in the eye.

I have four brothers, and my mom was always fighting for me to have more independence. My parents were divorced, and my dad was more protective. When I was nineteen, I spent the summer traveling alone in Europe. My mom said, "I think it's time for her to have an adventure." My dad said, "What are you doing?"

Like many budding entrepreneurs, Alexis pursued a number of passions until one really clicked:

I started modeling when I was thirteen. My mom said, "We'll do this as long as it's fun." My mom never put a focus on how I looked. She always said, "Pretty doesn't pay the bills." If someone said, "She's so cute," my mom would say, "Yes, but she's also very smart." I got on the cover of a magazine, and when I showed her, she said, "Great. Did you finish your calculus?" She always kept it in perspective. She told my brothers and me the most important thing that people could say about us was that we're kind. If I got a compliment, she always said, "Thanks, but my kids are great human beings, and that's what's important."

Sports were huge for me all through high school. I played volleyball and soccer. Eventually the modeling agency wanted me to give up sports to concentrate on modeling. They told me I was looking too strong.

I asked my mom what I should do, and she said, "Whatever you want. You choose." I chose sports. She said, "Great."

I was good in sports, but not great. And modeling was an avenue, not a passion.

I told the director of the modeling agency, "I'd rather be smart than pretty, and I want to go to college." And he said, "You are wasting your prettiness. Get out of my office."

I was also a camp counselor in the summers, and I loved telling stories by the campfire. Standing up and telling stories— that was a place where I shined in a way I didn't shine in other areas. My mom wanted me to try everything. And once I tried storytelling, and then writing, it was all over—I knew I'd found what I loved. Which led to acting, which led to my public speaking today. One passion led naturally to the next.

For Claudia, supporting her daughter's sense of freedom and choice never meant supporting laziness or a lack of focus. Alexis learned to work hard, like all the other entrepreneurs I talked with:

I was raised with a strong work ethic. I worked for a while in the entertainment industry. When I auditioned for a role, I'd tell them, "You can find prettier, you can find thinner, you can find more experience, but you will never find someone who works harder than me. I will be the first one here and the last one to go home."

I got cast for everything. My mom told me, "Put yourself in a race where nobody can compete with you." I took that advice. By sticking with activities I loved and working harder than anybody, I've been fortunate to achieve a lot of success.

My dream was to go to college, but we couldn't afford it. My mom said, "Never use a lack of money to walk away from your dreams. If you want it, make it happen." She told me, "Not having money is a terrible excuse for not following your dreams." Whenever I said, "I don't have something," my mom said, "Then go make it."

Alexis's mom supported her daughter in her chosen pursuits, from sports to modeling to storytelling to acting and finally to public speaking. She let Alexis choose her own path and make her own decisions, had confidence in her, supported everything Alexis wanted to do, and taught her daughter that financial limitations should not stand in the way of reaching for her dreams.

The Power of Stepping Aside

As we just saw in the story of Alexis Jones, parents can greatly influence their children's attitudes toward work. Many parents, aware of this responsibility, put a lot of effort, not to mention anxiety, into making sure their kids get the right messages. But in my interviews with entrepreneurs and their moms, I found that often the parents who made the deepest impressions were not those who constantly talked to their children about the importance of finding meaningful work, or who arranged their lives to accommodate their children's passions. In many cases, the deepest impressions were made by parents who took a more subtle approach of recognizing what their children wanted to do and giving them the space to do it.

Greg Gunn: Pursuing Different Passions

I've known Wendell Gunn for decades; we worked in government together thirty years ago. I spoke to his wife Linda about their son Greg, a Rhodes Scholar and one of the country's most successful African American tech entrepreneurs, who built and sold his educational software company, Wireless Generation, for $450 million.

Greg started to read when he was four years old. According to his mom, Linda, he also always liked math and computers:

> When Greg was only eight, and the first Apple computer came out, Greg insisted we get one. From then on, he learned about computers on his own, writing programs.

It may sound like a small thing, but when Linda and Wendell bought that computer, they didn't just give Greg a tool he could use to explore his passion. They also showed him they would provide tools he needed to advance his skills. Sometimes that meant letting him assemble Legos and play video games, even when other parents saw those activities as a waste of time.

As Linda also told me:

> Greg was always a leader. The other two kids weren't like that; he just seemed to be born that way. All the neighborhood kids would defer to him when they played games. I didn't raise Greg to be an entrepreneur; our kids have always done the leading, and we did the following; we support them in what they want to do.

It's true that Greg is the oldest, and was an "only" until he was five. When there weren't a lot of kids around, he spent his time mostly with adults. He also had strong internal motivation, a gift he seemed to come by naturally. His younger brother now works with him and his sister is pursuing her dream, poetry. According to Linda, he showed great grit and determination in whatever he was doing:

> *In high school, Greg wanted to get a well-rounded education, and he also started running track. He previously hadn't been interested in sports. Even though he wasn't a superstar, he always wanted to do his personal best in everything.*

Apart from computers, Greg had another great passion—education. In high school, he had a tutoring program to work with kids who were struggling in math. After graduating from the University of Chicago with a degree in physics, he took a gap year and taught in a tech-intensive magnet school.

After going to Oxford University as a Rhodes Scholar, he went on to MIT for an MBA and a master's degree in computer science, and started thinking about how to combine his two loves: education and computers.

With a friend he'd met at Oxford, Greg cofounded Wireless Generation, an educational software company that provides assessment and instructional products for three million children. After he sold Wireless Gen, he was named Entrepreneur in Residence at City Light, a venture capital firm that invests in high-growth U.S. companies.

Linda and Wendell Gunn had no idea their son would grow up to be an entrepreneur. But by supporting him wherever his interests led him, they left him free to pursue his passion to unexpected heights.

Robert Stephens: Mr. Fix-It

Robert Stephens founded Geek Squad twenty years ago in Minneapolis. He was twenty-four, and he had a bicycle, a white shirt with a nerdy black clip-on tie, and $200 of start-up capital. He built Geek Squad into a global brand with 20,000 employees and, after ten years, he merged the company with Best Buy, staying on for two years as chief technology officer before leaving to pursue new ventures.

The child of Depression-era parents, he grew up outside Chicago, the youngest of seven. His mom married at fifteen (she told his dad she was sixteen) and started having kids immediately. Robert is the youngest by five years, and he's the only one to go to college. His siblings include a bricklayer, a mechanic, and a truck driver. His dad spent twenty years in the Navy. Robert told me that he and his six siblings never wanted for anything, but they definitely weren't spoiled.

I find it fascinating that most of the entrepreneurs I talked with told me that their place in the birth order, whatever it was— oldest, youngest, somewhere in the middle—had contributed to their independence. Wherever they were in the family, and regardless of how many siblings they had, they thought their situation was perfect. As the youngest, Robert thought his parents had loosened up enough by the time he was born to give him more independence than they had given the others. They were the opposite of helicopter parents. He could build a raft, float down a creek, and come home in time for dinner with no questions asked.

Unlike other entrepreneurs I talked with, Robert had a passion for fixing things as he was growing up:

> *When I was three years old, I took off all the doorknobs in the house. When my parents saw me, I had them laid out neatly on the table, all organized—doorknob, screw, doorknob, screw. My parents weren't angry, though they did tell me to put them all back.*
>
> *This became part of our family mythology. I was the fix-it guy. That's who I was—"Robert can fix anything." It gave me a sense of pride and self-esteem. I loved taking things apart,*

finding out how things worked. I took apart a radio. I really could fix anything.

When I was twelve, I had a job repairing TVs in the neighborhood. Back then, lots of people had a fear of technology, but I didn't.

My parents got me a chemistry set and a lot of Lego sets. I spent a lot of time alone, in creative play, building rockets or making the sandbox whatever I wanted it to be.

Looking back, I think my parents were very thoughtful about how they supported me. I think that's key—recognizing and allowing my essential personality to emerge, and then giving me room to develop. I had freedom, but with fences. And my parents were always okay with whatever I wanted to do: "Sure, I'll drive you to computer club."

I was a really fast typist, so in high school I typed papers for people. I charged $20 per paper, and $25 with a bibliography. Then I started offering to write the papers also, for $45. I was making $250 a week. I kept a database, tracked the grades, rewrote papers to turn a B into an A. I did this for three years. My dad said, "This isn't ethical." I said, "I'm not cheating. They are."

Then I typed up Rolodexes for businesses like beauty salons and hardware stores and sent out cards for them. They didn't have an organized database. When I was seventeen, I got a job delivering mattresses. Then I built a database and a tracking program for them on my Commodore computer because there was no computer system. That was my pattern—I'd get a menial job, and then I'd start organizing it better. And then I started repairing computers.

Robert Stephens is a classic example of someone who turns a childhood passion into entrepreneurial success: the boy who loved to fix things started a company that fixes things. His parents consistently supported his passion and trusted him to make his own choices, and he learned to believe in his own abilities. And when he was ready, the fix-it guy made his entrepreneurial dreams real.

My Family

Each of the entrepreneurs profiled in this chapter grew up in a home where parents supported their passion. That might sound simple, but it's not as easy as you might think, and it's also not as common. In ways large and small, supporting a child's passion means letting the child take the lead in her own life. This is hard for parents! We know so much more than our children do about the world and how it works, right? And besides, we want to shield them from making mistakes or getting hurt. So we give them advice that we think will help them in their journey: help them get into the right college, help them get a career where they can support themselves. But our desire to help, based on our knowledge of how the world worked when we were growing up, may backfire if it prevents our kids from spending time on something they love.

So there comes a point when "supporting" your child means "stepping back." I'll end this chapter with some things I learned from writing this book about my own experience, as our two boys grew up and became who they are today.

Each of our sons had a passion outside school while they were in high school and college. And although I didn't realize it at the time, there was a serendipitous aspect to Elliott's playing competitive tennis and Austin's writing music. It was only when I started to speak to the moms of successful entrepreneurs that it hit me: both of them had passions in areas that my husband and I knew nothing about.

If they had been interested in politics or media or law or economics—areas in which my husband and I had worked—we would have gotten involved. We would have tried to help and offered advice. But we knew almost nothing about tennis or music. So Elliott had to decide without help from us where to train, which coach to work with, what racquet to use, what tournaments to enter. Austin had to decide without our advice what instruments to learn, who his piano, guitar, drums, and voice coaches would be, what music software to get, what microphone and mixer to buy, what songs should be on his album, and what producer to work with.

And that was a good thing. They had to take control, make decisions, figure it out for themselves. It wasn't a conscious decision on our part, but looking back, it was lucky that it worked out that way. I didn't know it at the time, but now I know that all children should be allowed to figure out their own passion, that parents should nourish and support and encourage that passion, and that parents should largely stay out of the way so that it becomes truly theirs.

RULE 2

Let Your Child Learn to Win—and Lose

I almost called this rule "Let Your Child Play Sports" because sports had a role in the lives of so many of the entrepreneurs I interviewed for this book. Sports can be crucial to developing an entrepreneurial mind-set. That's because kids who play sports learn how to compete, which also means learning how to lose and learning how to pick themselves up again—lessons that can be transferred to competing in business. Whatever sport your child plays, whether a team sport like basketball or an individual sport like tennis, it must be one your child loves.

And if your kid hates sports, that's not a problem. Lots of other activities will teach her to compete, strive for success, win, and lose. Just make sure the activity is the child's choice, not yours. You can advise your child on the pros and cons of a particular activity, but it must be your daughter's passion that drives her; it must be your son's choice to commit himself. A friend whose son is a serious chess player told me how he'd battled through an epic four-hour match only to lose at the end, and what he'd learned from it, and how he vowed he'd never lose to that guy again. So these lessons don't only come from sports. Any passionate pursuit that involves competition—playing chess, auditioning for roles in plays, submitting watercolors to juried exhibitions, participating in spelling bees—forces a young person to be tested on a regular basis.

The key is learning to compete, to fight to succeed, to learn how to win, and to learn how to lose. Much has been written on how the lives of economically disadvantaged children have been transformed through chess. University of Maryland Baltimore County President Freeman Hrabowski famously turned his largely African American commuter school into the nation's top chess powerhouse.

And much has been written about an impoverished New York City middle school, IS318, whose kids beat all the top private schools in the country in the national chess championships. As their coach Elizabeth Spiegel explains in Paul Tough's *How Children Succeed*, young people grow when they can take responsibility for their mistakes and learn from them without obsessing or beating themselves up.

She says, "[W]hen they lose a chess game, they know that they have no one to blame but themselves...you have to find a way to separate yourself from your mistakes or your losses. I try to teach my students that losing is something you do, not something you are" (Tough 2012, 115–116).

Steve Jobs talked about learning from failure in his famous 2005 commencement address at Stanford. He described his greatest failure, being fired from Apple, the company he had founded, just after he turned thirty. And how that failure led him to reorient himself, be brought back to Apple, and turn it into one of the world's most transformative companies.

How Children Succeed also quotes Dominic Randolph, head of the prestigious private New York Riverdale Country School, about the mistake many parents make in preventing their kids from failing. Randolph makes "a persuasive case that failure—or at least the real risk of failure—could often be a crucial step on the road to success." He worried that "his mostly affluent students…were being short-changed by their families and their school and even their culture by not being given enough genuine opportunities to overcome adversity and thus develop their character. The idea of building grit and building self-control is that you get that through failure…. And in most highly academic environments in the United States, no one fails anything" (Tough 2012, 177).

Though kids can learn about competing through many different channels, in this chapter I'm going to concentrate on sports. Many of these entrepreneurs played sports competitively through high school, and a surprising number continued in college. Their moms were like me—they didn't have their kids play sports to learn skills that would help them when they started companies or nonprofits—but looking back, we all realize that perhaps one reason our kids became entrepreneurs is that learning to compete in sports helped them understand how to compete in business.

Also—and this is really important—this is not about being a star athlete, or even a good or natural one. It's about learning to compete and learning to deal with setbacks. I remember speaking to a loving mom who worried because her daughter enjoyed sports, loved being part of a team, but wasn't particularly athletic. She had gone to a baseball camp the summer before, and had spent a lot of time warming the bench.

Remarkably, in the last game of the summer, deciding the county championship, her daughter came up to the plate with the game tied in the ninth inning. The bases were loaded, with two outs. Her mom gulped. Her daughter swung—and got a hit, winning the game for the team.

She wanted to go back to baseball camp the next summer, but her mom wanted to protect her from disappointment. "I told her, 'Don't go back. You will never repeat that moment.'" She worried her daughter could never live up to the expectations that dramatic hit sparked: "I told her to quit while she's ahead. Why should she go back to camp and do worse than she did the summer before?"

This mom loved her daughter so much and wanted to protect her from getting hurt, but I wondered what message that would send. Not to follow your dream? Not to try? That failure is bad? That not trying is better? There was risk in her daughter returning to camp, but so much opportunity for growth—and for grit.

The Importance of Grit

Another lesson children learn when they play competitive sports is the direct connection between hard work and results. Getting this connection leads to what psychologists call *grit*.

University of Pennsylvania psychology professor Angela Lee Duckworth studies what leads to success. She has popularized the concept of grit, which she defines as "passion plus perseverance toward long-term goals" or, in other words, working really hard to make dreams a reality. She studied West Point cadets, national spelling bee champs, effective teachers, business leaders, at-risk school kids, and Ivy League undergrads, and in all of them she found that grit is the best predictor of success. More important than IQ. More important than talent. More important than family income. More important than social intelligence, or good looks, or health. She says grit is living life like it's a marathon, not a sprint. It's having stamina. It's sticking with your goals day in and day out, not just for a week or a month.

Chris Wink: Unstoppable

One of the entrepreneurs I interviewed has a particular interest in Angela Duckworth's work on grit. Chris Wink cofounded the Blue Man Group in 1988 with his friends Matt Goldman and

Phil Stanton after their small shows on Manhattan city streets got noticed. The troupe has been playing to packed audiences around the world since then and is now a global entertainment company with ongoing theatrical productions in Las Vegas, Orlando, Boston, Chicago, New York, and Berlin. In 2011, BMG won the Off Broadway Alliance Audience Choice Award for best long-running show. Chris is also one 'of the co-founders of the Blue School.

Chris is passionate about innovation and creativity. He invited Angela Lee Duckworth to his school to talk about grit. When I asked him about it, he told me: "Grit was one of the topics we were interested in trying to teach at the Blue School. It also resonated with our own experience of having to work incredibly hard to make our show successful. The question is, is grit teachable? Or do some people just have it? Well, one thing is certain, you won't have it if you pursue things you aren't passionate about. People said I was lazy when I was doing stuff I didn't like. But when it comes to building cool shows, I'm an unstoppable force. I'm not saying all my ideas are good, I'm just saying I can't be stopped."

Kids with grit succeed, and all successful entrepreneurs have grit. People with grit learn that when they invest effort in something, they will see success. For many high achievers in careers such as medicine, law, and investment banking, that lesson is learned in school. Their hard work yields obvious rewards, enabling them to climb to the next level. To use the example of future doctors, the top high school students get into the top colleges, and then into the top medical schools, and then get the top internships and the top residencies, before getting positions at the top hospitals.

But many future entrepreneurs, especially those who aren't fully engaged by school, first learn about the power of grit on the playing field. Perhaps it's because they played sports, or perhaps it's just common to the current generation of young people, but it seems they all keep score. They want to know if they've won or lost. They're achievement-oriented, and they determine achievement by metrics. That's true even for those who don't seem to invest much effort in getting good grades. They all want to win: some at school, some on the playing field, and some performing. Benny Blanco, the songwriter we'll meet in the next chapter, wanted to win rap battles, not spelling bees. The common denominator: if it's something they care passionately about, they want to be the best at it.

In business, "the best" is often measured by money. The money is a scorecard; entrepreneurs tend to value it because it measures their success in business, rather than for what it can purchase. For the entrepreneurs I talked to, the money's not the goal: it's a marker for winning, creating, accomplishing, succeeding, building. For entrepreneurs who started nonprofits, money's important inasmuch as it lets them help people and transform communities—the real fruits of success.

That drive yields much more than the momentary joy of victory. We're so busy protecting kids from failure that they don't learn to compete with intensity, which builds character. We've become the country where everyone gets a trophy regardless of effort.

Riverdale Headmaster Dominic Randolph says, "[T]here was always this idea in America that if you worked hard and you showed real grit, that you could be successful... Strangely, we've now forgotten that. People who have an easy time of things...I worry that those people get feedback that everything they're doing is great. And I think as a result, we are actually setting them up for long-term failure" (Tough 2012, 56).

How can we raise our kids with grit—teach them a work ethic, keep them motivated for the long run? I think it has to do with letting them pursue something they love. If they love it, they'll work hard. If they work hard, they'll keep trying, despite failures, and they'll eventually succeed. If they see the connection between hard work and success in one part of their life, it can translate into hard work, and a willingness to fight past setbacks, for a different activity when they get older.

For another angle on the way kids learn from failure, I look to the work of Stanford professor Carol Dweck (2008). She studied four hundred fifth graders who took three tests, one of which was so difficult that they all failed. She found that those kids who had been praised for their *effort* recovered enough that by the next test they scored 30 percent higher, while kids who had been praised for their *intelligence* scored 20 percent lower. She concludes that when you praise kids for qualities they can control, like effort, they learn to work harder than those who are praised for just being smart. In other words, kids who are praised for their brainpower might think that hard work isn't necessary. Kids praised for hard work—by their parents or their coach or their music teacher—learn to work hard and to understand that they can learn and grow from failure.

Simon Isaacs: Disappointment ≠ Defeat

Simon Isaacs describes his work as "positive social disruption."

He climbed Mt. Kilimanjaro with a team of celebrities and global influencers to raise awareness of the need for clean water around the world. He worked to bring attention to Malala Yousafzai, the young Nobel Peace Prize recipient from Pakistan who was shot for her advocacy of education for girls. He led the Clinton Foundation's work on agriculture and safe water in Rwanda. He founded GATHER, a company that builds large-scale nonprofit organizations or campaigns, often with funding from the Gates Foundation, and with focuses like nutrition and voting.

When I met him, we started talking about the influence of sports on kids who become entrepreneurs. I asked him if he had played a sport when he was younger. He said, "Oh, yes, I was an All-American skier on the Olympic Development Team."

From the time he was six, Simon lived in the Vermont woods with his parents, Lisa and Henry (both artists) and his two sisters. His mom started a design agency, and she and his dad built a house that included an office and studio space.

Simon began cross-country skiing, and he started racing when he was eight. He was good enough to become an Olympics hopeful on the U.S. Development Team. "Between the ages of ten and fifteen," he told me, "I was skiing six days a week—Nordic combined, which is both cross-country and jumping. I trained at the Olympic Center in Lake Placid during the summers. At fifteen, I decided to focus on cross-country—it was really my life."

But for all his joy in skiing, Simon also knew great sorrow from an early age:

> My mom was diagnosed with cancer when I was ten. She died when I was eighteen. My dad was also sick. But they both worked really hard to be there for us as much as they could. The illnesses would come and go, and whenever they could, they were there and involved. But there were also times we were alone. Looking back, I'm amazed how involved they were in our lives, in our school, going to my ski races, while all this was happening.

Throughout this time, with the help and mentorship of his uncle, Simon continued skiing. He spent his final two years of high school in Colorado; after high school, he went to Middlebury College, where he raced and even spent a semester training with the Italian national team. He also graduated second in his class. "I was a real nerd," he told me.

As much as Simon loved skiing, he eventually decided that he wanted to do something different with his life. But he told me that devoting so much time to an individual sport had taught him three lessons, which he uses today as an entrepreneur:

First, you have a constant feedback loop—understanding your body, your fitness, your shape, your technique, your heart rate. You're always trying to figure out how you can improve. I'm still that way today. I'm always looking at myself, analyzing myself, trying to evaluate myself from that perspective. I'm always asking myself, How did that meeting go? How can I be better?

The second lesson is, how do you manage defeat when you aren't winning? How do you get yourself back up the next day, get back to the starting line and begin again? You're not going to nail everything, so you have to view the journey as one long race. I've had a lot of disappointments, but I look at it as one big feedback loop, and I just say to myself, How do I get back up on my feet? *I've learned it's not a defeat. It's part of the learning curve, part of the process.*

The third lesson I learned is always to survey the course before the race. Before I started, I was constantly thinking, Where is everyone else going to slow down? What stretch am I going to turn this on? *I've always done this throughout my career, tried to figure it out in advance:* Where am I going to be able to stand out? *Every good entrepreneur surveys the landscape, and the market, and asks, "Where is the opportunity?"*

In addition to running GATHER, Simon recently launched a media company and a nonprofit incubator that will provide funding to fledgling nonprofits for space, public relations, media, and operational costs. He also cofounded Fatherly, a parenting resource in the dad space. "Because of how intense my life was when I was competing," he said, "it's very normal to do all this stuff, to keep this busy, and to stay on top of everything."

Adam and Scooter Braun: Lessons from the Basketball Court

Adam Braun started one of the country's top nonprofits, Pencils of Promise, which is building hundreds of schools around the world. His older brother Scott, called Scooter, is one of the top talent managers in the country. He discovered Justin Bieber and Ariana Grande, owns a record label, a publishing company, a management company, and a tech incubator. Their sister, Liza, is a physician.

I talked with their mother, Susan, an orthodontist, to learn how she had raised two successful entrepreneurs. Susan told me that all three of her kids played competitive sports into college. When they were young, their dad coached three sports, but basketball became the boys' main focus. Through sports, Susan said, the boys made friends from all walks of life, and their coaches provided another level of adult supervision and mentoring And although they were both good students, Susan believes it was invaluable that each of them had something else so significant in their life.

Scooter went on to play basketball at Emory, and Adam played basketball at Brown. Playing competitive sports in college forced them to become very efficient and disciplined about managing their time, Susan said, and playing team sports forced them to live up to their teammates' expectations, while teaching them how to get along with others. She also spoke about how important it was for others to watch her sons lose—not just their teammates, but also the crowd—and for them to learn to pick themselves up, deal with their losses, move past them, and try not to repeat them. "Learning how to lose gracefully in a public way was so important," she said, "even though it was hard for me to watch."

I started thinking about the difference between playing team sports like soccer, basketball, and hockey compared to individual sports like tennis, golf, and swimming. Both teach you how to focus on a goal and how to win and lose; both teach you to strive and to compete; both force you to set priorities and to be organized with your time. Both team sports and individual sports teach invaluable life lessons, but they are different experiences. Team sports are more about learning to collaborate and realizing how your contribution can be critical to success, and about getting along with others. Individual sports are more about realizing there are no excuses, and that there's nobody else to blame—or credit—for success or failure.

I told a friend my theory about the different skills individual and team sports teach kids and he said, "Maybe parents should try to get their kids to play both." I replied, "No, that misses the point. The idea is that you expose them to everything, but then you support them in the sport *they* choose." The key to having it work for your child is that it must be a sport—or some other competitive activity—that your child loves. That is one of the most important lessons in this book. You can give your child your advice about the pros and cons of any activity, but it must be your son's passion for him to want to compete; it must be your daughter's choice to commit herself to it.

Alan Chan: Game Face On

I first met Alan in 2010, when he offered to sublet his sixth-floor walk-up in New York City's Chinatown to my son Austin, who had just graduated from college. He was the founder and CEO of Arbitrage, a stylish clothing company, and he gave Austin a couple of really cool shirts. He'd been a basketball player when he was younger, and he told me that playing sports taught him invaluable lessons he used as his business grew: to work hard, to be prepared, and to adjust his game when the competition changed:

> I was born and raised in Toronto. My parents are Ronnie Leung and Wing Chow Chan. My sister laid out a path for me to follow when she went to Stanford—my goal was to go to the U.S. Although I was always a good student, what I really cared about in high school was basketball. I also played soccer and baseball, but basketball was my passion. I was team captain my junior and senior years and won the Best Athlete award when I graduated.
>
> Basketball was a huge influence on my life, and very important in my becoming an entrepreneur. The leadership experience from being captain helped develop my entrepreneurial spirit. Motivating my teammates showed me I could motivate employees. I even think the fact that my coach really believed in me gave me the confidence to start a business.
>
> Playing sports teaches you preparation. I learned I have to have a game plan. I learned how to execute, how to prepare for the championship game. Because I had that experience, now I go into key meetings very calm, very prepared, ready to dominate and kill the meeting.
>
> Being an entrepreneur is the culmination of a series of successful meetings. The feelings I have today before preparing for a big meeting are the same as I had going into a big sports match. Because of that, I'm always ready now. As an entrepreneur, you get a lot of meetings, and you have two minutes to make the investor or vendor or client your best friend. If you can't win them over, you won't be successful.
>
> I was always interested in clothing and fashion. I collected sneakers and basketball shoes. I was fanatic about products I liked. And I loved great ads—I put ads all over my bedroom wall.

I went to Cornell for pre-med, but during my junior year I took a class on how to start a business. That changed my life.

When we were seniors and were thinking about life after college, all my friends needed new clothes—business attire. The only clothes guys could buy at that time were baggy and not very interesting, so I saw an opportunity to create a better-fitting clothing line for young guys.

I incubated the company my senior year of college, moved to New York, and launched my company, Arbitrage, in 2006 with two friends.

It was doing really well. We were in Saks and Nordstrom's. Then the recession hit, which hurt a lot of retail brands. All the department stores were losing money, and they started cutting the smaller brands. I had been doing the online marketing for the company, and I realized there was a need for better advertising on the Web. So we decided to pivot.

We hadn't raised outside capital, but had bootstrapped it, which meant we didn't owe anybody anything. So we decided we could put Arbitrage on hold for a while and pursue other ventures. I had two business partners, who went on to other things. We're still friends.

Alan went on to start Bread, a company that created a platform for distributing full-page ads on websites, tablets, and mobile devices. Its customers included Lady Gaga, 50 Cent, and Pepsi. It was acquired by Yahoo in 2014. He told me, "I love what I do, and I think one reason I've been successful is the confidence I gained and the habits I learned from sports."

Eric Ryan: Method and Moxie

Eric Ryan and a high school pal, Adam Lowry, cofounded Method in 2001 to make environmentally friendly household products that smell great and look cool. In 2006, *Inc.* magazine named Method the seventh fastest-growing private U.S. company.

Eric grew up in Grosse Pointe, outside Detroit, with two younger brothers—one of whom is now an advertising entrepreneur, the other in corporate finance. He told me he'd always wanted to be an entrepreneur:

> *I come from an entrepreneurial family. My great-grandfather moved to Detroit to work for Henry Ford for $5 a day and then founded his own machine-and-stamping company with my grandfather. My father kept it until the eighties, when he just couldn't compete anymore.*

His mother's side of the family also contributed to Eric's sense of determination and hard work, according to his mom, Pam:

> *We were blessed. My husband and I both came from families with strong values. I was one of six kids, and my father died suddenly of a heart attack when I was sixteen and the youngest was three.*
>
> *Both my parents had a wonderful work ethic—my mom worked so hard for all of us, and we all worked hard for her. Whenever I'd think, I can't do this, I'd think, Wait, my mother had six kids—I'd better get moving! She also had a passion for her family, and that passion for family was passed down.*

Eric told me that his mother's stories really resonated with him, and so did the ones from his dad's side:

> *I always loved listening to entrepreneur stories and reading books by entrepreneurs. Other kids built forts or space villages with their Legos. I built office buildings.*
>
> *I was always working on a business idea. In lower school I got a machine and made and sold buttons with funny*

sayings. I made and sold hockey nets. I sold stationery. I had a plan to launch English-muffin pizza.

I also worked at jobs through high school and college for my spending money. I ran the middle school bookstore. I bagged groceries. I delivered pizza. I shoveled snow.

I always worked. I was a terrible student, but I really enjoyed working and thinking up business ideas. There was never a time when I wasn't working on an idea.

It was sports that helped Eric develop the perseverance to see those ideas through. He grew up on Lake Michigan, so his passion was sailing:

I first sailed when I was in summer camp after fourth grade, and I loved it. I sailed competitively through college. My dad would drive the boat up and down the East Coast, to St. Petersburg or Newport, so I could race. He was always there to support me at regattas, even though he didn't know anything about sailing.

It's a very complicated sport. I tell folks if it's windy, it's very athletic, like rugby, but if there's no wind, it's more like chess.

It also teaches you a lot of independence. You have to be so well organized. You have to be a self-starter.

I wasn't a good student, but I loved sailing and worked hard at that. I chose where I wanted to go to college based on the sailing team, and I raced at the University of Rhode Island. I raced until a couple of years ago, when I had three kids. I miss the competition.

That competitive fire helped drive Eric's career. Unlike most of the other entrepreneurs I spoke with, whose passions were for particular areas of business, he looked around until he saw an area that needed disrupting. He realized that the cleaning industry hadn't changed in years—the products had an unpleasant smell, and they weren't environmentally friendly. So he decided to revolutionize the industry:

> I knew I was going to start a company, but first I worked at an advertising agency. It helped me understand cultural shifts and marketing.
>
> I spent a lot of time looking at different categories where I could start my business. I liked the idea of going into what appeared to others to be a boring category and finding a way to do it differently.
>
> The cleaning category caught my eye. Everything looked so similar. I knew I could do better. I thought it was a big opportunity to connect your lifestyle with your home.
>
> I thought my friends would laugh at me if I told them I was going to start a cleaning company. When I told my mom, she said, "I've never even seen you make your bed!" But my folks really believed in me and gave me $10,000 to get started.
>
> I knew Adam from high school—we were both sailors. So in 1999, I told him what I was planning. He said, "I have a degree in chemical engineering," and offered to help me, and we decided to become business partners.
>
> It was a classic entrepreneur story. We laid out our vision. It seemed so obvious that we couldn't believe nobody had done this before.
>
> We gave our business plan to twenty smart people and asked them what was wrong with it, and nobody could come up with anything. We went store to store to pitch the product. We'd get twenty seconds to make our pitch in the back of a store.
>
> We got it into twenty local stores. We hand-delivered the product. Then we went to independent premium stores, then to regional stores.

Eventually, after raising both an Angel round and Series A money from investors who, according to Eric, "believed in us more than they believed in the product," the two cofounders had their product in eight hundred stores in the Detroit area. At that point, Eric said, what they really wanted was to get their product into a nationally recognized chain:

> We met someone at Target who said we had a snowball's chance in hell of getting it into his store. We knew we needed to get to a certain size to start making money. We were still losing money on each bottle.

At every step of the way, Eric and Adam drew on the grit they'd developed in their sailing days. They knew that if they kept doing whatever the situation demanded, whether the wind was filling their sails or not, they'd eventually see success:

> Our first lucky break came in 2002, when we got a meeting with Target's marketing department. The buyer who had already turned us down was annoyed. Somehow, they agreed to do an eighty-store sample, but there was a sales number we had to hit. We started buying our product ourselves to make our number. We'd go to a store, buy it, and then ship it back. We knew we had to make the number, and we figured we'd do whatever it took. We knew if we could get national distribution, we could afford marketing.
>
> The buyer who didn't like us retired. Fortunately, the new buyer loved our product. He gave us national distribution. Target is now a huge customer.

In 2012, Method had revenues of more than $100 million, and in 2013 it was sold to Ecover, which then became the largest green cleaning business in the world. Eric is still involved, and he recently built a new Method plant, which is a living example of the company's mission and values. Everything about the new plant—its location on the South Side of Chicago, its practice of hiring local people, its wind turbines and solar trees, its rooftop greenhouse (the world's largest) built to bring fresh produce to a food desert—was designed with sustainability and social good in mind. Eric has also started OLLY, a company that aims to do for vitamins and nutritional supplements what Method did for cleaning supplies—make them fun, green, and easy to understand.

Erika Paola Gutierrez: Shifting into Drive

Erika Paola Gutierrez is the founder of epgPR, a public relations firm with scores of clients. The firm does marketing, branding, and media placement in dozens of magazines and newspapers as well as on TV.

I asked Erika what had motivated her when she was young: like Eric Ryan, it was athletics more than academics. Her story is another example that it doesn't matter what you compete in; it only matters that you learn to compete:

> For eighteen years, my life was just ballet and acrobatics. I competed seriously from the time I was ten.
>
> At first it came effortlessly. I was in third grade and walked into an acrobatics studio where girls were doing backflips. I said, "I can do this." My mom said, "Are you sure?" I went into the class. By the end, I was doing backflips and cartwheels with no hands.
>
> I started winning competitions. And then I really got into it. I was training for hours every day. Ballet classes, acrobatics, jazz, modern dance—I did that all through high school. Every weekend I'd be in competitions. I worked really hard at it, and I was so good at it. I loved it.
>
> My parents were so proud. My mom, Edilia, still talks about it to this day. They both were always so supportive of

whatever I wanted to do. Dad was busy at work, but he never missed a competition or a recital. Dad would always say, "Do whatever you want—anything you think you'll be good at." I got yelled at a lot about school, but my parents were proud about the dance and acrobatics.

I'm the middle of three children. We moved around the world for my dad's job as I grew up—Mexico, Austin, Canada, Michigan, Miami, and D.C. I have an older brother, Carlos, who's a lawyer, and a younger sister, Karina, who works with me part time. They're the insanely smart ones in the family; they always got straight A's.

I never did well in high school and didn't focus on school. My parents were always furious with me about my studies. My mom pushed me every day to do my homework, but I just didn't care.

It hurt my confidence level. I began to think I wasn't smart. My mom said, "There's no such thing as smart people. There are people who work hard and people who don't." My dad said, "Hard work always pays off."

I didn't get into a great college, didn't study, changed majors three times, and barely graduated after five years. Education was really important to my parents, but it just wasn't important to me then. I'm ashamed to say I just didn't care. I regret it now.

Erika's parents didn't understand why the grit she'd developed in dance and acrobatics didn't translate to her schoolwork. Eventually, though, Erika decided to apply the same hard work and tenacity to school that she'd been applying to the activities she cared about:

After college, I moved to D.C. and got a job at the Department of Labor. It was kind of overwhelming, being around so many educated people. I decided I had to change my life, and I knew that I was the only one who could do that. So I brought back my sports discipline and drew on it as if I was training again to compete. I worked my butt off studying for the GREs, and I got into Georgetown.

I got a master's in corporate communications and public relations. I graduated with almost a 4.0, because this time academic success was my decision, and I was studying things I cared about. For the first time, I felt like one of the smart ones.

I had always been good with people, and I knew I wanted to go into an industry where I could use my strengths. I got a job with a big PR firm and worked there for six months.

I saw so many people starting their own firms, and I remembered how I felt walking into the gym for the first time. I thought that if they could do it, I could do it, too. My parents were very supportive and gave me the courage to start my own firm. That was four years ago. I'm very lucky. I've done very well.

Seeing how proud my parents are of me, I realize it doesn't matter how smart you are or how good your grades were. All that matters is how much drive you have and how good an executor you are. That's the key to being successful. It's true in sports, and it's true in business. If you have ambition and you have drive and you can execute, you'll be successful.

You can't assume things will come to you. You have to go after them. You have to force yourself to work harder than other people, and harder than you ever have. You can't let yourself get discouraged. You can't ever give up. I did this with dance and acrobatics for years before I started doing it in other aspects of my life.

The kids who went to high school with me probably thought I'd be a failure in life. They'd be surprised.

My dad, Carlos, didn't have a college degree. He left Cuba when he was seven and started out driving a truck in

Mexico. Twenty-five years later, he was the CEO. He told me how he always set goals for himself. First he said, "I'm going to be the manager of the trucks," and then he said, "I'm going to be the manager of the Mexican group," and he just kept setting new goals. Now my dad says, "We're so proud of you. You've set such high goals."

Radha and Miki Agrawal: The Legendary Soccer Twins

Radha and Miki Agrawal are serial entrepreneurs and identical twins. The sisters have cofounded five projects. Their biggest is Super Sprowtz, a children's entertainment movement focused on healthy eating. They've produced more than twenty-five videos designed to show kids, in a fun way, how vegetables have "superpowers." Several of the videos feature Sam Kass, former chef at the White House, and Michelle Obama.

Radha is the CEO of Super Sprowtz. She's also a cofounder of Daybreaker, a global morning-dance movement, and Thinx, an underwear company that benefits women in developing countries (whose motto is "Change your underwear, change the world"). Miki is the CEO of Wild, farm-to-table pizzerias in New York City and Las Vegas. Miki is also the author of *Do Cool Sh*t: Quit Your Day Job, Start Your Own Business, and Live Happily Ever After.*

Radha told me, "We love to organize experiences that we hope will change the world. We were so influenced by our mom, who showed us, through her passion and determination and drive, how to make a difference."

They have one sister, Yuri, who's a year older, went to Harvard, and is a surgeon. The twins' mom, Mire Kimura, is from Japan; their dad, Raj Agrawal, is an aeronautical engineer from India.

I've known Radha for a few years, but I never knew that she and her sister were known as the legendary Soccer Twins. They played soccer in high school, and played all four years they were at Cornell. Radha was a striker, and Miki was an outside midfielder. Radha told me how they got started, and how important soccer became to them:

Yuri was enrolled in a soccer program when she was five, and one day we went to see her game. Miki and I were both so excited, we wanted to play, and we ran onto the field. The coach had to stop the game.

But our parents saw how much we loved it, so they organized a soccer team for us. Then they not only drove us to practice, they organized the practice and coached our team. For eight years, my dad was our coach and my mom was an assistant coach until we started playing on higher-level teams and doing travel soccer.

We had three hours of soccer practice every day, our whole life. You have to be so disciplined. You really learn to be organized and focused. And you learn the politics of teamwork, and what it takes to be the captain. It's not just all the work when you play sports in college—it's all the work you put in before you get to college.

But Radha told me that grit was something she and Miki learned from their mom's personal story even before they learned it from sports:

We were born and raised in Montreal. My mom told us that all kids go to school seven days a week. For ten years we went to Japanese school on Saturdays and Hindi school on Sundays. So we speak four languages. We didn't come to the U.S. until college.

My mom's story inspires me with her spontaneous adventurousness and her willingness to pursue her dreams. She went to Ottawa from Japan to go to grad school for a year, and met my dad there. He'd come from New Delhi to get a PhD. They were both supposed to return home after their education.

My mom came from a wealthy family. My dad came from a merchant family. He arrived in Canada with $5, which he spent on a winter coat from the Salvation Army. He got a loan from a bank to take my mom on their first date.

Despite knowing that her parents were adamantly opposed to their marriage—her mom didn't come to the wedding—my mom chose love. She drove herself to her wedding, and on the way she got a flat tire and changed the tire in her wedding dress. And she married my dad.

To me, that's hugely inspiring—that love is all that matters. My mom was always the woman who took a chance. If my mom saw a hole, she filled it. She showed me that if you want something done, you do it yourself. You don't wait for others to do it for you.

Blake and Paige Mycoskie: Sharing Support, Sharing Struggles

We met Paige Mycoskie, founder of Aviator Nation, in rule 1, about nurturing kids' passions. If Paige's last name looked familiar when you first saw it, maybe that's because you've heard of her older brother, Blake Mycoskie, the founder of TOMS, a shoe company that gives a pair of shoes to a child in need for every pair of shoes someone buys. They have a younger brother, Tyler, who works with Blake. We've already met their mom, Pam, who was unconditionally encouraging when Paige dropped everything in her twenties and moved back home to learn how to sew. Their dad, Mike, is an orthopedic surgeon in Arlington, Texas.

Pam told me that all three kids learned to compete and work hard when they were young. Like many other entrepreneurs, Blake and Paige grew up as avid athletes:

Sports played a big role in the kids' lives when they were in school. Blake played tennis, and our family was always there at tournaments to support him.

Paige played all sports, but her biggest sport during high school was volleyball. Her team won the state championship. Our family traveled all around with her.

And we all supported Tyler at his paintball tournaments.

It taught them the importance of supporting each other. We told them, "We're supporting your sibling. Your turn will come."

We lived in a tennis neighborhood in Texas, and when Blake was seven, he just decided he wanted to play. He started riding his bike to the club every day. Eventually we got some good coaches for him.

Blake wasn't the best, but he was always the most self-motivated. I never had to push him. He got the award for being the hardest worker on the team his senior year in high school, even though he wasn't the top player.

Blake's passion evolved from sports to business, and in this he was like many other athletes who became entrepreneurs. He had earned a tennis scholarship to SMU, but when an injury to his Achilles tendon forced him to quit, he started EZ Laundry, a campus-based dry cleaning business, which eventually expanded from SMU to other campuses in Texas.

According to Pam, "Blake kept looking for the next thing":

He founded an outdoor billboard company in Nashville called Mycoskie Media, which he sold to Clear Channel. Then he and Paige competed in the second season of The Amazing Race, *missing first place by four minutes. Next he started a reality cable TV network called Reality Central.*

Every time Blake launched a new business, Pam told me, she and her husband reacted somewhat differently:

Mike always said, "Maybe you should think about it." But I always said, "Wow, that's great!"

"I was always the cheerleader," Pam said, and she went on to tell me what I've heard from so many other moms whose kids grew up to become entrepreneurs:

Whatever the kids chose to do, I encouraged them. I don't think kids realize at the time how important it is to have your family support whatever you want to do. Just because your child isn't the valedictorian or number one player, it's your enthusiasm and support for them that matters.

Aside from her family's belief system and closeness, Pam thought another experience influenced her children's approach to life:

The kids saw me struggle with, but not give up on, a big project—writing a book. I found out that I had high cholesterol, and I had to change my diet. I wanted to share how I got my cholesterol down, so I wrote a book with recipes for how to cook with less fat, Butter Busters.

I didn't know anything about writing a book, and I didn't know anything about the publishing industry. The kids packed up the books with me on the dining room table. We started out borrowing $60,000 to self-publish it.

Another mom might have hidden how much she was struggling, not wanting to upset her children. But Pam chose to share her experience with them. Her kids learned that everyone has to deal with problems—and that, with grit, problems can be tackled head on.

The book ended up selling one and a half million copies. Blake went on to write a book, *Start Something That Matters*, and for every book purchased, he gives a new book to a child in need. "He wrote about my cookbook experience in his book," Pam told me. "When I read what he wrote, I realized that watching me struggle had had a positive impact. They thought, *If our mom can write a book and get it published and have it be a big success, then we can succeed with our dreams too.*"

LEARNING TO FAIL

A key difference between entrepreneurs and successful people in other fields has to do with their attitude toward failure. People in law, medicine, banking, government, and retail hope to avoid failure at all costs, but people who become entrepreneurs tend to view failure as a positive experience. They believe they've learned and grown from their failures, and that their failures have increased the probability of their success over the long term.

Athletes tell you how important it is to set "reach goals," even if they don't meet them, because it keeps them focused on the end result. Entrepreneurs know this too. They strive; they fail; they change their approach; they work harder. Athletes learn to be focused; they're disciplined. After each failure, they try again. They never give up.

As Billie Jean King put it, "I don't call it failure, I call it feedback."

People often are under the impression that successful adults experienced a lot of success as children. But much of the time, that's not true. Many *became* successful adults because they learned how to deal with failure. Goldman Sachs president Gary Cohn struggled in school and in his early jobs: "My upbringing allowed me to be comfortable with failure. The one trait in a lot of dyslexic people I know is that by the time we got out of college, our ability to deal with failure was highly developed. And so we look at most situations and see much more of the upside than the downside. Because we're so accustomed to the downside. It doesn't faze us" (Gladwell 2013, 123). In his book *David and Goliath*, Malcolm Gladwell observes that many other successful businessmen—Richard Branson, Charles Schwab, Craig McCaw, John Chambers—struggled with dyslexia, which helped them learn not to be afraid of failure. Many of the entrepreneurs I spoke to learned that lesson through sports.

In *Building Resilience in Children and Teens* (2015), Kenneth Ginsburg writes that many parents won't address the fact their kids have failed because they want them to feel good about themselves. They think they're helping their kids because they believe that shielding children from failure will keep them from feeling sad. In fact, it's the reverse. We don't do our children a favor by protecting them from realizing they could have done better.

As Dr. Ginsburg observes, "Most parents worry terribly when children fail at something...so we respond by saying and doing anything to brighten their moods. We deny it was a failure.... We blame someone else or reassure the child, 'It just wasn't your fault.'... Responses like these are...misguided because they send the message that feeling bad is a disaster." He goes on to say, "Rather than cheering up a child every time he experiences failure or disappointment, we should focus on resilience. We all have failures. Resilient people learn a bit from every failure. They learn how to do better the next time. They are persistent. They use those bad feelings to motivate themselves a little more" (2015, 114).

There is a great quote from Maya Angelou about failure: "Courage allows the successful woman to fail, and learn powerful lessons from the failure so that in the end, she did not fail at all."

Clemson management professor Wayne Stewart looked at serial entrepreneurs—adrenaline-driven men and women who start business after business (Bounds, Sporz, and Flandez 2007). He found that those who'd started three or more businesses share common traits:

- They had a higher propensity for risk, innovation, and achievement.

- They were less afraid of failure.

- They were more able to recover when they did fail.

I believe their attitude toward failure is traceable to how they were raised, and what their parents and their mentors—whomever they looked up to—taught them about failure: that it's just one step on the pathway to success.

Elliott Bisnow: Ready for a Rematch

This was my son Elliott's favorite quote, which he had on his wall during high school. He hadn't heard people talk about grit, but that's what it's about. It's Teddy Roosevelt's famous "daring greatly" philosophy:

> It is not the critic who counts;
> not the man who points out how the strong man stumbles,
> or where the doer of deeds could have done them better.
> The credit belongs to the man who is actually in the arena,
> whose face is marred by dust and sweat and blood;
> who strives valiantly;
> who errs;
> who comes short again and again...
> who at the best knows in the end the triumph of high achievement,
> and who at the worst, if he fails, at least fails while daring greatly,
> so that his place shall never be with those cold and timid souls
> who neither know victory nor defeat.

I thought I was raising a tennis player when he was in school, but as I look back, it turns out I was raising an entrepreneur. I just didn't realize at the time that playing a highly competitive sport like tennis at a serious level nurtures the same skills.

Elliott loved all sports growing up and played everything when he was young: baseball, basketball, soccer, football. Around the time he was twelve, he decided he wanted to focus on tennis. The key words in that sentence are "he decided." We didn't push it—in fact, we were surprised, and it was a bit of a hard sell. ("You want to take a private lesson every week for *how much?*")

But he pushed—to take more private lessons, to get into a more challenging clinic, to practice more frequently, to spend the summers in tennis camps, to start playing tournaments. We saw how focused and determined he was, and how much he loved it, and recognized that the daily grind of hours on the tennis court was what made his heart sing, so we went along with it.

When he started playing seriously, all the top kids his age were already playing regional and even national tournaments. I said, "I'm not taking you to an out-of-town tournament until you win a local tournament!" I didn't realize I was giving him a goal and inspiring him to work harder; I just didn't see the point.

Elliott single-mindedly fought his way up to a national ranking of thirty-five in the country in the juniors by the time he was eighteen. At first, he lost almost every match. But after each loss, he picked himself up and said, "I know what I did wrong; I'll beat him next time." I didn't appreciate it then, but that was perfect training to become a successful entrepreneur: learning to lose; figuring out why you lost; determining what lessons should be applied next time; changing your strategy; not getting discouraged; and trying again.

Maja Kermath: Learning to Live an Inspired Life

Sports teach every athlete differently. Elliott started a very competitive sport relatively late, losing many matches the first several years. It taught him resilience, determination, focus, the correlation between preparedness and success, and especially how to deal with setbacks. On the other hand, if you're really good, think of yourself as a star, and aren't used to losing, you learn very different lessons. Maja Kermath told me that one of her most crucial lessons was when she lost her college tennis scholarship.

Maja was born in Communist Poland, but her family left as refugees, emigrating first to Australia and then to the U.S. She and her parents and her younger brother lived in Spokane and Chicago before settling in Champaign, Illinois. "Our journey exposed me to different people, places, and environments," she told me. "I'm definitely a product of the American dream."

One constant for Maja, as she negotiated the twists and turns of adjusting to a new country, was tennis. "I was always athletic," she said. "In high school, I took two lunch periods so I could get my homework done and play tennis after school. I was the top player in the state, and I was getting straight A's." But she was also getting no small amount of flak:

> I was always fighting a battle. I thought I knew how we could change the way things were done in order to improve them. And I would tell people in charge how they could do things better.
>
> The school was furious with me and wanted to hold me back to punish me. But I always knew my parents had my back when I was fighting my teachers or my principal or my tennis coach. My mom sat down with the principal and convinced them to let me go ahead. It gave me the confidence to know I could do anything I set my mind to.
>
> Tennis also gave me confidence. There's nothing more powerful than to know you have all the tools you need to

control your destiny. I'll never forget the moment I realized this. It was quadruple match point to become the state champ, and I knew I was not going to fail. I had trained endless hours for that one shot. I knew I'd hit it. And I did.

After high school, Maja went to Creighton University and played D-1 tennis on a scholarship. That's where she learned for the first time about failure:

Suddenly I wasn't a star anymore. In high school, I didn't lose a match in three years. In college, everybody was better than I was, and I kept losing.

Looking back, I know now that I was very difficult. I had a really bad attitude. I had arrived thinking I was the best thing since sliced bread, and I didn't have the capacity to deal with that kind of failure.

The pivotal moment for me was when they pulled my scholarship. I reacted from my ego and said, "Then I quit the team!"

The thing that defined me—I was a tennis player—had just been taken away. I called my parents, and I was crying so hard. My parents told me to use what had happened as a learning experience.

It was a really painful time for me, but I learned that you have to be humble, and that you're always replaceable. If I had to do it all over again, I'd have sucked it up, earned the respect of the coaches, and played the last two years. It's one of the biggest life lessons I've ever had.

In time, the experience taught Maja not to be afraid to fail. She grew to realize that facing failure gave her courage and strength. And she needed plenty of both when she faced a critical juncture in her career. She had earned an MBA degree from the University of Illinois and gone to work for AT&T:

I kept rising in the ranks, getting promoted, and buying lots of stuff I thought I should have, including a Saab and a beach house. I always knew I wanted to start my own company. But I knew I needed to learn about how to run a company and thought I could do that by working at a great company and keeping my eyes open.

One day, I flew to another city to talk to a roomful of entrepreneurs about how they could try to land a deal with us. That evening, I got on a plane to fly home, and it was the first moment I'd had all day to be without anyone who knew me, and I just started sobbing. I was so unhappy with my life. I didn't understand where the tears were coming from. My whole life I'd done everything everybody had asked of me—the Division 1 school, the MBA, the Saab, the house on the beach. Why was I so miserable if I had what I should want?

I decided I needed to compare how I wanted to spend my time with how I actually was spending my time. I knew I needed to change what I was doing.

I wanted to be living an inspired life, from what I was putting in my body to what I was putting on my body. I wanted to achieve wellness, and to be happy.

Maja left Los Angeles—and AT&T—for Texas. In Austin, she launched Kor180, a lifestyle brand that franchises studios featuring Pilates, cycling, and wellness. She didn't know anyone there, she told me, but she had a "gut feeling" that Austin was the place for her to be:

From a sad moment, I created a modern wellness franchise. My dad was my first investor. He was the first person I called. I laid out my plan. He said, "Give me forty-five minutes while I talk to your mother." He called back and said, "We're in."

The six months after we launched were the most difficult of my life—emotionally, spiritually, and financially. Every day as an entrepreneur, you lurch from one extreme to the other. My family got me through. They believed I could do great things and always told me that I could do anything I put my mind to. Who am I to launch the next billion-dollar business? But then again, why not me?

In *David and Goliath* (2013), Malcolm Gladwell says, "Courage is not something that you already have that makes you brave when the tough times start. Courage is what you earn when you've been through the tough times and you discover they aren't so tough after all" (149). If you are not afraid to fail, you are more willing to risk everything for a big idea. You ask yourself, "What's the worst that can happen?" And after you analyze the worst possible outcome, you say to yourself, "Yeah, I can live with that."

An astonishing number of these successful entrepreneurs played sports at a very competitive level. Their dogged pursuit of excellence was a key ingredient in their later entrepreneurial success: they learned how to compete; they understood the direct correlation between hard work and results; they learned how to prepare, to "survey the course" or "review the game films"; and they learned to win with humility.

Other future entrepreneurs learned these lessons by competing in nonathletic pursuits: by acting or singing, or by entering art contests, academic contests, or sales competitions. Reggie Aggarwal learned it through debate and running for student office.

Reggie Aggarwal: Everything on the Line

In the space of less than a decade, Reggie Aggarwal went from being a thirty-three-year-old forced to move back in with his parents after his company failed to becoming a model leader who turned the same company around and raised its value to well over a billion dollars.

Reggie's company, Cvent, was founded in 1999 to provide companies with software to help them register people for events. Starting with $17 million in funding, Reggie grew the company quickly, and by 2000 had 125 employees. But when the dot-com bubble burst, the company had only $1.5 million in revenue. Reggie couldn't cover his costs, and he couldn't raise any more money.

Like many other successful founders, Reggie refused to throw in the towel. He decided it was time to pivot from fast growth to cost-cutting. He let 100 employees go, gave up his salary for two and a half years, and asked his remaining employees to wear multiple hats and even double up in hotel rooms when they took to the road on business.

"We were the walking dead for three years," he told me. "But I powered through it for my team. I refused to give up. I had 120 investors—I couldn't let them down. I was so focused on surviving, two years flew by."

Cvent turned the corner in 2003. By 2008, revenue was growing at an annual rate of 30 percent. In 2011, Reggie raised $136 million in venture capital and finally cashed out his original investors, who'd been waiting twelve years. Cvent went public in 2013, and today the company operates in more than ninety countries, has 2,000 employees, and brings in annual revenues of $200 million.

When I asked Reggie how he had found the courage to persist through that hard time, he told me that he'd first learned to deal with failure as a member of his high school debate team:

> I had played sports, but I wasn't great. For me, the real competition came from debate, where I developed the single-minded focus to win. I joined the team my freshman year and really experienced the thrill of competition. It was the first time I did something I wanted to that I didn't have to. The competition was one on one. It got me excited about learning, about winning.

He had two debate coaches, both women, who were hugely influential and became great mentors. Most weekends, he traveled with them to tournaments all over the country. Debating was his whole life for three years. He told me that he learned to analyze his losses and figure out how to improve. "Putting myself in a competitive environment trained me for the battle of business," he said.

In his senior year of high school, he ran for student body president, and won. He also ran for office in college and was elected vice president of the student body at the University of Virginia. He found running for office similar to debating. "You put everything on the line," he said. "You really have to believe in yourself to put yourself out there." These days, he said, when he recruits college graduates for his business, he looks for people who have run for office.

Reggie told me that he'd never really wanted to work for anyone else, and so to earn money the summer of his junior year in college, he bought a franchise that employed students to paint houses. Little did he know what good preparation the experience would be for running Cvent:

> I jumped right in, had twelve employees, and was working ninety hours a week. The first couple months, I was losing money. I didn't want to give up and disappoint my employees. Finally, the last weeks of the summer, I got a couple big jobs, and we made money.

Reggie said his parents encouraged him, too:

> When things didn't go well, my dad would always say, "You're measured by how high you bounce after you fall." And my mom was instrumental in helping me push through failure. She always said, "Failure is a life experience that makes you stronger, so just learn from it, and jump into the next adventure."

After graduating from college, Reggie went to law school at Georgetown and then joined a law firm. He found the courage to leave after meeting some successful entrepreneurs and realizing that if they could strike out on their own, so could he:

> I learned they were no different from me. They didn't have connections. They weren't smarter. But I saw that they were willing to take a risk and willing to stick with it, no matter how tough. So I walked away from eight years in law.
>
> My motto has been "Be persistent, be consistent." It gave me the strength to get through the tough times for four years. It was really trench warfare.
>
> Now nothing scares me anymore. I learned that whether you win or lose, you get confidence. That gave me the courage to power through.

Not all of the entrepreneurs I talked to were competitive: a lot of the "tech geeks" simply got really good at computers, while some of the artists were intent on perfecting their craft, or whatever their passion was. But for many entrepreneurs, learning to compete was key. It led to their desire to compete in their professional lives. And it led to their not being afraid to fail, which led to their willingness to take risks.

Starbucks founder Howard Schultz says, "The difference between winning and losing—or between success and failure—is that gray area of perseverance and will" (Graft 2012). When entrepreneurs learn while they're young to compete—and even more important, not to fear failure—it makes them stronger. It creates indefatigable competitors.

Don't Worry About Straight A's

Many kids, even though they're smart, don't do well in school because they have learning styles or interests or temperaments that are not a good fit with teachers' expectations. These issues can persist from kindergarten all the way through college. If a college student is smart but not in the right learning environment to succeed, the parents may exert pressure for the student to stay enrolled—and stay miserable. But as we'll see, parents can make different choices, and their child can find a different path.

Let me tell you about conversations I had with three loving moms who meant well.

The first mother's son had dropped out of college, but then, under pressure from his parents, had reenrolled and was studying history. His mother admitted that her son didn't even like history, but he'd needed to pick something.

"Nothing really motivates him," she told me. Her distress was clear.

"Nothing? There isn't anything he loves?"

"Only one thing," she said, reluctantly and with a hint of sarcasm. "Video games. He plays video games every second of his spare time." And then she added, "He's really, really good."

"So maybe he should pursue a career in video gaming," I said.

She looked at me as though I were speaking a foreign language—because, to her, it was.

This mother was trying, with good intentions, to get her son to walk the safe path of earning a college degree, but it never occurred to her that gaming is a multibillion-dollar global industry that employs people like her son in high-salary jobs. There are opportunities in game design, graphics, coding, software engineering, and other areas.

I tried again. "Would you consider taking the money you're spending on tuition and using it to support him while he works at Electronic Arts or Sony as an unpaid intern for a year?"

She had no idea that gaming technology has applications in traditional fields. She didn't realize that people her son's age have started their own companies on the basis of their passion for and expertise in gaming science and technology. She didn't know that many of these young people have become quite successful. She thought her son would be better off if he got a college degree in a subject he didn't care about.

The second mother's son had also dropped out of college, and he too had reenrolled under pressure from his parents. He had chosen Japanese as his major.

"Why Japanese?" I asked her.

She told me that their family had lived in Japan when her son was young, so he was already bilingual. Besides, she said, he couldn't think of anything else.

"But isn't there anything that he loves?"

"He loves cars. He tinkers with them every day in his free time."

"Then why is he studying Japanese instead of pursuing a career in the automotive industry?"

But I already knew the answer—we reward our children for conforming, even when they're failing, and even when their failure is making them unhappy.

"Tinkering with cars isn't a college major," his mother pointed out.

"But automotive and mechanical engineering and automotive design are often college majors," I countered. "What if your son contacted all the Japanese car companies in the U.S. to see if they have internships or programs for career development? Or what if he applied to colleges that offer a degree in automotive design?"

I hoped his mom would try to imagine what could happen if she encouraged her son to walk away and tinker with cars. The alternative was to force him into conforming to a standard that might look good on paper but would ultimately lead him to fail. What if, instead, she helped him find a life that he could love and excel in?

The third mom had a daughter in high school. The girl was a passionate and accomplished musician, and she was about to start applying to colleges. Her parents had been very supportive of her interest in music, giving her music lessons and sending her to music camps.

"So will your daughter major in music?" I asked.

"No," the girl's mom replied. "I told her she has to major in something *real* so she can get a job and support herself."

This mother wasn't trying to be mean. She wanted to protect her daughter from the cold realities of the job market. And that's perfectly understandable. But I think it's misguided. We all want our kids to have financial security, but why send them the message that they need to be protected rather than inspired? That they're not good enough to make a living doing what they love? That they have to settle?

Many future entrepreneurs grow up learning to pursue their passions and follow their dreams. This mom—again, with every good intention—was teaching her daughter a very different lesson.

These three moms wanted their kids to follow a conventional academic path. That's fine for some, but their kids weren't thriving. They thought their kids should major in subjects they didn't care about and had no aptitude in. They thought their kids should prepare themselves for a traditional career they probably wouldn't be very good at. There is another way.

SCHOOLS DON'T ALWAYS NURTURE ENTREPRENEURS

Some children who grow up to become entrepreneurs have habits that most schools don't value. They question the rules and challenge authority. They want to do things their own way. They get bored and lose focus when the task at hand doesn't interest them. And what does that mean?

- It means they often aren't happy in school.

- It means some teachers may not like them very much.

- It means nobody at school is mentoring them, because they don't see how special they are.

- It means they aren't getting a lot of positive feedback at school.

Schools, of course, teach necessary academic and social skills, but to some extent they also reward behavior that is diametrically opposed to what's needed for entrepreneurial success. And, as one mom I talked with pointed out, schools often put more emphasis on remediating kids' weaknesses than they do on finding and supporting kids' strengths. That approach can be devastating to a youngster with an entrepreneurial mind-set: a kid who learns in ways that are determined by her passions, rather than by an academic schedule, a teacher's checklist, or a standardized test.

Some children do have serious learning issues. They may need medical attention or even a special type of school. But other kids, particularly boys, may simply have a lot of energy. After all, five-year-olds haven't always been labeled "hyperactive" or been medicated with Ritalin or made to feel there was something wrong with them just because they didn't feel like sitting still in a circle and hanging on their teacher's every word.

Benny Blanco: Not a Problem

Benny Blanco, whose given name is Benjamin Levin, is one of the top pop songwriters and music producers in America. He was one of three people named Songwriter of the Year at the 2013 BMI Pop Music Awards. He's a multiplatinum songwriter who has written and produced over twenty number-one hits, such as "Moves Like Jagger."

Benny and his older brother Jeremy, who now manages songwriters, producers, and artists with Benny, were born in Plano, Texas, and moved with their parents to L.A., where Benny went to a Montessori preschool. Then the family moved to Reston, Virginia, outside D.C., where Benny, by then a kindergartner, enrolled in public school. Their mother, Sandy, a social worker, is the admissions director at a senior assisted living facility.

Sandy told me that his kindergarten teacher wasn't happy with his inability to sit quietly in a circle. Sandy told me, "His teachers used to call me every day complaining that Benny couldn't sit still."

Sandy's response was succinct: "So?"

This, of course, is not a normal parental response. Most parents who receive a single report like that, even for a child still in kindergarten, quickly fall into line and try to "fix" the "problem." But Sandy didn't mind that Benny was different, and her response to his kindergarten teacher is typical of how she raised her son for the next twenty years. When Benny couldn't do something (and often he couldn't), or when he didn't conform to the expected norms, she said, "So?" And she meant it. Then she focused instead on what Benny was doing well.

Unsurprisingly, Benny was later diagnosed with ADHD. And so Sandy, who had been willing to stand up to Benny's kindergarten teacher, also spent many hours trying to help him. She took him to doctors, to meetings for kids with ADHD, to meetings with his teachers and counselors in the hope of getting him more engaged in school, and to special meetings where she fought for kids with ADHD to be allowed extra time on standardized tests. And she kept trying to redirect his boundless energy—into the theater, into music lessons—even listening to the lyrics and music he was writing, including rap music, which she hated.

What do you think when you hear that a twenty-five-year-old has twenty-five pop hits under his belt? You may think he's a musical prodigy, or that he has industry connections, or that something extraordinary must have catapulted him to the top of his field. But Benny was anything but a child prodigy, and he didn't have an easy go of it. What was extraordinary was how his mom anchored him.

What Sandy did was assure Benny that there are more important things than mastering a specific skill by a specific deadline, and she didn't question him for not conforming. In fact, she sent him a reassuring message when she reacted to the "problem" by saying "So?" It was clear that she really believed what she was saying, which meant that Benny believed it, too. How many careers require the skill of sitting quietly in a circle? How many careers require the fine-motor skills of coloring between the lines and writing neatly?

Sandy's unwavering belief in Benny gave him permission to feel good about himself even when he came in for criticism at school. And later on, when she supported his songwriting talent, she sent him that important message again and again. Benny's mom didn't know it at the time, but even when he was five years old, she was laying the foundation for his future success by not letting him see his perceived deficits as problems. Incidentally, by the time Benny finished kindergarten, his teacher had come to recognize that he was a truly special kid. She told Sandy that she wouldn't be surprised if he became president one day.

Today, even though Benny didn't graduate from college, he's a frequent guest lecturer at the Clive Davis Institute at NYU's Tisch School of the Arts. As Sandy told me, Benny likes to say that he always knew he'd do something with music if he just kept at it and was annoying enough.

Dhani Jones: Stealth Superstar

Dhani Jones was an All-American college football linebacker at the University of Michigan, earning All-Big Ten honors for three straight seasons, as he, Heisman trophy winner Charles Woodson, Brian Griese, and Tom Brady were an unstoppable combination for the Wolverines. After Michigan, Dhani went on to play in the NFL for eleven seasons, with the Giants, the Eagles, and finally the Cincinnati Bengals, where he made his permanent home.

When his football career ended, he started a series on the Travel Channel, *Dhani Tackles the Globe*, which followed him around the world as he learned to play various international sports while exploring the culture in each location. And as if that weren't enough, he opened the Bow Tie Cafe in a historic Cincinnati neighborhood. He is also a founding partner of VMG Creative, a New York creative agency with clients like Michael Kors, Capital One, and Estée Lauder.

Impressive, right? So when I talked with Dhani's mom, Nancy, an anesthesiologist, the first thing I wanted to know was whether Dhani had always been a superstar.

"No," Nancy said. "There were so many talented kids in his class, he didn't really stand out."

I was stunned. Dhani Jones didn't stand out in high school?

When Dhani was younger, Nancy explained, he'd mostly participated in individual sports like swimming, tennis, and wrestling. He didn't play football until high school. He started on the varsity team as a sophomore, and he played steadily. His team reached the state championship twice, and Dhani himself was recruited by top college football teams.

"His high school coach must have loved him, right?" I asked.

Nancy said she didn't know. A player could tell how much the coach valued him when the coach gave him the day's "game ball," she said, which meant that the coach recognized him as the day's outstanding player. Dhani had always hoped to get the game ball, Nancy told me. It became an important symbol to him, but during three consistently great seasons, he never got it—until the last game of his senior year. According to Nancy, Dhani's coach explained the oversight by saying, "He's so consistently good, I guess I forgot to recognize him."

But Dhani wasn't just a good football player. He was a good student, too—good enough to be accepted at the University of Michigan on the strength of his academic performance alone. Was he a favorite of his teachers?

"No," Nancy said, "not really. You see, he always asked a lot of questions. Sometimes you're not a favorite of the teachers when you ask a lot of questions. You'd think that wouldn't be a problem with teachers or coaches, to have a kid who always questions them."

Looking at things differently, wanting to shake things up, may not make you a teacher's pet, but it can help make you a great entrepreneur.

WHAT PARENTS CAN DO

I want to reiterate that many successful entrepreneurs were also very successful students. Lots of the entrepreneurs in this book breezed through Ivy League schools and got advanced degrees. This is for the parents of the kids who aren't doing well—or who are, but who aren't happy.

None of this is to say that you shouldn't help your children succeed in school—education is important. Many of the entrepreneurs in this book were great students, and didn't need help, but for those who weren't, I saw that there's plenty you can do to compensate and help them grow up in a confident and fearless way. As we'll see, a lot depends on why a child isn't doing well in school, and on what parents are doing for them outside school. When moms get it right, their kids thrive.

Jeff Marx: Not By the Book

Jeff Marx is the cowriter of *Avenue Q*, winner of the Tony Awards' triple crown—best score, best book, and best musical. Years after it opened, *Avenue Q* is still playing in New York and around the world. A song that Jeff cowrote for the "It Gets Better" campaign was featured in an episode of *Glee*. He also cowrote four songs for *Scrubs*, one of which, "Everything Comes Down to Poo," was nominated for an Emmy.

Jeff, born in Chicago to a pediatric dentist (his dad) and a dental hygienist (his mom), was raised in Florida with three younger sisters who did well in school (Traci, who has a PhD in psychology; Jamie, who has a master's in education; and Julie, who has a master's in counseling).

For all his success as an adult, Jeff struggled at school. Here's what his mom Wendy told me:

> *If there's one mistake I made when Jeff was little, it's that I let him start kindergarten when he was so young because he was already reading. That meant that all through school he was always the youngest, the smallest, and the least coordinated, and nobody ever wanted him on their team. He always found an excuse not to be on the playground because he was always the last one picked. He says he's going to write a book someday called "And You Get Jeff." He didn't really fit in and didn't have many friends.*
>
> *When he was in sixth grade, we were called in to the principal's office, and all his teachers were there. They were preparing to "counsel him out." Jeff had the highest grade in his math class, but his math teacher said he was going to fail him anyway. He said, "I give him a zero every day because he won't do the homework." Jeff said, "If I'm already getting the highest grade in the class, why should I do the homework? It's a waste of time."*
>
> *Jeff's science teacher said, "If he were a sponge sitting on the counter, he'd absorb more than he does in my class." Jeff said, "I don't care about science!"*
>
> *Then his history teacher complained about Jeff's lack of interest, and Jeff said, "I don't care what the Sumerians did in 3000 BC!"*
>
> *For reading class, each student had been told to pick a biography and, as part of a book report, to illustrate the person in front of the class. Jeff wanted to read a book about John Lennon, and he was incredibly excited. He was going to dress like him, play the guitar, and sing "Imagine." But the*

reading teacher said she wouldn't allow it, that Lennon was completely unacceptable, and that Jeff had to pick another person. Jeff was devastated—Lennon was one of his heroes. He said, "There's nobody else I'm interested in."

The principal felt sorry for Jeff and suggested that if he wanted to sing, he should enter the school's talent show in a couple of weeks.

That changed everything, Wendy told me. It was Jeff's first public performance, and it was one of the highlights of his mom's life. He sang "Annie's Song" and accompanied himself on the guitar. Everybody was spellbound, Wendy said—people had tears in their eyes:

All of his teachers who had been so mean two weeks before came up to me and said, "We had no idea that he is so talented. We really apologize." The school's founder, who had never talked to me before, told me, "Jeff has the most perfect pitch I've ever heard."

Suddenly his classmates saw who he was and wanted to be his friend. After that, he found his place in the school through music. He was in the chorus, in the school musicals, and accompanied other performers.

Wendy wanted to nurture Jeff's talent, so she got him voice lessons with someone who had a musical group called The #1 Bar Mitzvah Band, which he invited Jeff to join. Jeff performed several times every weekend for nine years:

Girls at the shows would run after him, wanting his picture or phone number. He was like a rock star. It was a huge confidence booster.

Jeff had always loved music. I took him to lots of shows. He grew up knowing the scores of different musicals, and lots of pop music.

I'd played piano as a child, and I wanted all my children to play an instrument. But after Jeff had a few piano lessons, he said, "I have no interest in learning this, Mom. It's a waste of time."

Jeff also didn't want to learn to read music. So when he was a sophomore in high school, I bought him a fake book—it has the melody line and chords. I found two songs in the key of C. One was "Getting to Know You." We sat down at the piano. I said, "I'm going to play the melody line, and you play the chords."

A few hours later, Wendy said, she found Jeff at the piano, playing the songs with full orchestration up and down the keyboard. "I couldn't believe it," she told me. "It was better than I could ever play." Jeff had found his calling. "Just like that, he was a pianist," Wendy said. She soon got him started with a new piano teacher, who said, "Once in a generation, a kid comes along like this." A week later, Jeff accompanied his school choir on the piano, and a week after that he was playing for tips at a local restaurant.

But Jeff, like many kids who veer from conventional, school-approved paths to success, still had obstacles ahead of him. His mom supported him through all of them.

In high school, as in elementary school, he refused to do homework for subjects that didn't interest him. As the time drew near to apply to colleges, he knew that he wanted to major in musical theater so he could sing and act. "He still couldn't read music," Wendy said, "but he played brilliantly by ear." As part of his application to a scholarship program in the arts, he submitted a tape of himself playing four piano pieces. On the basis of that tape, several colleges wrote to Jeff and invited him to apply. Wendy told me what happened next:

I had an appointment with his school's college counselor. I went in with a list of the schools that had written to him and told her where Jeff was planning to apply.

She laughed at me and said, "Why would you think he'd get in there? We have honor students who get rejected by those schools."

I said, "They wrote and asked him to apply."

She replied, "You must be mistaken. Schools like that wouldn't want him."

So I showed her the letters. She was stunned.

To her surprise, he got into the University of Michigan musical theater program, but he was the worst dancer in the class. He had trouble remembering the routines because he had never danced before. Piano was also hard because he'd never learned to read music. And he never got cast in any of the plays, so he graduated with no acting experience. One professor told him he'd never make it in theater.

As a result, Wendy said, Jeff decided to become an entertainment lawyer, and he enrolled at the Cardozo School of Law. But he didn't like law school any more than he'd liked any other school, except when he wrote lyrics for *Law Revue*, the school's annual musical, which spoofs the professors and legal topics. One of the deans, Frank Macchiarola, worked with Jeff on his songs, saw his talent, and eventually became an investor in *Avenue Q*. "Without his encouragement," Wendy told me, "Jeff wouldn't have finished law school. Basically, *Law Revue* was all he did. He told me, 'I'll finish, but I don't want to do it after I graduate.'"

Jeff passed the New York bar exam and then decided to apply to the three-year BMI Lehman Engel Musical Theatre Workshop in New York. He was accepted as a lyricist, and finally found himself in an academic program where he could thrive, and where he began to write music and lyrics. It was here that he met Robert Lopez, and together they won a portion of the $150,000 annual Ed Kleban Prize for promising lyricists.

"I always believed in him," Wendy told me:

> Jeff brought me as his date on the red carpet at the Tonys, at the Emmys, and at the Grammys. My life is so amazing, I have to pinch myself. He took us onto the Paramount lot when they taped Glee. We went to a church where the Gay Men's Chorus of L.A. sang one of his songs. He arranged for us to meet President Obama.
>
> I'm so proud of Jeff and the person he is—a generous, thoughtful, multitalented, brilliant, creative person. We always supported what he wanted, and somehow he found his own route.

Jaclyn Mason: True Grit

Jaclyn Mason is the owner of Charm Georgetown, a success-ful boutique in Washington, D.C. Growing up, she had a terrible time in school. In fact, she told me, she was always changing schools because the schools were always asking her to leave.

Jaclyn's academic troubles were due to her learning disabili-ties. When she was young, she said, learning specialists told her mom, JoAnn, that her daughter would never be able to succeed in a mainstream school.

But JoAnn refused to accept that conclusion. Jaclyn told me that her mom was always a very involved and proactive parent who decided to help her daughter catch up with her classmates. Almost every day after school, JoAnn took Jaclyn to speech and language therapy specialists to help her learn to read. Jaclyn was pushed to the limit, she said, but she persevered, and she did finally catch up.

Today Jaclyn does all the buying for her store, which features jewelry, accessories, decorative gifts, and other items. She keeps up with fashion trends, and she's in charge of marketing and social media for her business. She earned her success by working hard, but she also had a mom who believed in her and did what was necessary to help her.

Jenna Arnold: Different Learning

Jenna Arnold is a highly successful entrepreneur in her early thirties. She's so confident that it's hard to believe she ever struggled while she was growing up. But Jenna's mom, Lauren, talked openly with me about raising Jenna:

She was such a challenge—always a force of nature—but I knew her gift would reveal itself at some point. I learned that even though you only think one week at a time so you don't get overwhelmed, you have to keep the big picture in mind—children have their own life purpose.

On the day Jenna was born, she came out screaming, and she didn't sleep for eighteen months. I knew it would take more than me to make it work. I'd import cousins, friends, an extended family of forty to keep her soothed and entertained. I used to say to everyone, "Come help me out!" She was two years old, and I went to my room and cried my eyes out and thought, I can't do this.

I chose mentors early on. I also leaned heavily on my husband because I had my own active career. She was independent and self-sufficient as a result, and she saw a mother who worked hard to pay the bills, to contribute to society, to educate herself, and to raise a family.

When Jenna was in second grade, I realized she had learning differences. She'd been a leader among her friends before that, and she was in the most advanced reading group. I went to the parent-teacher conference not knowing anything was wrong. The teacher said, "She can't read like the others." I said, "Then why is she in the highest group, if she can't keep up?" The teacher said, "I want her to be popular— that's where her friends are. Don't worry. She's pretty. She can always be a model."

So I pulled her out of that school. We recognized her learning differences, embraced them, found the right schools, and built a network to support her. We helped start a lab school. Jenna credits her ability to manage a project, organize, and delegate to that school. They taught her the techniques to conquer her learning disability. After two years, we put her in a Quaker school because I knew that would protect her self-esteem.

She has one brother, Thomas, two years younger, also an entrepreneur, who lives in Dubai and does private equity projects in the region. Jenna went on to major in education at the University of Miami, where she won the top teaching award for her class, and then earned a master's in international peace education from Columbia. When she was twenty-five, she founded Press Play Productions, a content creation company, to educate people about important social issues through media.

Lauren recognized that she could meet only a small fraction of Jenna's needs, so she engaged others—a whole village—to help. Not all parents can start alternative schools when their children are floundering. But they can support their children by making sure they're getting the kind of help they need, and by being proud of what they are doing well.

Erica Ford: Voice for the Voiceless

Erica Ford, born in New York City, is regarded as one of her generation's top self-empowerment and antiviolence activists. In

2002, she cofounded LIFE (Love Ignites Freedom through Education) Camp and she serves as CEO. LIFE Camp's mission is to improve the lives of Black and Latino youth by providing them with tools to promote critical thinking and personal accountability. Erica also heads an antiviolence program in the South Jamaica neighborhood of Queens, and she works to build public-private partnerships to create summer jobs and reduce violence among young people, since homicide is the leading cause of death among New York City youth.

She grew up in Queens with one brother a year older. Their father died in Vietnam when Erica was only three, and from that time on, their mother, Doris, raised her children on her own.

Erica told me that every year, her mom got a note on her report card that read, "Erica talks too much." The school didn't know how to deal with her. Even so, "I was always a leader," Erica said, "whether hanging out on our bikes or in the community— maybe because I had a big mouth."

Doris did a lot to inspire confidence in her kids:

My mother allowed us to experience the world, to experience a lot of different places and things that allowed me to feel hope. She's from Panama, which we would visit in summers when we were little. We went to a lot of different countries in North and South America. I was always confident. Even hanging out in the community, I would walk through the drug dealers and gangs with confidence that nobody would do anything to me.

In all her years at school, Erica said, she had only one teacher who believed in her, but that teacher's encouragement had a huge impact:

My sixth grade teacher, Miss Landrum, convinced us that we could do anything and stand up to anyone if we did it right and were organized. It made a big difference in my life. That's why I do what I do today. Even in a small way, I know I can have a positive impact on kids' lives.

Erica has been an activist since she was eighteen years old. When she was twenty-one, she went to Geneva with the December 12 Movement International Secretariat, an organization that consults with the United Nations. There, she said, she was treated as if she were a head of state: "I suddenly realized that I really could make a difference."

Erica always knew that her mom supported her, even if her mom didn't always support her choices:

When I started doing what I do, my mother wasn't enthusiastic about it, but she supported me financially, which showed me she believed in me. When my mother would see me on TV doing a rally, since she was afraid of it—she came from a place of fear—she tried to convince me to do something else. But still, she kept supporting me. I couldn't have gotten where I am without her financial support.

She helped me survive financially, even though her mission was to protect me. I appreciate it even more now, knowing that even if my path wasn't her choice, she supported me anyhow. She wanted me to have a safe job, but she was still there for me.

My father was a sergeant in the Vietnam War, and I feel that willingness to fight for what he believed in—to fight for a better life—transferred to me.

In addition to the support of her mom and one teacher, Erica said, she had guidance from a lot of women in the community who were surrogate moms and helped mold her into the person she became:

I owe a lot to those women who looked after me and made sure I grew on the right path. They were the ones who really made me go back to school, because when I was talking in the back of the class, I wasn't learning what they were teaching in the front of the class. They helped me realize how important that was for me. So many different mothers contributed to my life!

Erica's mom always supported her, even when her teachers found her annoying. She encouraged Erica to find and use her voice, even if it was in a way she wouldn't have chosen.

For the last ten years, I've been so busy organizing! People always saw me with a bullhorn, and I was still the kid who got in trouble for talking too much. But if I'd listened to teachers who wanted me to be quiet, I wouldn't be what I am today—a voice for the voiceless.

WHAT SCHOOLS CAN DO

Some schools are beginning to realize that if students are allowed to pursue their passions instead of being forced to spend time studying subjects they hate, they will be more successful. This is the principle behind Blue School in Lower Manhattan, an independent progressive school for kids from age two through grade eight. Blue School was cofounded by Chris Wink, whom we met in the last chapter, and his friends Matt Goldman and Phil Stanton. The three of them are the cofounders of Blue Man Group, which they started to inspire creativity in their audiences and in themselves—for mutual learning and growth—and they transferred those values to a school where creativity is encouraged so that children can fall in love with the joy of learning. The school's credo is "It will be impossible to convince Blue

School children that their aspirations are unattainable. There will be no talking them out of pursuing their passions. There will be no way of fooling them into believing that the stirrings in their hearts are unimportant." Matt Goldman sees innovation as key to Blue School's mission. "Innovation does not happen in a vacuum," he says. "It typically requires people who have extraordinary skills, knowledge of the rules of diverse disciplines, and an added desire to integrate and break those rules. It is from this rule-breaking, 'trickster' energy that I believe true innovation grows" (Goldman 2013).

Most schools aren't like that. An article in *Brain, Child* by Rebecca Lanning (2013) talks of her struggles with her son whose learning issues made finishing high school a serious challenge. The author was extremely smart, well-informed, thoughtful, proactive, and involved. She took her son to specialists, had him tested, tried various medications, changed his school, helped him so much she had to cut back on her own work, and eventually got him through high school. He was brilliant but never became interested in any of the subjects, so he didn't do well. After graduating, the kid was so exhausted, he took a "nap year."

I couldn't help but wonder as I read the article what might have happened if the school had let Lanning's son pursue something that interested him, as Blue School does. Or if his mom had let him spend some of his time on something he loved, as opposed to the all-out assault on grinding through subjects he hated. Maybe he'd have barely graduated high school or only gotten a GED, but maybe he'd also be writing music or making movies or taking photos or writing computer code or drawing pictures or cooking or fixing appliances or fighting for social justice or selling lemonade. And maybe then he'd figure out a way to pursue his passion financially, instead of napping and dreading going to college.

Many parents believe that if their child doesn't get into a good college—and then graduate—they will not have a successful career. That was true in the last century, but it definitely isn't true today. Thacher School head Michael Mulligan (2014) says one reason so many teens are depressed is that all they've done is try to get into an elite college, rather than work to learn something they love. Some careers require a graduate degree; others don't even need a college degree. Most start-ups value knowledge, not degrees. And, of course, if you start your own business, you write the job description.

Until more schools adopt the Blue School's philosophy, there are a few things to keep in mind if you think you may be raising a future entrepreneur.

A stellar academic career simply isn't a prerequisite for entrepreneurial success. Some of the entrepreneurs I talked with had always been great students—a third of them graduated at the top of their class from top universities, and a quarter of them earned advanced degrees. But others who are just as successful decided not to finish college and chose instead to get on with what mattered more to them. Mutual Mobile founder John Arrow, whom we'll meet later, made an interesting point. He said that among some entrepreneurs, especially in San Francisco, there's a view that you have to drop out of school to be an entrepreneur, but that this is not quite true. He explained: "It's just that, at some point, you have to be fully *in*. You can't run a company— especially a start-up—and have another job or be a student. It's not about the hours in the day, it's about the mental bandwidth. It's about where all your focus is. And if you have a safety net, you're less likely to give it that extra push."

This is why, when they got a great idea, many entrepreneurs quit school to give it their all. Many were good students, some were not, but almost 20 percent of the entrepreneurs in this book left school before graduating from college because they were eager to get on with the next phase of their life.

Whether these entrepreneurs graduated from college or dropped out, never went to college or were academic stars, their formal schooling was all but irrelevant to their ability to achieve success in the real world.

Most of the people who have raised extremely successful adults probably didn't realize what they were doing, and may have been horrified when their kids dropped out. Bill Gates, Sr., says, "As a father, I never imagined that the argumentative young boy who grew up in my house, eating my food and using my name, would be my future employer" (Guth 2009). Many of the entrepreneurs loved school and thrived in every academic situation. Many were miserable in school but finished to make their families happy. Many were miserable and didn't finish.

The key is this: If your child is thriving in school, that's fantastic. But if they aren't, you have to deal with it. Forcing a child to stay in a situation where she feels stupid isn't the solution. Don't accept her current school and its values as the only possibility. Question approaches that haven't managed to engage her. Consider changing schools, switching to a charter school, or homeschooling. And if your kid hates college, don't make him finish. As we'll see in the next chapter, another possibility that can be invaluable to a child, whether or not she's academically oriented, is to help them connect with a mentor who counteracts any negative feedback they may be getting from their teachers or classmates.

Whatever you decide to do, make sure your children know that you support them in finding, exploring, and mastering something they'll love.

Here's one last thing to remember. Records show that when John Lennon was in high school, he was punished for being a "nuisance" and having "just no interest whatsoever." He was described as "an extremely cheeky boy," and two times, he got three detentions—in a single day. Those detention sheets reportedly sold for $3,000 at auction (Strauss 2013). And even though no one can prove it, Lennon is reputed to have said, "When I went to school, they asked me what I wanted to be when I grew up. I wrote down 'happy.' They told me I didn't understand the assignment, and I told them they didn't understand life."

RULE 4

Mentors Can Be Great

To a restless, creative kid, the world can seem rigid and rule-bound. It can feel as if everything's designed to prevent them from exploring what's truly interesting, or from even figuring out what that might be. But an adult who demonstrates that it's okay to do things differently, to color outside the lines, can be powerfully validating. When that adult also trusts a child enough to hand him the tools he needs to start creating something new, he can be launched toward great things. A mentor can also broaden a young person's view of available possibilities—many doctors' kids go into medicine, and lawyers' kids go into law or public policy, but a mentor can show kids a whole world beyond the world of their parents.

There are many important reasons for a child to have a mentor. Some are obvious—a mentor offers you help and guidance, teaches you, and promotes your growth. There's another, less obvious reason—if a mentor believes in you, it will boost your belief in yourself. That can be especially important if a child is receiving less positive messages from others in her life.

A mentor's belief in a child gives them confidence in their skills. That leads to resilience—and without resilience, it's almost impossible to become an entrepreneur. Building something new means you won't always be appreciated. Your early efforts might even be laughed at. You might work as hard as you can and still find that your project doesn't catch on. Most people would take that experience as a sign that they should pursue a safer path. The entrepreneur just modifies what he has or starts a new project.

Mentors have one major advantage over parents. A mentor, unlike a parent, isn't responsible for keeping a child safe. The ideal mentor is driven by a different impulse—to expose the child to challenges and equip her to handle them. A mentor can also give a much-needed kick in the pants that parents are reluctant to give. And a child, especially a teenager, may listen to a mentor precisely because the mentor isn't a parent. At some point, as we all know, many kids start treating their parents' advice with automatic skepticism, and so a mentor with the right values becomes even more important.

Most of the entrepreneurs profiled in this book had one or more mentors. A mentor doesn't have to be famous or important. A mentor just has to be someone the child respects, someone who comes into the child's life and shows her a new way of looking at the world, or who validates a child's self-worth by understanding the way he looks at the world.

FANNING THE FLAME

Mentors are good for everyone. But if a child feels underappreciated at school, few things do more to boost his confidence than having someone who appreciates his talent, especially if that person is skilled in the area he loves most. It brings him joy and rejuvenates his spirit. If you're not an academic star, or if your teachers find you annoying because you can't sit still or you ask too many questions, what could be better than having someone who excels in the thing you love think that you're incredible?

Benny Blanco: A Second Vote of Confidence

Remember Benny Blanco's mom, Sandy, who used rule 3 in responding to teachers' reports of her son's difficulties at school by saying "So?" She also decided she had to find another adult who believed in Benny.

She was divorced from her sons' father when Benny was in middle school, and the boys had a very difficult few years, but it was an important part of their development. "Ben was forced to take on a more mature role in the family," Sandy said, "and I think it made him the compassionate, good boy that he is today."

During this time, Sandy and her ex-husband often disagreed about whether the boys should attend a private school with a special education program, since Benny's brother had also been diagnosed with ADHD. But Sandy told me that she was determined to keep the boys in a regular class so that they would fit into the "real world." Which meant that when Benny got serious about music, he was a white Jewish boy going to largely Black middle and high schools. He made friends with kids from dramatically different backgrounds, and those friendships influenced his musical tastes.

He was a white rapper before Eminem made that acceptable. By his own admission, Sandy says, he was "horrible" at rapping. But instead of discouraging him, Sandy encouraged his growing love of music. She didn't care what his teachers thought. She didn't listen to her friends. She got him drum and guitar lessons outside school, and she found someone else who believed in him—a music teacher who said that Benny was the most talented student he'd had in thirty years. This meant everything to Benny.

By the time he was in eighth grade, Benny was winning rap contests. He sold his first song when he was a teenager. It was set to the beat of a soft-core porn video called *Hip Hop Honeys*, one that he insisted on showing to everyone. Sandy must have taken a big gulp. When Benny wanted to take five-hour weekend bus trips from Virginia to New York City so he could try to meet with rappers and producers, she must have taken an even bigger gulp. And when he wanted to drop out of college after a year to pursue music full time, she must have taken the biggest gulp of all before she finally agreed.

Ultimately, though, Benny's mom let him do what he wanted, and he went all the way to the Grammys, where he earned nine nominations by his mid-twenties. Without the one-two punch of a parent and a mentor who believed in him, who knows whether Benny's remarkable talent would have flourished? It's clear that he understands the important role his mentor played in his life, because now Benny, who's been nominated for the Songwriters Hall of Fame, mentors young musicians all the time.

Jesse Genet: Trusted to Do It Right

Jesse Genet is a pioneer in the do-it-yourself world, thanks to Lumi, the company she cofounded. It's based on an innovative photographic print process for textiles that offers an alternative to screen printing and lets people easily design their own clothes. One friend described Jesse admiringly as a "make-it-happen science geek."

Jesse's mentor was her stepfather, Doug, whom Jesse met when she was a teen:

I grew up in a suburb outside Detroit, with one sister six years older, so in some sense I grew up almost like an only child. My mom, Laureen Sue, was a schoolteacher. My dad was a lawyer. They divorced when I was twelve. Mom remarried when I was fifteen, a sophomore in high school.

Mom treated us like little adults, so I was always comfortable around them. Whether I was three or thirteen, she'd

110

let me come with her. She'd say, "This is an adult place, so you have to act like an adult." She taught me never to be afraid to deal with any situation. She trusted us and gave us a lot of freedom.

But I'd never met anyone like Doug. He was a technology developer and, unlike my parents, he had never had a normal job. He let me hang out at his shop after school. I'd do my homework there and watch how he ran his businesses. He'd humor me, let me sit in on meetings, let me be a fly on the wall. I sucked up this whole new world like a sponge. My sister was already in college when they got married, so this wasn't part of her experience while she was growing up. She didn't understand why I would hang out in Doug's shop instead of with my friends. She's much more traditional, with a master's in engineering—ironically, she now works for me part time.

For Jesse, being trusted to create in a grown-up way was a transformative moment:

Doug was very hands-on. He'd show me how to do anything I wanted to do—build a cabinet, refinish the floors. It was all very exciting to me. And he had so many tools—woodworking, metalworking. He'd give me a demo, and then I'd go weld something. He trusted me to do it right.

Doug was the first person who wasn't a direct family member who I asked for help and who said yes. This opened my eyes to how much you can get by asking. My dad was very traditional. Everyone in his family is a doctor, lawyer, or dentist. Everyone went to the University of Michigan. Doug showed me that rules didn't have to be so rigid.

I'd been kind of a loner kid. I skipped my senior year in high school. I didn't want to spend nine hours a day sitting in

*a class when there were so many other things I could be
doing. I convinced my principal to let me take college classes.
I spent a lot of time at the shop and took some online classes
and some from a community college.*

Although Jesse got into the University of Michigan, she chose
to break the family tradition and went to the Art Center College
of Design in Pasadena:

*I decided to study something I felt I didn't have an aptitude
for. I was creative but didn't know design. I knew that there
was a lot I didn't know, coming from middle-class America,
and thought this was one way I could catch up. I began
working toward a BS in product design.*

*I didn't finish college. I met Stephan Angoulvant, with
whom I cofounded Lumi. I'd been working on the concept for
a while. I knew there must be a better, cheaper way to do
printing.*

*Stephan has a lot of design talent. I have marketing talent
and could translate the technology into what people want to
use, and could communicate why the idea mattered. It was a
good match.*

Jesse started Lumi on the crowdfunding site Kickstarter in
2010, when she was still a student.

"I love what I do," she told me, "and it's been well received.
Revenue should double next year."

Jesse credits her mother with making her "confident and
wise." Her mom, she said, "teed up" her success with Lumi.

"But it's only because of Doug that I became an entrepreneur," she said. "Nobody else in my family understood my passion.
I'm so happy I started spending time in Doug's shop, even though
everyone except him thought I was wasting my time."

ENCOURAGING BOLD CHOICES

Kids who get plenty of recognition from their teachers and peers may not seem to have a great need for mentors. But even though stellar students and popular kids may not struggle with self-confidence, they still need encouragement to pursue their dreams. In a way, conventional success at an early point can actually hamper entrepreneurial success. An excellent student may be tempted to follow the well-worn path that is clearly laid out—the right activities, the best school, the most stable career, the highest salary. To get off this track and start laying their own tracks, accomplished kids may need a mentor's encouragement.

Tom Scott: A Nudge in the Right Direction

Tom Scott, cofounder of the juice company Nantucket Nectars, sold it for tens of millions of dollars and went on to start other companies. Much has been written about Tom and the companies he's started. His latest organization is The Nantucket Project, a gathering of people from all walks of life, from world leaders to small entrepreneurs, all of whom want to give back and make the world a better place.

I interviewed Tom's mom, Jane, whom I've known for many years, about her son. She told me that he was always popular and a good student. But to become an entrepreneur—to avoid the safest route and take a chance—he needed a nudge from a mentor.

Tom was born in Chevy Chase, outside Washington, D.C., the third of four children, all born within five years. Jane told me that the first two kids were more difficult and took up a lot of her time and energy. Tom, on the other hand, "didn't need a lot of parenting," and she "kind of left him alone" because he always "seemed to know what to do":

Tommy would do things out of the norm. He was always a leader, always the one who organized all the games, and all the others went along with it.

Tommy always wanted to work because he wanted money. His senior year in high school, we spent the summer in Truro, on Cape Cod, because his grandpa who lived there was sick. The kids wanted to stay home with their friends, so I said they could bring them. We had bought an old Boston Whaler with an engine, and Tommy took the boat thirty miles to Nantucket and started a painting company there. His first job was painting a bank.

After high school, Tom went to Brown, where he met Tom First, who became his business partner and eventually the cofounder of Nantucket Nectars. Jane told me:

They started their first company in Nantucket together while they were still in college—AllServe. Their motto was they'd do anything. They serviced boats in Nantucket that didn't have a space on the dock. They did solid waste disposal, laundry, getting newspapers, lobsters—anything anyone needed. They brought their friends up from D.C. and Brown. They worked really hard.

After college—they graduated in 1989—they lived in Nantucket. Tom First had spent his junior year in Spain and had fallen in love with the peach juice there. The boys decided to start a juice company, and to put Nantucket in the name.

Tom First's family was upset. They said, "This is what you're doing with a Brown education?" They wanted him to get a real job and get on with his life.

The boys lived in their Suburban that first winter. They poured their life savings into the business. Tom First was the business side, and Tommy was the marketing/PR side. It was slow going.

About a year later, Tommy was trying to decide what to do. Lots of his friends were headed to jobs in finance, or to law school, or to business school. Tommy applied to Harvard Business School and was accepted.

He was on his way to a prestigious business school, which would lead to a job on Wall Street, at a time when that seemed to be every young person's dream. At that point, shifting away from his struggling business and toward an MBA looked like a reasonable move. His parents were thrilled, especially his dad, a successful lawyer, who really wanted Tom to go to Harvard. All his classmates had jobs where they wore a suit to work. Rejecting an MBA to start a business, working out of your house, was almost unheard of back then. Without a mentor's advice, he probably would have made the conventional choice.

But then, Jane said, Tom sought his favorite teacher from Brown, Barrett Hazeltine, who had become his mentor. Tom Scott and Tom First had both taken Dean Hazeltine's course in entrepreneurship. "He was basically an ethics teacher," Jane told me, "and he had tremendous faith in the boys. He'd helped them prepare their business plan for Nantucket Nectars." Now, Jane said, her son sought his mentor's advice:

Tommy asked Dean Hazeltine whether he should go to Harvard Business School. His professor answered, "You've got a great thing going here. Don't waste your time going to business school. But don't turn it down—defer for a year, and think about it. Also make sure the school knows about Nantucket Nectars."

Jane told me that she and her husband trusted Dean Hazeltine to give the boys great advice. They agreed it was okay for Tommy to put the decision off for a year and see if the boys could make a go of their struggling business.

In the end, Tom Scott didn't go, but he didn't burn his bridges, either. Now the story of "the two Toms" is a case study at Harvard Business School (Lassiter, Sahlman, and Biotti 1998), and they speak there about Nantucket Nectars every year. In fact, Jane said, they were the first in a long line of superstar entrepreneurs to be inspired by Barrett Hazeltine. He taught them to live passionately, do what they love, and have the courage to do something different.

On Dean Hazeltine's seventy-fifth birthday, his former students put together a book of tributes. Here is Tom Scott's letter to his mentor:

Dear Dean,

I've recently turned forty, have two children and a wonderful wife. In other words, I'm sort of a grown-up now. Just using simple math, I'm pretty much middle-aged and have lived a significant portion of my life. One thing is certain—there is a very short list of people who have most significantly, and positively, influenced my life. I would put my parents, my high school football coach, and Dean Hazeltine at the top of my list.

Life is full of details. However, there are very few significant truths that can guide one's life. The one I think you gave me is spirit. It is really such a simple concept. However, the message comes in some complex formula of qualities/emotions, etc. You have them. I can't say much more than that—whatever that is, you have it and it greatly influenced me. I am very grateful. Furthermore, you are kind and make people feel good. I can only hope I can deliver some of what I learned from you to my children.

Happy birthday! But, more important, thank you!

Tom Scott
Class of 1989

Alan Chan: Three Wise Men

While some kids had a single mentor who made a dramatic difference, most of the entrepreneurs and moms I spoke with mentioned several mentors as the kids grew up.

Alan Chan, whom we met in the chapter on competing (rule 2), cofounder of the clothing company Arbitrage and founder of the online ad distributor Bread, told me he had three mentors who changed his life:

My first mentor was my basketball coach. He picked me out from almost all the other kids, believed in me, promoted me. He chose me to play for the JV team as a freshman, which was almost unheard of in my school, then put me on varsity my junior year, so I was the team captain for two years. That made a huge difference in my perception of myself and my abilities.

A mentor can show you that there's a big world out there, beyond that of your parents. It was another mentor who helped Alan realize he didn't have to become a doctor:

My second mentor, Craig Frances, was even more influential in my becoming an entrepreneur. I met him the summer after my junior year at Cornell. I was supposed to be a doctor. Both my parents are doctors, as is my older sister. There was always huge pressure growing up to get good enough grades to get into medical school.

I was always on the honor roll in high school and on the dean's list at Cornell with a 3.9 average. I felt a lot of pressure to be a doctor. But I also think that the necessity to excel was part of the driving force that made me become an entrepreneur.

By the end of my junior year in college, I had already gotten into med school, but I was also starting to be interested in business. I thought I might be able to be a doctor who also did business. I had learned a little about venture capital and private equity and thought that might be interesting. I Googled Cornell alums who were working in those areas, and then I e-mailed a letter with my résumé to eighty firms. I got only two responses, and only one interview.

Craig hired me as a summer intern, which turned out to have a huge impact on my life. He was the head of the health care and consumer products group at Summit Partners, a private equity firm. He invested in hospitals. He had gone through med school, had practiced medicine, and then quit to go into business. He said to me, "If you want to go into business, don't waste your time and money by going to medical school." I listened.

Coming from a parent or a teacher, that advice might not have meant much. But because it came from a mentor who had gone down the same path Alan was considering, it was powerful.

Alan went on to tell me about his third mentor, a real estate developer who was the father of his girlfriend that summer:

I saw that he had a much better work-life balance than doctors, and I knew I wanted that for myself. So I decided I was going to start a business, not become a doctor. First, I told my parents I was going to defer my med school acceptance to start my first company. After a year, they saw the writing on the wall and accepted it.

"If I hadn't met those three men," Alan told me, "I'd probably be a doctor today." Having a doctor for a son is not exactly every parent's worst nightmare, and I'm sure Alan would have made a wonderful physician. But he also always would have wondered what he had missed by not pursuing his passion. His mentors emboldened him to make what turned out to be the right choice.

The Gift of Inspiration

Some entrepreneurs were helped by a mentor in ways even more fundamental than nurturing confidence or encouraging bold decisions. For these fortunate entrepreneurs, a mentor provided not just guidance, but guiding principles—attitudes and beliefs to be drawn on over a lifetime, especially in adversity.

Elizabeth McKee Gore: Figure It Out

Elizabeth McKee Gore has never founded a start-up or a non-profit organization. Instead, she has launched groundbreaking projects within existing organizations.

It's scary to start an organization from scratch. But it can take just as much courage, confidence, and persistence to come up with an idea for a project, sell it to colleagues, implement it, and stake one's professional reputation on its success. Elizabeth has done all this half a dozen times.

As executive director of global partnerships for the United Nations Foundation—admittedly not the world's most entrepreneurial organization—Elizabeth was an "intrapreneur" who created three significant grassroots projects: Nothing But Nets, which raised $50 million, with an average donation of $60, for bed nets that offer protection from mosquitoes that carry malaria; Girl Up, which raises funds to provide girls with education, training, and mentors; and the Shot@Life global vaccines campaign. Elizabeth was also the foundation's first resident entrepreneur, and she chairs its Global Entrepreneurs Council.

For the typical successful entrepreneur, a mentor is a professional who has already succeeded in the entrepreneur's chosen field and now helps the younger person along. But Elizabeth's mentor was a woman of modest means and no formal education—her grandmother, Opal. I've heard Elizabeth speak often of how much her grandma meant to her, but until I talked to her for this book, I didn't realize how big a role she had played. She taught Elizabeth what was truly important. She taught her how to solve problems. She taught her to grab opportunities. She taught her never to give up:

> My grandma inspired my brother and me our whole lives. I grew up in Whitesboro, Texas. My grandma lived six hours away, and I spent every summer and many weekends with her. My brother is five and a half years younger than I am and, like my grandma, he fishes every day. That's not his job—he's a tech salesman—but that's his passion.
>
> She wasn't an educated woman, but she was always very wise—that's why I named my daughter after her. Whenever I had a problem, I called her, and she always had a very grounding truth to share.
>
> If there was a problem, my grandma always figured out how to fix it. I remember there was an old abandoned filling station near her home that she wanted taken down. She called the mayor's office every day for three straight months until they finally did.
>
> She and my grandpa were both products of the Depression and World War II. In fact, she was a riveter during the war. My grandma was always busy, but she spent most of her time on us. She'd take us to mud pie contests, fishing, youth activities, and church activities. With her, we were always going, going.
>
> My parents started their own cattle ranching business, but most of my direction came from my grandma. I learned tenacity from her. She'd say, "Don't sit there if you have a problem—solve it!" She also gave me her sense of community. She'd always tell me, "Use your powers for good."

I was the first woman in my family to graduate from college. My grandma really pushed me to do that.

At Texas A&M, one of the most significant things that happened was that one of my friends had to drop out because she had a baby, and there was no support. I asked my grandma what I should do about it, and she said, "Well, figure it out."

Those four simple words—"Well, figure it out"—contain the essence of what would become Elizabeth's approach to work, the principle that would guide all her efforts. Elizabeth continued the story:

I researched the problem and discovered that our school was the only one in the Big Twelve without any child care. So I decided to raise money for a children's center. I worked so hard at it, I almost flunked out of school. But it got me excited about the nonprofit world. I had been planning to work on my family's ranch—I'd been studying animal science. But this opened my eyes to another career path.

While I was getting my master's in financial development, because of my fundraising experience for the children's center, I had an opportunity to raise funds for a foundation for the Bush School of Public Policy, which got me involved with the Points of Light Foundation, which took me to Washington, D.C. Then I met Billy Shore, who ran Share Our Strength, and I launched their anti-hunger initiative, The Great American Bake Sale. And that led me to the head of the U.N. Foundation, who inspired me to join her. I just let one thing lead to another.

After college, I joined the Peace Corps and went to Bolivia. It was the hardest thing I ever did. My grandma and

I wrote letters back and forth. In one letter, I wrote how hard it was to get the farmers to work together and to trust me. I saved her answer: "Keep your head held high, and give 'em hell."

That was her philosophy—have integrity, but give 'em hell. She was so committed to her community, and nothing would ever stop her from something she thought was right. She was always polite, but she never backed down.

My grandma taught me the entrepreneurial spirit. It's why I'm able to build things today.

WHERE YOU COME IN

The best mentors are often the ones children find on their own. After all, as we've seen, part of mentors' value is that they're not you! A mentor's attention shows a young person that an adult who isn't obligated to care for her thinks she has potential, is worth an investment of the mentor's time, and has something special to offer.

But that doesn't mean you can't help your child connect with a mentor. Encourage your child to reach out to successful people in the field he's passionate about. You can make specific suggestions, but be careful not to limit your suggestions to people you admire. One way a mentor can serve as a bridge to the adult world is by giving your child a different perspective from yours. Even though it may not be easy, you need to trust your child to make the most of that different perspective, because it's a key part of letting him create his own perspective—the one he'll keep refining for the rest of his life.

RULE 5

Instill Confidence

I remember reading a story in *The Washington Post* about Alex Len, a basketball phenom from a small coal-mining town in Ukraine who headed to the NBA from the University of Maryland (Prewitt 2013). Nobody from his town had ever done anything, but when he was little he used to dream of playing at Madison Square Garden. "You'll make it," his mother told him. "I know you will. Dreams can come true."

That's what it's all about: a mom who believes in you, who tells you that you can do anything you set your mind to. If there is one thing all of these young entrepreneurs have in common, it's someone who believes in them. And that person was usually their mom. Of course, most also had dads who believed in them. And/or aunts, uncles, stepparents, or grandparents. And I'm sure there are entrepreneurs who succeeded against all odds with parents who didn't believe in them—but I haven't met them.

Every one of the entrepreneurs profiled in this book is confident. Every one had a mom—and generally an entire family— who believed in them and supported their choices. They all said to me, "My mom believed in me, so I believed in me." They weren't afraid to try. They weren't afraid to fail. Every one of these entrepreneurs believed they could succeed in their mission, no matter how improbable.

Kids aren't stupid. They know the difference between phony praise and praise for something real. According to Carol Dweck, psychologist and author of *Mindset: The New Psychology of Success*, when kids are praised for something they've *done*, not for something they *are* (smart, or beautiful, or talented), they're inspired to work harder and achieve even more.

Your daughter won't gain confidence when everyone on her team gets a trophy. Your son won't gain confidence when you argue with his teacher for a higher grade if he doesn't deserve it. They won't get confidence for being praised when they know they didn't do their best. A kid gains confidence by working hard and doing better than last time. Kids gain confidence by mastering skills they care about. They gain confidence when they see that results are produced by their own efforts. And they gain confidence when their parents are proud of their achievements, even when those achievements are in fields the parents might wish their kids hadn't chosen.

THE POWER OF BELIEF

To believe in themselves, most kids need someone else to believe in them first. It's probably no coincidence that every one of the successful entrepreneurs I talked with is supremely confident. Every one of them had a mom and/or other family member who believed in them and told them they could do anything they set their minds to.

Michael Saylor: Best Paperboy in Town

Michael Saylor is the founder and CEO of MicroStrategy, a software company with more than $500 million in annual revenue. He also established the Saylor Foundation to provide free online education, and wrote *The Mobile Wave*, about the next phase of computer technology.

The entrepreneurs in this book come from a wide socioeconomic spectrum. Michael was definitely not born with a silver spoon. He grew up in Ohio with an older sister and a younger brother. He was valedictorian of his high school graduating class, and went to MIT on an ROTC scholarship. He's a middle child, and neither his younger brother nor his older sister became entrepreneurs—again showing that you can't make a child an entrepreneur; you can only nurture those tendencies.

When I talked with Michael, I asked him what he had learned from his mom, Phyllis, who died five years before our conversation:

> There was no way I should have succeeded. I grew up a poor Southern Baptist—three strikes against me in my small Ohio town. But my mom told me I could do anything.
>
> When I was in seventh grade, I was a newspaper delivery boy. That summer, there was a contest for best newspaper delivery in the area. I didn't realize it at the time, but there were only about twenty of us. But somehow my mom convinced me that winning that little contest meant I was the best in the world. I started eighth grade with this outsize sense of confidence—I was the best delivery boy in the world, so I could succeed at anything.
>
> Different parents can interpret the same situations differently. If lightning strikes near you and misses, your parents could say three different things to you:
>
> "Lightning almost hit you. You're in trouble. It's amazing you escaped this time."
>
> "Lightning almost hit you. You are a lucky person. You're so fortunate always to escape. You'll be lucky your whole life."
>
> "Lightning almost hit you. God saved you because he has important things in mind for you to accomplish in your life."

Each of those responses affects you in different ways. Depending on what your parents said, you'd come out a different person. Against all odds, I knew I could do anything, because she said so. She believed in me—so I believed in me.

Michael makes a wonderful point, but I think there are other things a parent could say, too:

"You put yourself in a very risky situation. How did you analyze it?"

"What made you decide to go out in a lightning storm?"

"Is there anything you learned from this experience that would make you evaluate risk differently next time?"

"You obviously made some very smart last-minute decisions that saved your life. In other words, you didn't stand against a tree. What thoughts went through your head?"

"How did you decide what action to take?"

"How did you make such a wise decision in such a risky situation?"

Smart questions show that you respect your child's judgment, and that creates confidence. You encourage children to make smart choices, and you applaud them for doing so. You build their confidence by teaching them how to manage risk and how to make choices among different possibilities with various trade-offs and different outcomes. You help them learn by inviting them to answer your questions, not by telling them what they should do. These are some of the most important things parents can do— show their children how to make choices, praise them for their analysis, and congratulate them for following through on the decisions they've made.

Jessica Jackley: Learning to Think Globally

As cofounder of Kiva, Jessica Jackley is a microfinance pioneer. Since 2005, Kiva, an online lending platform, has worked to end poverty by directing sums as low as $25 to small businesses, usually in developing countries. To date, Kiva has channeled $750 million in microfinance loans to more than 325,000 struggling entrepreneurs outside the U.S. In 2006, Springwise, an innovation-discovery website, named Kiva one of the year's top ten financial service ideas. Jessica went on to cofound ProFounder, an online crowdfunding platform for U.S. small business entrepreneurs to raise start-up capital.

Jessica has an MBA from Stanford. She was a visiting practitioner at its Center for Philanthropy and Civil Society. She has taught global entrepreneurship at USC's business school, sits on lots of boards, and has worked extensively in Africa.

She grew up outside Pittsburgh with a younger brother, who's a pastor in a church near where they grew up. Today she's married and has three young sons, including a pair of twins.

Here's what Jessica told me about her mother:

My mom built my confidence every single day. She always told me I could do anything I wanted to do, and in very specific ways we would talk about different opportunities that came up along the way—leadership opportunities—and both my mom and dad would talk through it with me and encourage me to pursue those things.

Mom also taught me to love learning. As an educator herself, she is extremely gifted at this, and she has instilled this love in countless kids, but she brought this into our home and into everything we did together.

We were never bored. We were always learning things together or playing games or exploring or having little adventures. I think that this spirit in some way prepared me to be an entrepreneur—to be proactive and see opportunities in the world.

Her dad was also instrumental in getting her ready to succeed. When Jessica was in high school, she told me, her dad would have a conversation with her at the beginning of each school year. Together they would chose a theme for the new academic year, such as "Keep your head" or "Ask the right questions." Now, she said, she realizes that these "mission statement warm-up exercises" showed her how to approach different projects with intention and purpose. When she started Kiva, she drew from that experience to prepare its mission statement: to connect people through lending to alleviate poverty. That is what defined and differentiated the organization and enabled it to be so successful, she told me.

Again, we see how the small actions of parents can produce big outcomes. Because Jessica was encouraged to try new things, and because her parents showed her that they believed she could accomplish them, she has spent her life enabling countless other budding entrepreneurs, first in the developing world and now in the U.S., to achieve their dreams, too.

Tania Yuki: Encouraged to Be Curious

The belief in a child's abilities doesn't have to be evidence-based—or even conscious. In some cases, it might spring more from a mother's attitude toward life in general than from a rational confidence in her child's abilities.

Tania Yuki is a native of Australia and an attorney who is the founder and CEO of Shareablee, a company that analyzes what works on Facebook and Twitter and helps companies improve communication with their customers across social media. Here's what Tania told me about her journey:

> The reason I became an entrepreneur was definitely because of my parents. Always having the perspective that everything I did was going to turn out great was the key. Looking back, I think I had this perspective because of my mom's optimism rather than her observation that I was special.
>
> I think this because my dog is really stupid, but recently my mom [Yukiko] said, "Billy is such a smart dog." I said, "Mom! Do you really believe that, or are you just saying it? Because Billy is not smart!" Based on her view of Billy, I don't know if she based her view of my intelligence on any sort of proof. But it doesn't matter—what matters is that I believed it growing up.
>
> I always knew I would turn out great—I was sure of it. And having that belief made me sure that I would do really great things. I believed that none of my ideas were wrong— that I should pursue them and they would turn out great.

Tania also learned from a very early age that curiosity isn't dangerous:

> I never learned the word "no" growing up. One of my earliest memories is when I was four years old. I was with my dad [Ante] in a high-end gift store, like Tiffany's, which had many breakable things. A sign said NO TOUCHING, but I was still touching everything. A salesclerk walked over to us and snatched something out of my hand. I remember that moment clearly, as I was afraid I'd be in trouble. She looked terrifying—I was so little. I looked at my dad. He glared at the woman and said, "She's just curious. If she breaks anything, I'll pay for it!"

Tania told me that this early experience led directly to her confidence:

At that moment, I knew my parents would always trust me, would always have my back. They never had any reason to discourage anything I was curious about. They never wanted me to feel limited, to think there was something I couldn't do. I never felt I would suffer consequences for being curious. Now, today, when I hear "no," I always want to push until I get "yes" or at least "maybe." That moment set me on my journey.

The memory of that moment also really helped her, she said, when she moved to the U.S. after college. She told me that she thinks she had ADHD, though she was never tested. But she said that she had all the traits—she was bored easily, she liked doing a lot of things at once, and she needed lots of stimulation. She found that in New York, where she went as a film producer with a documentary she'd made. She started working in digital media and data, and later she launched her company:

My confidence and belief in myself that I got from my parents was critical when I started doing things at first, and then even more so as I moved to a bigger and bigger pool, and finally when I moved to the U.S. and didn't know anybody.

Today, this successful company founder traces her willingness to experiment, her fearlessness, and her confidence to an episode that occurred when she was only four years old. Her experience shows that it's never too early to let kids know you believe in them.

So, parents, don't wait until high school to start thinking about your kid's attitudes toward work; the die may be cast long before then.

The Power of Trust

Entrepreneurs are risk takers, but they weren't all born that way. Many grew up with a fundamental sense of safety, which let them know that even if they took a risk and failed, it wouldn't mean the end of the world. It's much harder to take a leap if you're not on firm ground to begin with. When a child has a strong, secure home base and is trusted with responsibility, the results can be spectacular. Children who are given responsibility learn that they can do important things. And those who love that discovery so much that they want to experience it again and again, may well grow up to become entrepreneurs.

Susan and Anne Wojcicki: You Can Do It

Susan Wojcicki grew up as the oldest of three girls, and her sister Anne is the youngest. Janet, the middle sister, is a pediatrician.

They grew up in a house on the campus of Stanford University, where their dad Stanley is a physics professor, and Google was started in the family's garage.

Susan and Anne are two of the country's most successful entrepreneurs. Susan, Google's first marketing manager, helped persuade the Google board to acquire YouTube, and became its CEO in 2014, the same year she was named number 12 on the *Forbes* "100 Most Powerful Women" list. Anne, married for eight years to Google cofounder Sergey Brin, quit her job analyzing health care and biotech investments and, after six years of research, cofounded 23andMe, a personal genomics and biotech company named for the number of pairs of chromosomes in a human cell. In 2013, *Fast Company* named Anne Wojcicki "Most Daring CEO."

Their mom, Esther Wojcicki, has been a terrific role model for her daughters. The first in her family to go to college, she became a journalist and has taught journalism at Palo Alto High School for more than thirty years, building the program into one of the country's biggest. She was named California Teacher of the Year; has inspired hundreds, including actor James Franco, who returned to his high school to teach a few classes with her; and authored a well-received book, *Moonshots in Education*.

When I talked with Esther about her remarkable family, it was clear that she had given her kids a rock-solid home, raising them in an atmosphere of trust and independence. Esther was always working, and her kids had to be independent. They grew up knowing that she trusted them to behave responsibly. She told me the key to success is developing a particular mind-set: "If you think you can, you can. If you think you have the ability to do it, you do it."

Anne told *Inc.* magazine (Bercovici 2015) that her mother is the main reason she became an entrepreneur. "Without a doubt, the number one thing that influenced me is her saying, 'Just get it done. It's all within your control.'"

According to Esther, the Wojcicki girls were given freedom that some parents, especially today, would balk at:

> I'm very independent and gave my children the opportunity to be very independent early on. I had three children in four years, and no help, so I put them to work out of necessity. For example, we used cloth diapers, and the girls were responsible for folding them. It was play, but they also knew it made a difference to our family.
>
> We had a two-story house. There were no baby monitors back then, so the two-year-old had to come down and get me when the six-month-old was crying. It taught them responsibility from a very young age.
>
> When the two oldest were five and three, we lived in Geneva for a year, and they would walk to the boulangerie

to get bread. *They walked down six flights of stairs and around the building—they didn't have to cross a street—paid for the bread, and came back upstairs. They walked to school when they were five. I walked with them a few times, but then they were on their own.*

We talked about the current debate over helicopter parents versus free-range parents, and about two Maryland kids, six and ten years old, who had been picked up by the police after neighbors saw them walking home alone a few blocks from their neighborhood park. It reminded me, for the first time in many years, how I walked to elementary school and back every day, and how my brother and I went out to play in the evenings, with the instruction to come home when the streetlights came on.

Esther said, "Today it's the same place, and the walk to school is just as safe, but parents won't do that. Their view of the world has changed. When I was young, I walked one and a half miles to school every day by myself. I thought it was great." She went on:

We were a very close family, but we also gave them a lot of freedom. I would let my seven- and eight-year-olds ride their bikes a couple miles to Woolworth's to spend their $1 allowance. They loved the sense of freedom, and I think it gave them a lot of confidence. My mother lived in L.A., and I put my five-year-old daughter on a plane to visit her and sent her there with a tag around her neck. And then, when Susan was twelve and Janet was eleven, they flew through JFK to Geneva by themselves. They had traveled enough with us. They weren't intimidated. Today everyone's afraid, which I think is a shame. But even if you're afraid to give them the kind of freedom I gave my girls, you can still give them things to do around the house to contribute to the family. You can still give them chores to make them responsible and to develop their confidence.

Esther told me that even she hadn't been fully aware of how rare and powerful trust can feel to a child:

When I was awarded the California Teacher of the Year, I wondered for a long time what was so great about what I was doing. And then I realized that, just like with my own children, the number one thing is that I trusted my students, and many don't get trusted anywhere else.

I taught them how to do something, and then I trusted them to do it. I sent them the message, "You can do it. If you fail, do it again. But you can do it, and that's the end of the discussion." Of course, sometimes they screwed up, but so what? My kids and my students knew it was okay to fail, and they just kept trying, because I knew they would get it right eventually.

It's interesting to me that most of the families in this chapter raised their kids the way they did, in part because they were working moms and had to give their kids a lot of independence.

A recent study by Harvard Business School professor Kathleen McGinn of 50,000 people in twenty-five countries found that daughters of working mothers were more educated, more likely to be employed and in supervisory roles, and earned higher incomes than daughters of stay-at-home moms. This was especially true in the U.S., where daughters of working moms earned 23 percent more (Miller 2005).

According to the author, "Part of this working mothers' guilt has been, 'Oh, my kids are going to be so much better off if I stay home,' but what we're finding in adult outcomes is kids will be so much better off if women spend some time at work."

One can speculate about the reasons why the entrepreneurs in this section were such competent, confident kids and retained their competence and confidence as adults. But working moms should take heart: your kids will be fine.

Karolina Kurkova: A Model Upbringing

Karolina Kurkova is a supermodel. By the time she was thirty-one, she'd been on the cover of *Vogue* twenty-five times, been named MTV's Model of the Year, and had gotten a star on Hollywood's Walk of Fame.

But Karolina is more than a beautiful face. She campaigns for the welfare of children through organizations like AmFar and Feeding America. She's also done work on behalf of the Injured Marine Semper Fi Fund and Wounded Warriors. She's married to Archie Drury, an investor, and they have a five-year-old son and a baby.

Karolina grew up with a younger brother in what was then Communist Czechoslovakia. Her father, Josef Kurka, was a professional basketball player as well as a policeman—even star athletes had day jobs back then. Her mother, Eva, worked halftime in a bank while Karolina was growing up, and she's also an artist; Karolina's younger brother Josef works while getting his master's degree. Her family still lives in the Czech Republic.

Karolina told me:

> My parents had grown up in a very strict, traditional way and took what they didn't like about their upbringing and changed it. They gave us a lot of trust and a lot of freedom. They wanted us to experience everything. They told us never to be afraid to speak to anyone. There were a lot of rules, but a lot of freedom to explore what we liked and to figure out what we wanted to be. And they wanted us to have the skills to survive.

She told me that watching her dad play basketball contributed to her becoming a driven person:

> Every weekend we would travel to his games. He wanted us to learn discipline, passion, hard work, teamwork. But he

didn't force a sport on us. They wanted us to decide what we liked. They never pushed us to like what they liked.

I trained to be a professional gymnast from the time I was six until I was thirteen. I had to audition to be in the program. I trained for hours every day, before and after school. I loved it. It taught me to work hard, to be committed and focused, and to be really tough. I wanted to be the best. I learned to compete against others who were better than I. It taught me so much.

My parents never pushed me. It was my own drive and determination, though I was influenced by their work ethic. Then I got too tall and started playing basketball. I did that for two years until I started modeling.

Whatever she wanted to do, her parents supported her. And her parents gave her a lot of independence:

At five and six, I walked to school by myself. I took the bus by myself. I grew up very quickly. I was always very responsible. I picked up my younger brother from school and watched him till my mother got home. I helped out around the house, did dishes, cleaned my room.

And she was given even more freedom when the family visited her grandparents on weekends. "We just ran around in the countryside, completely free," she said.

When Karolina was sixteen, she started working full time as a model and traveling. That wasn't what her parents wanted, she said, but they let her do it because it was what she wanted. "They said, 'If you try it and you like it and you're working hard at it and it's what you want, we'll support you,'" she told me. When she was seventeen, she went alone to New York to pursue her modeling career, and within two years was on the cover of *Vogue*.

Karolina's parents still live in the small town where she grew up, a place without many opportunities. She observed:

My parents allowed me to go and travel the world to have opportunities they didn't have. They had to have so much trust in me. And now that I have children of my own, I realize it was not easy to let me go.

D. A. Wallach: Freedom to Choose

Rochelle Lamm is another mom who worked full time and raised her son to be confident and independent, but in a more hands-on way than some of the other working moms. Her son, D. A. Wallach, or David-Andrew, as she calls him, is best known for having been a member of Chester French, the critically acclaimed pop band that D. A. started in college with Max Drummey. Chester French was one of the first bands to use Facebook for promotion and fan interaction because both boys were at Harvard when Mark Zuckerberg launched it. Today, in addition to having released a critically acclaimed solo album, *Time Machine*, D. A. invests in tech start-ups and advises them about using social media for marketing. He is also Artist in Residence at Spotify and directs ten music ambassadors who help him develop artist relations around the world. *Forbes* included him in its "30 Under 30" list in 2011, and *Fast Company* named him among its "100 Most Creative People in Business" in 2013.

D. A. has two stepsiblings, twenty years older than he is, who are now married with kids, and a sister ten years younger, who's in college. So for his first ten years he was basically the only child at home. His parents divorced, and then it was just D. A. and his mom at home through his middle and high school years.

Rochelle told me that she was raised in a small town in Canada, where her parents still run a large hunting and fishing lodge. She became a nun but left the convent and went to college. To avoid gender discrimination at work, she decided to make her mark in sales, because whoever sold the most came out on top. She climbed the ranks, became CEO of two different mutual fund companies, and then started her own company.

As a passionate and accomplished executive who worked hard and traveled a lot, Rochelle also expected D. A. to excel. He was very smart, she told me—he read a lot, spent a lot of time talking to adults, and went with her on work-related trips.

In third grade, she said, he became interested in investing. She gave him $5,000, opened an account for him, and told him he had complete authority over the money. She wanted him to think through what to invest in, and why. D. A. spent hours researching companies and reading their quarterly reports. Rochelle discussed his choices with him, and she gave him her opinions, but he chose his own investments. They included high-risk companies in fields like satellite tech as well as a maker of electric scooters. He lost most of the money within six years, but Rochelle told him that losing was part of the learning process. It also prepared D. A. for the kind of venture funding he does now. Of course, not everyone can afford to give their child $5,000 to learn about investing. But Rochelle nurtured his talents in other ways that didn't cost money: analyzing, discussing, and debating choices with him; treating him like a grown-up; letting him make his own decisions; and not agonizing over failure.

D. A. was a poor athlete, Rochelle said. He tried many different sports, but one day he said to his mom, "I really suck." She agreed, and D. A. turned to his strengths. He had always liked to perform, she told me, and began putting on magic shows, which he did all through elementary school. He also distinguished himself as a good student.

Rochelle supported D. A. when his actions weren't popular:

His junior year of high school, he decided there wasn't enough diversity at his school. He campaigned about it.

The school wasn't happy, but he wasn't afraid to take it on. The school headmaster told him to stop. I told him he could pursue it if he wanted. I told him he could handle it, but I never interfered.

I always encouraged him to be adventurous. After that year, he traveled with five of his friends and one parent to India for eight weeks. I thought that as he learned to do adventurous things, the experience would allow him to take on challenges in life and in business that others might be hesitant to take on.

His senior year, after 9/11, he wanted to have a low-key prom. He thought it wasn't appropriate to spend a lot of money and that they shouldn't use limos or hold it at the country club. He wanted the class to save $20,000 and give it to the victims' families. He got a lot of calls from angry parents saying, "You're ruining the prom!" We talked about it, and I told him to do what he needed to do. He didn't prevail completely, but they did save some money and send it off.

D. A. was a percussionist in the high school jazz band, but he went to Harvard to major in African American studies. I got a call one day: "Mom, I'm in a band! There's four of us, and we've got a drummer!" I said, "But you're a drummer. So what do you do?" He said, "I sing." I said, "But you don't sing!"

He was incredibly lucky. They put out a CD, his band took off during his senior year, and he signed with Pharrell Williams at Interscope.

Rochelle told me she had suggested to D. A. that he postpone becoming a full-time musician and work at Goldman Sachs first, to get some experience. He just laughed. But she supported his choice, and it turned out he was right:

I've never expected him to agree with me. I knew it was important to defer to his judgment. I wanted him to make his mistakes and to learn from them. I knew when he was making mistakes, but I thought he would learn so much from the experience.

Chester French opened for Lady Gaga before the superstar was famous. Most bands don't achieve that kind of immediate success. But D. A.'s experience illustrates how letting a child pursue a passion can lead to a career that a parent would not have been able to imagine.

Kathy Roth-Douquet: Walking the Walk

Kathy Roth-Douquet, a U.S. Marine Corps wife and mother and a former aide to President Bill Clinton, is the cofounder and CEO of Blue Star Families, a nonprofit that has served almost a million military families by generating twenty-five million hours of volunteer community service. In addition to her work as an attorney and political activist, Kathy has coauthored two books.

Now that she's raising two kids of her own, Kathy told me, she realizes that it's okay to do a lot of things wrong if you do a couple of key things right. She said her mom got those things right:

The most important thing is that I knew that she really, really loved me. It was so clear to me that it was always a pleasure for her to be my mother. If there was something I wanted to say, she wanted to hear it. If there was something I wanted to do, she wanted to do it with me.

Kathy told me that when she was in school, she wanted to protest apartheid at the South African embassy. Even though her mom, Debbie, wasn't really the type of person to protest, she not only gave Kathy her support, she went to the embassy with her:

> My mom thought that if I was doing it, there must be a reason, and that if I thought it was important, there was something worth thinking about. So she came along, and she got arrested with me.

Showing her daughter—not just telling her—that what she thought mattered and what she did was important, was the ultimate expression of trust. And ultimately it gave Kathy the confidence to go out on her own.

Michael Skolnik: They Let Me Fly

Trusting children with independence isn't always a deliberate parental strategy designed to instill confidence; sometimes it's simply the result of circumstances. That doesn't make it any less powerful.

Michael Skolnik, a civil rights activist and filmmaker, has led national conversations about race and violence. He's the cofounder of Dot2Dot, an annual summit for concerned young leaders. He's also the president of GlobalGrind.com, an entertainment and lifestyle site cofounded by Russell Simmons with almost five million views a month. One of the biggest differences in how the entrepreneurs I talked to were raised was how much freedom (versus supervision) they were given. I have to admit I was on the more involved end of the spectrum. Michael was definitely raised as far as you can go on the other end.

Michael grew up with an older brother in affluent Westchester County, New York. His dad was a construction manager and engineer, and most of his other relatives were engineers, too, so that was the career path he was expected to follow. Michael's brother, two and a half years older, runs the D.C. office of the Taproot Foundation. His mom pursued many occupations—chef, bakery manager, plumber, photographer, editor, nutritionist, and museum director. In what free time his parents had, they were involved in the arts and acted in community theater.

Because Michael's parents were so busy, he was given freedom that many kids never have. His experience should be encouraging to parents who work exhausting schedules and wonder if missing out on many of their children's activities means their children won't turn out as well as those raised by full-time moms.

Michael's parents weren't around a lot, he told me, but they always provided emotional support:

> I learned about what an entrepreneur was from my mom, who could do anything. She was an art student while she was pregnant with me, and she studied photography with Ansel Adams. We had a darkroom in the house.
>
> Both my parents were political. My father protested in Chicago in 1968. My mother grew up in the South and rode in the back of the bus to protest.
>
> When I was a kid, I acted in commercials, and I loved the theater. When I was only fourteen, I wrote a letter to fifty Broadway general managers and producers to see if I could intern, and forty-nine said no. But the general manager of Blue Man Group said yes.
>
> My parents said, "We support you 100 percent, but we can't help you. We both work. We can't spend an hour every day to take you back and forth to the city."
>
> My best friend's family had an apartment in the city that they only used on weekends, so they let me live there by myself for the summer.

From the time I was fourteen, my parents let me live by myself to chase a dream. They trusted me enough to let me live alone in an apartment in New York City. I honored their trust.

I also got a job as an usher at the summer theater in Central Park, Shakespeare in the Park, where I worked every night and weekends. I was one white kid among thirty-five Black and Latino kids. It shaped my life, my view of who I am today, and everything I believe about race and privilege.

So for all four years of high school, I went back and forth on weekends and during the summers. I worked at Blue Man all four years.

I also worked with Michael Moore on his first book when I was eighteen.

My parents' friends in Westchester said they were crazy to give me so much freedom. It was the mid-nineties, and hip-hop was just emerging, hitting suburban America for the first time. Most of the parents I knew there were afraid. My parents were the opposite. They said, "Go for it!"

Michael told me that he often felt like a fish out of water, and that his high school years were tough because he didn't fit in—when he wasn't a white kid from Westchester living with Black and Latino kids in New York, he was a suburban football player who was into hip-hop. But he told me his parents were always there for him, even if they weren't physically present:

Whatever I did, my parents supported me. Every step of the way. They never questioned what I was doing.

There's no doubt in my mind that letting me fly is a huge part of my success in what I do now. I'm thirty-five, and I've been working for twenty-one years.

To give you an idea of how much my parents let me run free, I was also on the high school basketball team, and at the end of the semester, one of the moms called my mom and said, "We're having an end-of-season potluck dinner for the team. Would you like to bring something?" And my mom said, "Michael plays basketball?"

It wasn't because she didn't care, but because she was so busy. So she let me run free. I wasn't resentful. I appreciated my freedom.

I always believed my mom had my back and didn't want me to fail. I always believed she wanted me to fly.

My parents took a huge risk in how they raised me. They rolled the dice, and it worked. I don't know if that much freedom and independence at such a young age would work for everyone, but it worked for me. Their trust in me let me mature a lot earlier than my peers and allowed me to achieve professional success a decade earlier than I would have if I'd been raised like most kids.

Standing Up for Your Child

The more freedom you give kids, the more freedom they have to come into conflict with other people about the way things should be done. When that happens, it's crucial for someone to show them that they don't have to fear conflict, and that it's okay to challenge conventional ways of thinking and doing things.

Many of the mothers and entrepreneurs I talked to described a combination of freedom and support. Without support, freedom can feel to a child like indifference; without freedom, support can feel restrictive. When the two are combined, kids gain the confidence to pursue their dreams. Few things give kids more confidence than seeing their parent stand up for them.

These moments also teach them to stand up for themselves. A future entrepreneur learns how to argue for her own interests— and eventually, as she makes her way in the business community, she learns how to stand up for her vision, her employees, and her organization. By standing up for a child, you not only give the child confidence, you also model how to be an advocate when it's called for. This skill is one that translates into becoming a great boss who empowers people to try, doesn't express anger when employees make mistakes, and is there to help when it's needed. It's also important when they are dealing with investors, clients, customers, and board members. This skill is one aspect of what psychologist Robert Sternberg (1997) calls instilling "practical intelligence," which includes showing children effective ways to talk back, negotiate, and question adults.

Giving your child these tools by showing them how you do it when you stand up to authority on their behalf is what I call being an advocate and what Malcolm Gladwell (2008) calls teaching a sense of entitlement (in the best sense of the word). Whatever it's called, giving your child the tools to stand up for themselves by standing up for them when they are young helps them navigate the world successfully as an adult.

John Arrow: His Biggest Champions

John Arrow dropped out of the University of Texas a few credits short of his degree to work full time on his company, Mutual Mobile, which solves mobile technology problems in high-stakes fields like medicine. By the time John was in his mid-twenties, his company had 350 employees; he was named to both *Forbes's* "35 Under 35" list and *Inc.'s* "30 Under 30." The day before I talked with him, John sold a minority stake in his company to London-based WPP Group. It had been just four and a half years since he'd founded the company. That's about the time it takes to go to grad school for a JD/MBA.

The conventional wisdom about entrepreneurs is that they all start out selling lemonade on the street corner, but John is the only one I talked with who actually did. "I was always selling something," he told me; his parents always supported him:

> When I was five or six, growing up in Austin, I was always the kid on the street corner selling lemonade in the summer and hot chocolate in the winter. By the time I was nine, I was tired of selling lemonade and decided to look around for something else to sell. One day I saw these beautiful plants in what I thought was a field. I dug them up. We had a wonderful elderly neighbor who always bought everything from me that I was selling, so I took these plants to her, rang her bell, and delivered my sales pitch, but this time she said no.
>
> When I got home, my mom sat me down. She said, "I got a call from our neighbor. She said you just tried to sell her own plants to her." Our neighbor had planted them that morning. My mom wasn't angry, but I did have to replant them.

This is a great example of why entrepreneurs grow up unafraid to try things and why they aren't afraid to fail—John didn't get scolded for screwing up when he was young. He may have been told he had to fix something, but he wasn't punished for experimenting.

John told me another story that has stayed with him throughout this career:

> When I was in fifth grade, we had a school newspaper. I decided to create a competing paper that included a section on who likes whom.
>
> My friends and I wrote it up and printed a couple dozen copies, which sold out immediately. I hadn't had any journalism classes and didn't know anything about attribution. I didn't know that you can't just guess about facts and make statements that you don't know are correct.

The principal was furious. He told us that he was going to tell our parents, expecting that they would punish us. The other conspirators got in a huge amount of trouble. But my parents thought it was hilarious.

I realized that they were willing to support me even when an authority was against me. Knowing that they would stand up for me made me double down and work harder, to show them they were right to believe in me.

John traces his confidence to his parents' belief in him:

I always knew I didn't want to work for anyone else, and I always had the optimism to believe that I'd succeed. I had a mind-set from an early age that anything is possible.

I think it's because of my parents. Especially as I got older, I noticed that my friends' parents were different. They were always giving their kids a signal that they should make choices that had a higher certainty. If your biggest champion is telling you that you probably shouldn't do something, why should you believe you can do it?

My parents, Judith and Lloyd, didn't go out of their way to make me become overly pragmatic, which is something I've noticed with parents of non-entrepreneurs—they want their kids to do something safe, even if it doesn't have as high a potential. All parents want what's best for their kids, and they assume that what they had wanted when they were that age will be right for their kids, too. My parents were always incredibly supportive of whatever I wanted to do.

I have a younger brother, Zach, who's also an entrepreneur. He's nineteen and is working on starting a mobile advertising company. My parents were big believers in higher education. I remember when I told them I was going to drop out, even though I only had to take a few classes to graduate.

My cofounder and I could see the potential of our idea, and we wanted to pursue it with 100 percent of our energy, so we both dropped out. Most of the people we knew didn't see that potential and thought we were nuts. My parents were incredibly supportive. It was important to have someone on my side who recognized the magic of what could be created.

John was willing to take risks because, when he made mistakes as a child—pulling out his neighbor's plants or printing inappropriate things in the school paper—his parents didn't punish him for experimenting. They told him how to fix the situation, which he did, learning and growing. It paid off:

Yesterday I closed a big transaction. It was an incredibly gratifying conversation to be able to call my parents and share my success with them. They've always believed in me and were so aligned with whatever I wanted to do. I was so proud to have earned their support.

Dhani Jones: I'll Find Something

As we saw earlier in our discussion about entrepreneurs and school (rule 3), Dhani Jones, the NFL linebacker who went on to host a TV show and cofound a creative agency, wasn't always a superstar, nor has he always been as confident as he is today, according to his mom, Nancy. And yet, she explains, confidence is one of the most important attributes of an entrepreneur.

"Entrepreneurs are fearless," she told me, adding that they'll risk putting everything on the line to achieve what they think is important:

Money doesn't drive them. Passion does. They believe they'll always have enough money to survive. A lot of people are frightened to let go of what they've attained, but if parents have instilled enough self-confidence that the child believes they'll manage, the kids can approach life fearlessly.

That kind of confidence doesn't just develop on its own. When Dhani was still in high school, his mom played a pivotal role by standing up for him. It was Dhani's senior year, and as a successful linebacker he was getting recruited by lots of colleges including Navy and Washington. But he wasn't being considered for the football team at the University of Michigan, where he'd always wanted to go.

So Nancy and Dhani went to Ann Arbor one weekend, and they stopped in to talk with the head football coach. He told them that the Wolverines weren't looking for linebackers, and that they'd already given out all their scholarships. But, the coach said, because Dhani had already been admitted to Michigan on the strength of his grades, he could try to "walk on" the team, which meant that he would play without a scholarship, and without the status that goes with it.

Dhani didn't say anything, but Nancy could see that he was crushed. She had a strong sense that the coach hadn't bothered to look at Dhani's football tape and had no idea how talented her son was. And so Nancy turned to the coach and said, "I'm not paying to go here, when Washington has offered Dhani a full scholarship. But, just so you know, when he's playing in the Rose Bowl for Washington, he'll sack your quarterback, and you're going to be really sorry."

Nancy knew Dhani was so good that the coach would want him if he looked at Dhani's tape, and apparently her comment caused him to review it. That was on a Sunday. On Tuesday, Dhani got a call from the Michigan coach. Two days later, the Wolverines sent their quarterback coach to watch Dhani play for his high school team. Twenty-four hours later, Michigan offered Dhani a full scholarship. Getting All-Big Ten honors his last three years playing for the Wolverines proved Dhani's mom had been right. The best part of this story is that Nancy was more prescient than even she could have imagined: when Michigan played in the 1998 Rose Bowl, Dhani sacked Washington State's quarterback—twice.

By the time Dhani graduated from Michigan, he had developed a steadfast faith in himself. When he was drafted by the New York Giants in the sixth round, several people told him not to count on making the team. But he packed up all his belongings anyway and prepared to drive to New York.

"How do you know you'll make the team?" Nancy asked.

"I think I'll make the team," Dhani said, "but even if I don't, I have a degree from Michigan, and I'll find something."

I'll find something—I can't think of three words that better capture the entrepreneurial spirit. They don't show arrogance, or a belief that it's impossible to fail, or to be wrong, or to make mistakes. They show the self-confidence to meet challenges, solve problems, and handle anything that comes up. Without that kind of confidence, no budding entrepreneur can get very far. When he was younger and less confident, Dhani's mom's belief in him helped build his confidence. Five years later, his mom could relax, knowing her job was done, and he was ready to take on the world. He actually did make the team, and played for the Giants for four years, then moved to the Eagles and the Bengals. And when his football career ended, Dhani turned his considerable talents to becoming an entrepreneur.

RULE 6

Embrace Adversity

I think there's a common perception that successful entrepreneurs have had a straight-line path to success. People look at Bill Gates, Jeff Bezos, and Mark Zuckerberg and think, of course, their future success must have been obvious to everyone, their path must have been smooth. Yet for many of the entrepreneurs I spoke to, it could not have been more different.

When I speak with the mothers of enormously successful kids, I often hear more about challenges than an easy road. More about struggles and obstacles than brilliance or intellectual gifts. More about parenting strategies than raw talent. More about financial issues than wealth. More about death or divorce or illness than fairy tale childhoods.

Of the entrepreneurs profiled in this book, many faced tough situations: some grew up poor; some struggled with learning issues or other problems in school; many came from difficult family circumstances; several had parents who divorced; some had parents who were struck by major illness. In fact, ten percent had parents who died before the kids finished college, an astonishing number. Even if they didn't face major crises directly, often their parents taught them about their ancestors' struggles. And they learned to overcome adversity. As Winston Churchill said, "Success is not final...failure is not fatal...it's the courage to continue that counts."

In his book *The Gift of Adversity: The Unexpected Benefits of Life's Difficulties, Setbacks, and Imperfections* (2013), Norman Rosenthal says that our most important lessons are learned from life's challenges. He discusses different types of adverse situations and shows how each kind of challenge can lead to its own form of wisdom. In chapters such as "Don't Hold On to a Grudge" and "Hold On to Dreams," he shows how people gain resilience from confronting difficult situations.

Of course, most entrepreneurs don't learn how to overcome challenges by reading a book. They learn it by watching their parents—and especially their moms—do it, day after day.

The fantasy about entrepreneurs is that they're geniuses who can do anything with the snap of a finger—even conjure up whole industries out of thin air. In reality, though, most entrepreneurs face enormous adversity before they achieve success. What sets them apart from other people is their combination of vision and resilience. Vision isn't completely teachable, but I learned from my interviews with entrepreneurs that resilience most definitely is.

OBSTACLES AS OPPORTUNITIES

None of us would knowingly choose adversity, but I believe that we get to choose how we meet it. We can choose resilience, or we can lower our expectations and even retreat into blame, self-pity, or fantasy. We can settle for being unhappy. One thing entrepreneurs seem not to have learned is how to settle for less than they want. That's an effect of resilience, a quality that many of the entrepreneurs I talked with trace to their parents.

At its core, the entrepreneurial spirit isn't about parlaying gifts and advantages into wealth, power, and prestige. It's about refusing to back down, no matter what.

Sean Stephenson: Outcome Oriented

Sean Stephenson was born with osteogenesis imperfecta (OI), or brittle bone disease. He's three feet tall and uses a wheelchair. But after you've heard him talk a few minutes, you realize he doesn't think he has problems. And then after a few more minutes, you yourself begin to think he doesn't have problems either. He's as mesmerizing, charismatic, and inspirational a speaker as you've ever heard. You stop seeing the wheelchair. You start to see instead one of the coolest people you've ever met.

By the time Sean was eighteen, he had broken two hundred bones. Then he went on a plant-based diet, eating food that kept calcium in his bones. He got stronger, and now he's even able to work out, which he does every day in the home gym he designed.

I spoke with his parents, Gregg and Gloria, who told me that when Sean was born, a doctor told them that all children with OI are bright and outgoing. That turns out not to be so, but they didn't know that until Sean was ten. And maybe it was because they believed it, but in his case, it was true.

Besides vowing to create as normal a childhood as they could for Sean and his older sister, Gloria and Gregg encouraged him in all his pursuits. They told me that if something didn't work, they tried it another way. And when someone said, "He looks different," they said, "No, he looks memorable." When someone called him "a wheelchair person," they said, "No, he's a person in a wheelchair." And when people said he had a handicap, they said, "Everyone has a handicap. You just can't always see it." They always told him, "It's okay to be different. It's okay to be who you are."

Sean experienced a lot of discrimination when he was young. One school wanted to transfer him to a school for children with disabilities, but his parents refused. And in college, when he applied for a job, he was told, "We've already hired our

153

wheelchair person." But he kept his sense of humor and didn't let those incidents discourage him.

Since there were lots of things Sean couldn't do while he was growing up, his parents let him play video games, more than they would have if he'd been more mobile. Sean loved sports, and so he loved playing sports video games. One day, he was sad because he couldn't play any sports except the ones on his game console. To cheer him up, his dad said, "You can always make a lot of money and own a team one day."

Often, when Sean was young and couldn't play with other kids, he spent his time watching adults and making mental notes. He loved to figure out what makes people tick. He realized that everyone has fears about the same things, and that everyone experiences joy about the same things.

It isn't often that someone three feet tall wheels into a room. Sean knew he could easily command attention. He never had stage fright, and he learned that once you have people's attention, you have to keep it. He always had compassion, and he knew he wanted to help people. In fact, the first time I heard him talk, he said, "Guys, why are you afraid to ask a girl to dance? Look at me. If I'm not afraid, you shouldn't be, either."

Sean began his career as a public speaker when he was in high school. One speaking invitation led to another, and soon he got paid—$200 the first time. It hadn't even occurred to Sean that he could get paid to speak. He kept it up through high school and college. But one thing he refused to do was speak only to people with disabilities.

It was through the Make-A-Wish Foundation that Sean met his mentor—Tony Robbins, the famous motivational speaker. Tony told Sean, "You can do this, too. And you have an advantage over me. When I tell people that they can overcome anything, they reply that it's easy for me to say. But they'll never say that to you."

Sean became outcome-oriented. He told his parents, "If I can't do it myself, I have to figure out a way to get what I want," and that taught him to keep trying different approaches until he solved a problem. When he broke his arm in high school and couldn't write out his math solutions, he learned how to come up with the answers in his head. Then he had to argue with his teacher so he wouldn't have to submit the worksheets.

Though he was generally optimistic, there were still times when Sean felt dejected. His parents never discounted his feelings, but they also encouraged him not to wallow in them. When he was sad, his mom told him, "You get to choose how you're going to feel. All emotions are valid. But feeling sorry for yourself isn't a good place to live. You have to decide how long you're going to feel that way. If you can't decide, I'll decide for you and set the egg timer. You can feel sad for twenty-five minutes."

Sean spent more time with his family than other kids did because he couldn't do some things on his own. So the family became very close and traveled a lot, visiting forty-seven states together. Gregg and Gloria tried to show their kids how other people lived, exposing them to as many places and people as possible.

Sean's parents told me that the choices they made as a family gave him opportunities to do many things. But they never directed him toward any career: "We let him do what he wanted. We never told him what he could and couldn't do from his chair. We let him figure it out." So that's exactly what he did.

While enrolled as a student at Chicago's DePaul University, Sean worked as a White House intern for President Bill Clinton. He published *Get Off Your "But": How to End Self-Sabotage and Stand Up for Yourself*, with a foreword by Tony Robbins. He became a therapist with a private practice working with top executives from all over the country, who consult with him in day-long sessions to learn how to be happier. Oh, and in 2012, the Three Foot Giant married lovely, successful, five-foot-tall Mindie Kniss, a business coach and former *Fortune* 100 entrepreneur. They live in Arizona.

Did Sean's physical limitations result in his being entrepreneurial, because he had to figure out his own ways of accomplishing his goals? Or would he have accomplished just as much if he'd been three feet taller? We'll never know, of course. But we do know that with his parents' help, he learned to view his challenges not as a burden, but as an opportunity.

Most children don't face obstacles as imposing as Sean's. But the more common difficulties of childhood—getting bullied or teased, failing to fit in, having a hard time making friends—can feel powerfully intimidating to a kid. Those challenges present the same choice that Sean faced—to give up or keep trying. That's important for everyone, no matter how tall.

Ellen Gustafson: Outlasting the Mean Kids

Today Ellen Gustafson is beautiful, happily married, successful, and very involved with her causes. In 2007, she cofounded FEED Projects with Lauren Bush after Lauren created the FEED Bag, a tote whose proceeds feed one child for a year for each bag sold, through the World Food Program. Ellen has cofounded other food programs and initiatives since then, including the 30 Project, a food policy research center in New York that also operates a health and fitness program in public schools; Food Tank, the "food think tank" she cofounded with Danielle Nierenberg; and the Change Dinner campaign and HealthClass 2.0, both intended to change attitudes toward food at home and in schools. But, as she told me, life wasn't always easy for her:

I was very big when I was young, and really teased for that. They called me Cow and Big Bird. I stood out because I was so tall. In late elementary school and middle school, I had a lot of trouble with friendships.

All parents struggle with how much to help their children in difficult situations. Should they fix them or let their children struggle and learn to fix the problems themselves? Ellen's parents did a little of each:

It got so bad that my parents moved me from a small, sheltered school to a big public school after fourth grade. They wanted to take me away from kids who were mean and they thought I might find more friends in a bigger school.

At the time, I wanted my parents to fix the situation for me, but they couldn't. I realize now parents can't do that for you. You have to do it yourself.

So they gave me the tools to handle it myself. They told me I was talented and good enough, and that I didn't need to be hurt by those mean kids.

And then it was sink or swim, which in retrospect helped prepare me for the big wide world. My mom was very good at balancing being comforting and making me solve problems on my own. She made me feel I wasn't a big ugly monster, even if the kids called me that, but she didn't try to make friends for me. She taught me that life won't always be fair. People won't always be nice to you. Things won't always turn out the way you hope.

This has really helped me in my professional life. It's helped me understand that my convictions and what I thought about the world were right, even if others didn't agree with me.

Her mom's approach enabled Ellen to transform a potentially damaging experience into an attitude toward challenges that later propelled her entrepreneurial ventures. Ellen also gained some important insights into human behavior:

In eighth and ninth grades, when the other kids started growing, it all worked out. I had the classic "ugly duckling" transformation, as suddenly I wasn't taller than everyone else. But it was interesting for me to observe because I saw how differently people treated me when they thought I was attractive, compared to when they thought I wasn't.

The love and support from my parents got me through those difficult times. I didn't care as much that those kids in my class were mean to me, because my parents kept telling me I was a smart, capable person—and I decided they were probably right.

No Time for Self-Pity

Parents have a powerful instinct to shield their children from trouble and protect them from the pain the world can inflict. I'm confident that mothers who raise entrepreneurs don't feel that impulse less strongly than anyone else. But the mothers I talked with chose to let their children experience and respond to difficulty. They knew, consciously or not, that for their children to reach their true potential, they would have to learn to meet adversity head-on.

Sean Carasso: Solving It Together

Sean Carasso was backpacking around Africa in 2008, when he went to the Democratic Republic of Congo. There he met five child soldiers who had been abducted from their homes, subjected to unimaginable conditions, and forced to kill. And then he learned that young children who were too small to carry a gun were sent to the front lines armed with only a whistle—to distract the enemy or to act as cannon fodder.

He helped the children escape, wrote about the experience, and sent it to eighty friends and family members. People forwarded his e-mail to others they knew, and it went viral. The next day, he had thousands of e-mails from people asking how they could help. He realized he had the power to do something about it, so he formed Falling Whistles, a campaign for peace in Congo. They raise funds by selling metal whistles people wear as a necklace to let the world know they're whistleblowers for peace. The whistle has been converted into a voice to stop the warfare that continues to grip parts of Congo and its neighbors in the aftermath of the Second Congo War (also known as the African World War)—the deadliest war of our time, with millions dead and displaced.

Sean told me about something momentous that happened in his family when he was young: his family lost all their money. Other families might have been crushed by this—or at least tried to shield their children from it. Sean's family embraced it—and even learned to have fun with it. It's another example of taking something positive from adversity. Sean told me:

I still remember the dinner conversation with my parents, my grandparents, my brother, and me. My father's business partner had absconded with all the money. My dad sat us down and said, "We have nothing left." I was in third grade.

Glow-in-the-dark necklaces were brand new then, and my grandpa thought we could sell them. So we bought a load of them and went to parks and sold them to kids. I loved it. And I was a really good salesman—probably because I was selling to kids my age. We did this a few times a week for the next few years while my dad was in a lawsuit to try to get his money back.

And now I think back to when I was twenty-six, completely broke, and wanting to raise money to help the people in Congo. I think that there must have been something in my subconscious that told me to start selling necklaces.

The other thing we did when we didn't have any money is my mom ran a swimming camp in our backyard. It was great, full of fun and laughter. I loved that everyone was at my house. So when we started selling necklaces for Falling Whistles, I started holding events in my backyard in Venice, and bringing in the community, just like my mom had done. We'd educate them about what was happening in Congo; we had a musician, a fire, live art. It wasn't combative, as activism often is; it was inclusive and warm.

This spirit of survival and resourcefulness has deep roots in his family, Sean explained. His father is descended from Holocaust survivors—his great-grandmother was smuggled onto a ship in Greece as a stowaway at the age of fourteen, but the rest of her family perished.

Sean learned early that hardship didn't have to send a person into isolation or despair. Instead, it could be used as fuel to connect with, and serve, others who faced adversity.

Sean's parents didn't hide the family's problems from their children. They let the boys participate in solving them, in creative and playful ways. What could be better training for entrepreneurship than that? Sean learned one response to problems can be to create, laugh, and play.

Jenna Arnold: There Are Many Paths

We met Jenna Arnold, founder of the content creation company Press Play, when we were exploring how schools aren't always the best incubators of future entrepreneurs (rule 3). But Jenna's mom, Lauren, told me that learning issues weren't Jenna's only challenge while she was growing up:

When Jenna was ten, her hair fell out. One day I noticed a bald spot. I took her to a doctor, who told her she had an advanced case of alopecia. Within a month, she was completely bald.

Jenna somehow found the strength to get through it. She wore a wig for the next five years—she didn't want her friends to know. I washed it every day.

We finally took her to the Cleveland Clinic. They told us that she had autoimmune issues triggered by environmental and emotional conditions.

She was taking all sorts of medication. After two years she said, "Mom, let's sit in the hot tub and talk." Then she said, "I want to heal myself."

I couldn't see past the baldness. I couldn't see the future.

My husband said, "Let her have this adversity. She will grow from this."

And he was right. I grew from it, too. A friend told me, "It's time for you to get out of her hair so it can grow back." A light bulb went on.

I agreed to let Jenna spend the summer with an aunt she liked.

Two years later, she spent the summer with her uncle in California. Before school started, she came home still wearing her wig and said, "Mom, I have to show you something." She took the wig off. She had a gorgeous full head of hair. She said, "I'm afraid to take my wig off, because what if it falls out again?"

She decided to take the wig off anyway. She thought nobody had known she'd been wearing one. When she arrived at school the first day, all her friends hugged her and said, "Your hair grew back!" They had all known the whole time but had never said anything, because they hadn't wanted to embarrass her.

But Lauren told me that Jenna's struggles didn't end there—sometimes her classmates were unkind:

In the middle of high school she said, "I can't take these girls anymore. I've found an international exchange program, and I'm going to Spain. I don't like the focus on makeup. I don't like that my sixteen-year-old friend wants a boob job. I need to see what else there is in the world."

Some parents would have balked at the idea of letting a struggling teenager go overseas. But Jenna's mom embraced it:

We trusted her instincts for herself and her survival during those difficult teen years. When life got tough for Jenna, we recognized the importance of getting her into a different environment so she would see that the world was bigger than the world she'd known. We allowed her to leave the country for an international year to remove herself from the mean girls.

As my husband and I realized who she was, we supported her so that she would fulfill her potential and find her life's purpose, which, based on her compassion, we thought would be philanthropic.

She wrote about her hair in her college admissions essay, and about the lessons she'd learned coping with adversity. I always knew that she was such a special person, and that I needed to trust her instincts because she knew herself, and what was best for her, better than I could ever know her.

Lauren also told me that she talks with young women all the time about the things that matter when it comes to raising children.

"It's easiest in hindsight, of course," she said. "In the throes of parenting, it's sometimes hard to see a path forward."

She told me that as she watched Jenna grow, she embraced certain insights that became mantras. Here are the hard-won observations Lauren learned to live by:

- Perfect is the enemy of good.

- With every problem there is a gift; our life lessons are wrapped in those problems.

- Everything happens for a reason; trust the process.

- There are many paths to adulthood.

- People peak in their own time. I had an adult peaker; her best days are still ahead.

- Adversity is natural for a soul with such a purposeful mission.

- Gratitude and grace are the way; be grateful for your child's differences.

Lessons like these stand in stark contrast to the approach of some of today's parents, who try to shield their children from adversity, not realizing that learning to deal with it can help children become fearless, resilient adults.

RESILIENT FOR LIFE

Some of the entrepreneurs faced their biggest crises after their childhood years. Only in the wake of those challenges did they realize the full power of their upbringing.

Nyla Rodgers: Turning Grief into Action

Nyla Rodgers is living testament to the effect that a resilient parent can have. Her mother, Stephanie Moore, died while Nyla

163

was in grad school, and Nyla redirected all her energy to starting a nonprofit to honor her mom—Mama Hope, which has established thirty-four health, education, agriculture, and water projects to help 150,000 people in four African countries. She's also been inspiring people with her Stop the Pity campaign, the spirit of which can be traced directly back to her mom's approach to life. Here's what Nyla told me:

> The main lesson I learned from my mom was that I was a global citizen—I wasn't just an American. I was part of the whole world, and what I did affected the whole world, not just my community. We're interconnected, and what you do matters. She taught me that when I was really young.
>
> I grew up in the Bay Area, an only child raised by a single mother. She was a hotel concierge. One day she took a dance class for fun and realized she could teach the class better than the teacher. So she studied videos, and when I was six and she was the age I am today, she opened a dance studio. She taught every kind of ballroom class—swing, jitterbug, tango, waltz, two-step. She did this so she could be with me during the day. She taught in the evenings.
>
> She showed me I could do anything I set my mind to. I never realized we were struggling financially, although looking back now, I can see that we were. "No" was never an option. Not being able to do what we wanted was never an option. Even if my mom didn't know anything about it, she always figured it out. She hadn't finished college, but at a time when other moms generally weren't starting their own businesses, she did that, too. She wanted to do something she loved, and she raised me on that income for sixteen years.
>
> When she got older, she decided she no longer wanted to put on a sexy dress to teach dance, so she started teaching creative writing out of her home. She had taken a couple

classes and decided she could do it. She was even more successful than she had been teaching dance.

Nyla's mother taught her, both by example and through her advice, that the way to do something is to go out and do it. Her mom never paused to reflect on the difficulty of raising a child as a single mother, or to worry that she lacked the proper qualifications to do something she wanted to do.

Then, Nyla said, her mom got cancer:

When my mom was sick, her students were all there for her. People signed up on an hourly basis to spend time with her. She was never alone. My mom was a shining beacon of what's possible when you follow your heart.

She was the opposite of parents who tell their kids to finish everything on their plate. She was adamant that you should only take what you need. She would say, "Don't take any more than that. When you leave something, you make it possible for others to have something, not just for you to have something. When you're not taking everything, there's more for everyone."

And she also taught me to do what you can. We delivered food on Thanksgiving. We always did service work during the holidays. We were always giving back, even though we didn't have very much. It set up the feeling for me that no matter who you are, you always have something to give.

That sense of generosity was combined with a spirit of self-sufficiency and a belief in hard work. If you wanted to do something, you worked to make it happen:

I always wanted to do international work and see the world. I would watch National Geographic *stories with my grandmother.*

I took my first overseas trip when I was fifteen and my French class was going to France. I really wanted to go, and my mom said if I could raise half the funds, she would match me. That's what started my entrepreneurial work. I babysat, mowed lawns, walked dogs, taught swimming, did data entry. I worked fifteen hours a day, seven days a week, for a month to raise the money. By the end of the summer, I'd raised enough to go.

Nyla went to UC Santa Barbara, she told me, and she majored in global studies. As a freshman, she was asked to write about the career she wanted, and she wrote that she wanted to do international community development work. Nyla continued her story:

When I left for college, my mom had an empty nest. She had a phobia about flying, so she never left the U.S., but she still managed to help people around the world. In her mind, she was a global citizen, and she always tried to do something bigger than herself.

So she started sponsoring an orphan in Kenya named Benard. He became her son. I had just finished college and started grad school, studying international relations with a focus on peace and conflict transformation. She and Benard kept writing letters to each other, back and forth. They'd never met, but my mom had a picture of each of us on her mantel. When she first got sick, it was her dream to go to Africa and meet him.

Nyla's mother died before she could go. But she continued to provide inspiration:

Two weeks after she passed away, a friend of my boyfriend's mother was planning an environmental trip to Africa with her students and said she was looking for someone to go with

*her. Incredibly, it was in the same village where Benard lived.
I told her I'd love to go, and I wrote his sponsoring organization to say I wanted to meet him.*

*When I arrived in Benard's village, there were five
hundred people holding a memorial service in honor of my
mom, singing "Amazing Grace" under a canopy. I hadn't
known that while my mom was sick, she had held a fundraiser
and raised $1,500 for the women there to start businesses.
They had wanted to start a community bank, and the seed
money my mom had raised had transformed their community.*

*I was struggling with what to do with the leftover love I
had for my mom. I think that's what grief is—we don't know
what to do with our leftover love. When we're children, we
send love to our parents every day, and if they die, we have no
place to send the love. It gets stuck, and that's what grief is.*

*The people in the village presented me with a statue of
two giraffes with their necks intertwined. They said, "We're
giving you this statue because your mom had the vision to see
her feet and the vision to see far beyond. And it's obvious you
are a giraffe as well."*

They were right. What the giraffes symbolized—the rare
combination of down-to-earth, practical humility and visionary
perspective—shaped Nyla's next move:

*I had been working for international aid organizations like
the U.N. In that moment, I realized I'd never seen anything
as impactful as my mom's $1,500. In bigger organizations, it's
always about the organization, not the community. I decided
right then to dedicate my life to finding other communities
like this one, by asking what they needed and funding it. I
would do it in honor of my mom, and I'd call it Mama Hope.*

*What separates it from other organizations is that it
started from love because I was so inspired by how ten women*

had taken that funding from my mom to start businesses and, by putting the profit back in the community, helped the whole community.

When I talk to a community, I ask about their vision, what they need. We create a partnership. I don't create dependence—it's not a handout. Often, communities have the tools to be a success. They just need the funding. I believe a community can solve its problems if it has the resources it needs.

Nyla took her mom's approach to life and turned it into an organization that is changing the way the world sees poverty. Her mom's influence lives on in other ways, too. Stephanie Moore's writing students still meet every week. Three of the group's members have published books, and all of them have had their work published in literary magazines. And they get together at a monthly poetry reading, Pints & Prose, to raise money for Mama Hope.

Deena Robertson: Live Every Moment

Deena Robertson, who cofounded Modo Yoga with her sister Jess, experienced a devastating injury as a young adult. She turned her rehabilitation into an opportunity to change what she was doing with her life.

Deena, Jess, and their sister, Shauna, grew up in a small town outside Toronto. Shauna, three years older than Jess, spent twenty years in the film industry and now raises money for charities through an online crowdfunding website she cofounded, CrowdRise. Deena told me that there was nothing for the three of them to rebel against, because everything they did was okay:

My mom had told us, "We believe in you as individuals, and we believe in your choices." Because my parents trusted me to make good decisions, I wanted to honor that. They said, "If you drink, call us." So I didn't drink.

Deena was passionate about three things in school—photography, English, and, especially, sports. When she was in fourth grade, she was put on the eighth grade basketball team, and by the time she reached eighth grade, she was really good at a lot of sports. Her teammates were her best friends.

When she was a junior in high school, however, her school dropped the sports program.

"That's what I lived for," Deena said, "so what was the point of staying in school?"

She was uninspired by her classes—and, in a terrible turn of events, her best friend committed suicide.

"I realized I was using school for a distraction," she told me. "I think so many kids are in school for the end goal. I wasn't getting what I could get out of it. I didn't want to go back there."

So she talked to her mom, Janet, who's called JJ. Deena told JJ that she hated school and wanted to leave. JJ had been a teacher at that school for many years, but she told Deena, "I'll support you. If you're not interested, drop out."

When I talked with JJ about Deena's not wanting to stay at her school, she said, "I felt she was my child, not the school system's. What my children learned in the world was more important to me than school."

She then arranged for Deena to enroll in an alternative school that allowed home study, and Deena, through a college program, was able to condense her last year in high school to a single semester. She was thriving.

Deena next enrolled in an acting program in Vancouver. But while she was there, a large blackboard fell on her and fractured her back. Suddenly the super-competitive athlete could barely move and was told that she might not walk again.

169

Deena flew home and began rehabbing with yoga. It healed everything and changed her life. She decided that instead of acting, she would open a yoga studio. She and Jess started Modo Yoga, and they now have more than seventy-five hot-yoga studios across the U.S. and Canada. The sisters are committed to promoting ethical, compassionate, environmentally conscious living through their studios, and their motto is "Calm mind, fit body, inspired life."

Deena's response to the accident—working hard, through yoga, to heal—didn't come out of nowhere. She told me that family members before her had experienced plenty of adversity:

> My mom lost her dad when she was sixteen, and then, when she was twenty-one, she lost her mom after a three-year battle with a massive brain tumor. My sister Jess had severe scoliosis and was told she'd need a metal plate in her spine. My dad broke his neck two weeks after Jess was born and was told he'd never walk again.

Today, happily, every member of Deena's family is strong and healthy, physically and emotionally. Deena told me that's because learning from challenges has always been integral to her family's life:

> The cool thing is, we really are all deeply grateful for this so-called adversity that happened to our family. Those experiences have been our greatest teachers, the long-term gifts that have made us who we are today. Adversity has a way of placing you in front of a crossroads. Either you die in the habit of pain and suffering, or you dive into the power of an empowered life through choice.
>
> All of our life is just made of moments, and we can label them good, bad, happy, or sad, but they are all moments in time. So why do we give so much attention to the pain in our

life? Imagine if we spent as much time thinking about a beautiful sunset as we do about our pain!

Deena told me that with yoga she rehabbed her mind as well as her body. Today, not only is she strong, graceful, and athletic, but one of the most joyful people I know.

Hooman Radfar: Focus and Keep Going

For Hooman Radfar, the most striking experience of adversity came after he'd become an entrepreneur. His mom's example, and her advice, helped him figure out how to deal with it.

Hooman, born in London shortly after his family emigrated there during the Iranian Revolution, grew up in Pittsburgh. He graduated magna cum laude in computer science and economics from the University of Pennsylvania before earning a master's in engineering from Carnegie Mellon, where he researched social networking. In 2004, with his younger brother Cyrus, he cofounded Clearspring Technologies to create products and platforms based on their research into web services and social networking. Hooman later acquired AddThis, a social infrastructure platform reaching one and a half billion users monthly across a network of fourteen million publishers. He subsequently sold it and joined the cofounders of Uber and Foursquare at Expa, which works with proven founders to launch new companies. Their parents are both psychiatrists, and got divorced when Hooman was twelve years old. The boys also have a much younger brother, Darius. Hooman told me that he believes he and Cyrus became entrepreneurs because of their mother:

> *I have a very strong mom who was so influential in my life. She's a very persistent woman who knows how to take a punch, which is so important for entrepreneurs, because you get a long string of no's before you get some yesses.*

171

Some parents are so determined for their kids to succeed that they foist their own interests onto them. But Hooman's mom, Soraya, took a different approach, by supporting her children's passions:

My mom always promoted and supported whatever we were interested in. From a young age, I was constantly drawing. I would steal my dad's computer paper and draw with a pencil for hours. My mom recognized my talent and asked a colleague at her job who was also an art teacher to work with me. So from fifth grade through high school, her friend gave me art lessons.

Mom always wanted to help us unlock our potential. When she saw that my brother and I were interested in programming, she arranged for us to go to a computer camp for the summer. The first time I saw the Internet was at computer camp, and I was blown away. From then on, we were hooked.

She thought we were unstoppable, so we decided we must be. When I left for college, I was intrigued with day trading. Trading in my dorm room, I was making real money—tens of thousands of dollars on paper. When the market crashed, I followed it down and lost most of the money I'd made.

I was so depressed. I called my mom, crying. "I've lost all the money!"

I've never forgotten what she said. "I have news for you. That's not the only time you'll lose money. Do you know how many times I've had to start over? When I came to this country, I had nothing and had to start again and keep applying to hospitals until I got a position. Focus on school. Keep going."

She was so calm, so confident, so reassuring. I never looked at failure the same way again.

But it wasn't the last time she'd teach Hooman that lesson:

I had started a company after grad school. We pitched it to some early investors, who were supportive. Then we went to Silicon Valley, and no one was interested.

We were upset, but we decided to change direction and focus on the social area instead of the technological. We told our investors, who said, "We'll support you if you change, but we won't fund you."

I was wrecked. I called my mom, so upset, and said, "It's over. They won't give us any more money!"

She was so calm. She said, "You're going to be okay. You'll get more money. Go in the direction you want."

This time, the lesson seemed to stick:

It was so powerful for me, because I had seen my mom battle and persist and come out on top. I had watched her on her journey.

My parents were divorced by then, and she was a single mom who was on her own, but she had done it. She was the master of her own destiny, and we had watched her take hits and bounce back up. So we knew we could do it, too. She was like a metronome—she always brought me back to the center.

We only had a few months of cash left, but we walked away from our first investors. We pitched new investors, and they gave us $2 million, and we moved to D.C. to be near them. And Clearspring became a huge success.

Hooman and Cyrus grew up in difficult circumstances, with parents who struggled. The parents didn't shield their sons from adversity, and the boys learned to grow stronger from it. Hooman told me it helped shape them. He also shared his own ideas about the essential ingredients of entrepreneurship:

> I think you need three qualities to be an entrepreneur.
>
> First, you have to be willing to take more hits than the guy next to you. You have to be willing to run head first with all you've got. And you have to be willing to run into failure. That persistence is the key.
>
> Second, you have to have a passion.
>
> Third, you have to be creative and be able to run down the path with that idea for a very long time.

Watching his mom cope with adversity, and then learning to cope with it himself, helped Hooman become an entrepreneur. Whether or not your own children ever do so, the lessons you teach them about responding to adversity will help shape what they do when life doesn't go their way.

RULE 7

Nurture Compassion

As we've learned, the path to entrepreneurial success often isn't as smooth as some imagine. An entrepreneur's development can be forged through difficulty—a common theme of my interviews with entrepreneurs and their moms.

As my interviews proceeded, I began to notice another common theme. It turned up in conversations with people who had overcome great challenges as well as in conversations with people who had enjoyed great advantages. Most of the entrepreneurs I talked with, competitive though they are, weren't raised just to look out for number one, or to win at the expense of others. And they definitely weren't raised to think only about money. They were raised to give back, to help others, to think about how they can contribute to their communities, and to be conscious of the positive impact they can have on the world. They were raised to have compassion and to let it fuel their work. Their parents nurtured that attitude with their words and their actions.

Consider Ellen Gustafson, who was cruelly teased at school but grew up to cofound FEED Projects (rule 6):

"My mom always told me that the most important thing in your life is what you're doing for the benefit of others," Ellen told me. "It's not about money, clothes, or cars. Both my parents had leadership positions in organizations that were involved in giving back, and they talked to me about why that was important. They were involved with Catholic church clubs, and my mom volunteered with the Girl Scouts and, later, at a women's shelter."

And Ellen's mom, Maura, told me about the deliberate choices she made to nurture her daughter's compassion: "We worried about Ellen being an only child," she said. "I wanted to be sure she wasn't self-centered or self-focused, so we always did a lot of volunteer work. She'd help me make meals for the homeless. I'd say, 'If you're going to do something for your fellow man, you'll gain more from that experience than the people whom you're trying to help.' She saw us doing that, and I think it had a huge impact."

Compassion may not be the first quality you associate with entrepreneurship, but I found it again and again in the entrepreneurs and moms I talked with. It became clear to me that the desire for wealth or power isn't enough to sustain the effort it takes to forge your path and change the world—a genuine desire to better people's lives can take an ambitious person much farther. And that desire doesn't fade after the IPO, or with the first million. It may even be the reason why many top entrepreneurs seem so urgently driven by the knowledge that there are always more people to help, more communities to improve, more lives to change. And for most of these entrepreneurs, that urgency was instilled in them when they were children.

A CARING VISION

Children whose parents show them how it feels to help others who are struggling, whether across the world or across the kitchen table, get a head start in developing a compassionate outlook. Early awareness of others' problems can also encourage kids to start asking entrepreneurial questions: "Do things really have to be this way? How can I make them better?"

Scott Harrison: Sweet Charity

Scott Harrison is the founder of charity: water, a nonprofit that digs, restores, and maintains wells to give millions of people around the world sustainable access to clean water. In only eight years, charity: water built sixteen thousand wells in twenty-four countries, brought clean water to five million people, and raised $170 million for the cause. These accomplishments put Scott's picture on the cover of *Inc.* magazine.

If you watch any of the videos on the nonprofit's website (charitywater.org), you'll be awed by Scott's compassion and his ability to motivate and inspire. In a relatively short time, he's improved the quality of life for millions by developing a solution to a life-threatening global problem, a solution that eluded many others who had more experience, scientific expertise, money, and political clout. But Scott had two things going for him—vision and determination—and they were integral to the mind-set he learned from his mother, Joan.

He had grown up in a small town in New Jersey and graduated from NYU. Scott's mom told me that before Scott started charity: water, he spent ten years as a New York nightclub promoter. But, she said, in spite of his financial success, her son was miserable and felt "spiritually bankrupt." Joan tells me that when he was "living a life of excess with no meaning," she referred to him as her "prodigal son."

Joan now delights in telling the rest of Scott's story:

In October of 2004, Scott turned his back on his life in New York City and boarded Mercy Ship for a year—it's a hospital ship that gives free medical care to people in West Africa. After a second tour as a volunteer, he returned with a clear vision to start a charity designed to meet a desperate need he had encountered there: the need for clean water.

Using the resources he had—dramatic photos from his Mercy Ship experience, an A-list of his former nightclub patrons, and an ability to motivate people, Scott visited night-club owners and friends and asked them to become donors. They did.

Meanwhile, having no income now, Scott lived on the sofa in a friend's apartment—the apartment that became charity: water's first office. The kitchen table was the desk, the employees were mostly volunteers, and the Internet and telephone were the main connection to donors. To hear over the workplace noise, Scott would lean out the window when he talked on the phone.

The first event was a birthday party held at the nightclub Tenjune in September 2006. Guests purchased a $20 bottle of water to get in, and Scott raised $15,000. He used the money to fix three wells and build three more in Uganda. Months later, the donors received a picture of the well that had been built with their money, and charity: water was launched.

A few years later, when the nonprofit had experienced phenomenal growth and success, a supporter came over to me at one of the events. She shared with me that in the early stages of starting charity: water, Scott had told her that his mom always said he could do it.

I asked Joan how she thought Scott had found the courage to walk away from a life of financial and professional success to start a nonprofit to make a difference in the world.

She believes it was the parenting foundation she set early on, built on spiritual community and disciplined hard work, that got Scott through tough times when she became very sick. She believes that same foundation helped him make a change years later, when he was unhappy with where he was in his life.

She gave me examples of how she instilled those values. When Scott was in elementary and middle school, she would help him sort through his clothes, books, and toys, and they would give some away to kids who could use them. On Thanksgiving and Christmas, the family delivered turkeys or canned goods to needy families. And when Scott was in high school, his church youth group spent a week helping build a youth center in a low-income neighborhood, where the group also established a vacation Bible school for children. Whenever Scott earned money, Joan said, he was free to spend, give away, or save as much as he wanted—after he had given ten percent to the church and put ten percent in savings. But Scott, touched by all the need he saw in that neighborhood, sent them all the money he had.

When Scott was a teenager, Joan became seriously ill. "He was called upon to help his dad keep our house running and take care of me, since I was completely disabled," she told me. The family's spiritual community helped reinforce the lessons that Scott had already learned, and he was able to see the positive impact of others' kindness during a difficult time.

"Because of my illness," Joan told me, "Scott saw compassion in action. Our church would supply meals, clean our house, and take care of him when I had to go to the doctor. One woman even shopped for clothes and shoes for him when I wasn't able to go to stores." It was this experience, Joan said, that led to Scott's becoming such a compassionate person, someone who would walk away from a life of comfort to save lives by bringing clean water to far-off corners of the world.

Adam and Scooter Braun:
Room for Compassion

We learned about Adam and Scooter Braun in the chapter on competing (rule 2). Adam left his high-powered consulting job to start a nonprofit called Pencils of Promise with only $25 in the bank; it now builds schools around the world. ABC News called it "the hottest nonprofit in the country." Scooter developed some of the most successful musical acts of our time. They have a sister in medicine.

The success of these two brothers can be traced to the sense of compassion and global awareness instilled by their parents. When Adam and Scooter were in their teens, their parents adopted two boys from Mozambique. It created a bond of adoptive brotherhood, which in turn led to Adam's desire to build schools around the world, and to Scooter's inviting Justin Bieber and his mom to live in a home in Atlanta that he paid for while he helped structure Justin's rise to stardom. In effect, the family members' commitment to one another spread across the globe when Bieber donated one dollar from every ticket sold on his *Believe* concert tour to Pencils of Promise, which built fifteen more schools with the proceeds.

"Our family is big on family lore," says Susan, the two entrepreneurs' mom. "Our children learned a lot about their forebears, and it frames who they are. Their grandparents and great-grandparents were people who came from Europe and pulled themselves up by the bootstraps."

Although the Braun kids didn't grow up with much adversity, they learned about it from the experiences of their parents and grandparents. Susan explained that her kids were taught from a young age to appreciate what they had, and to be aware of the suffering and hardship others had faced:

> *My father died when I was young. My mother was only thirty-five when she was left to raise three young kids alone. On my husband's side, both grandparents were Holocaust survivors who had lost most of their families. Hearing their stories had a profound impact on the boys.*

So both sides of our family had experiences where things didn't work out as they had planned. It's ingrained in us that you may have to change your plans. The safe path may not be so safe suddenly, and you'll just have to figure it out and move forward.

That perspective seems to have had a powerful effect on the boys, Susan said. Instead of making them wary, it fueled their sense of exploration and ambition:

They're not afraid of failure. They view it as a learning experience. They're not afraid of falling off the edge. Our sons have a much bigger safety net than we had, even though we told them that once they finished their education, they'd be on their own. They're more secure, more confident than we were.

Susan is another example of a full-time working mom who raised independent kids:

I was twenty-four when my first child was born, and I always worked outside the house. I didn't have a lot of free time. I couldn't have been a helicopter mom even if I'd wanted to. Because I couldn't do as much for my kids, I think it benefited them. By the time we got home from work, they'd figured stuff out they probably would have asked us to figure out for them. It made them independent, resilient.

That's not to say the boys did whatever they wanted. On the contrary, they learned early on to respect authority:

Since I'm an orthodontist, I see a lot of kids between the ages of eleven and fifteen. To me, a lot of them were over-supervised when they were young, and then their parents disappeared once their kids got to middle school. Not us. We had definite rules, with strong expectations for behavior—show respect, do your homework, go to bed on time. We had lots of rules that the boys found miserable. But, as my grandmother would say, "Better you should cry than I should cry."

There was no room for self-pity in the Braun household, nor was there room for selfishness, period. The members of this remarkable family didn't just talk about opening their hearts to others. They actually opened their lives to them:

My husband coached basketball in the summers. One summer, Sam and Cornelio were visiting from Mozambique on an exchange program and joined our son's basketball team. They were sixteen and seventeen. We took them home for a couple weeks to help them—and they never left.

One of the boys was just older and one was just younger than Adam, who was starting his senior year in high school. He had to help them academically and socially, which put extra demands on him. But what he gave them led him to see the world differently, and to appreciate everything that he'd taken for granted—simple things like having his own textbooks. Everything that Sam and Cornelio saw shocked them. The 9/11 terrorist attack occurred shortly after they came, and they were amazed that people could write critically of the government and not be arrested. They were incredulous at the idea of an anorexic girl. They couldn't believe someone could have enough food to eat and choose not to eat it. And it affected my kids as they watched their new brothers' reactions.

Taking Sam and Cornelio into the family was just one way they showed their kids—by the values they instilled and the example they set—that they could make a difference. But it wasn't the only way Susan exposed her boys to a broader perspective on life. She encouraged self-reliance for her sons from the time they were young:

> We expected the kids to have summer jobs. Both boys worked summers from the age of fourteen, starting with being life-guards and camp counselors. Adam ran basketball camps in high school and, in college, sold T-shirts and threw parties to raise money for a Cambodian children's fund. Scott was a party promoter in college, and always helped his brother.
>
> Adam went on Semester at Sea during his junior year in college. He went overseas with friends the next summer, traveling around Southeast Asia for six weeks. Then he did one more semester abroad in Australia. He landed a consulting job with Bain that would start six months later, so he back-packed his way through Central and South America for three months by himself.
>
> Adam worked at Bain for fifteen months, and then he got a sabbatical and started Pencils of Promise in 2008, when he built a school in Laos. He found he couldn't juggle both, and Bain said he had to choose. So he chose. He's built over 350 schools now in developing countries.

A WIDER WINDOW

Before a child can develop a strong sense of compassion for the world, the child needs to be shown that there's a world out there to begin with. If that sounds obvious, it's also true that the daily pressure of protecting and nurturing their kids can cause parents to lose sight of the big picture. But parents can encourage a broader, more inclusive worldview in their children by exposing them to different cultures, circumstances, and concepts. And yet, to judge from my interviews with entrepreneurs and their moms, the mothers of future entrepreneurs sometimes take an additional step. They seem to have an uncanny knack for striking a balance: they encourage their children to see themselves as capable, powerful, and able to do anything they set their minds to, but they also teach them that they belong to an interconnected whole.

Blake Mycoskie: Compassion in Action

You'll recall Blake Mycoskie, founder of philanthropic shoe company TOMS, from the chapter on letting kids learn to win and lose (rule 2). Blake's mom, Pam, told me that after he had started several businesses, something happened that changed his life:

Blake had decided to take a month off before starting a new job with one of his mentors. There were two things he'd always wanted to do—learn to sail, and learn to play polo—so he went to South America to do both.

He had just spent two weeks in Brazil, learning how to navigate a large sailboat, and now he was living at a polo academy in Argentina. He met some Americans in a café who had some old shoes they were going to deliver to an orphanage. They asked him if he wanted to go with them, and he said, "Sure!"

It broke his heart when he went to the village. It was filthy. He'd never seen such poverty. Most of the children had never even had a pair of shoes.

Many outsiders might have felt sad about that impoverished South American village and then gone on with their lives. Almost nobody would have figured out a new way to get shoes for these kids, let alone to give shoes to needy kids all around the world. Even fewer would have done what was required to execute such a plan. But not everyone was raised the way Pam Mycoskie's kids were. She told me that instilling compassion was an important part of bringing up her children:

We always adopted three or four families at Christmas through our church and bought clothes and toys that we delivered together to the kids. I adopted three children from Compassion International and was even fortunate enough to travel to Ethiopia to meet one in person. This has always been our family policy—to help those less fortunate. The kids have seen this practiced their entire lives, and it's just the way we are.

That day in Argentina, Blake's first thought was, "I'm going to go back and raise money and buy them shoes." His second thought, she said, was to start a charity. But then, Pam told me, he began to wonder if there was a way to make it sustainable, so he wouldn't have to depend on grants and donations. He discussed the idea of giving away a pair of shoes for every pair sold with Alejo Nitti, an Argentine entrepreneur who also happened to be his polo instructor. And Alejo said, "You're loco!" Alejo ended up becoming Blake's business partner. They found a garage that had been turned into a small factory for manufacturing *alpargatas*, the classic Argentine slip-on canvas shoes, and Blake determined to make them stylish. He decided to call the company TOMS, to represent the idea of "shoes for tomorrow." Pam continued the story:

That was in February. He came home with his alpargatas and worked around the clock. He finally got his first retail client, American Rag, which realized they weren't just selling a shoe, they were selling a story. The Los Angeles Times *heard about it and wrote a prominent article. We were all helping him pack up shoes on the dining room table of his apartment. He sold ten thousand pairs of shoes that summer. That meant he could give away ten thousand pairs.*

The first shoe drop, when we went back to Argentina, was that October. We gave away all the shoes. It was thrilling. He's now given away forty-five million pairs in seventy countries. Later, Blake also started selling sunglasses, and for every pair sold, a child gets the gift of sight—an eye exam or a pair of glasses.

TOMS is now valued at over $500 million, and Bain Capital bought half of the company in 2014.

But for Pam, the important thing has never been money; it's always been her family. She told me:

Our family is very close. We all still take family vacations together. To me, that closeness is one of the best things you can give your child and that's what we've always tried to do; we just loved them and supported them.

And Pam told me she discovered something astonishing about her kids:

Blake writes in his journal almost every day. One day, when he showed it to me, I realized with a shock that he and Paige had started their companies on the very same day, Paige's birthday, February 26, 2006! He was in Argentina. In his journal, he had drawn a picture of a shoe, and written, "buy a pair today, give away a pair tomorrow; TOMS is short for tomorrow." That day I'd gone to L.A. to spend Paige's birthday with her, and she told me she'd decided to buy a used sewing machine with her birthday money. They started TOMS and Aviator Nation on the very same day.

Sean Carasso:
The Allegiance of Your Conscience

Earlier, when we met Sean Carasso, cofounder of Falling Whistles, we saw that one of his primary life lessons was that hardship doesn't have to send a person into isolation or despair (rule 6). Instead, it can be used to connect with and serve others who face adversity.

People who know Sean now as a caring and compassionate person are surprised to learn that those words hardly describe who he was when he was young:

I was a very angry kid, always arguing with authority. Perhaps it's because of my bloodline—Italian, Greek, Spanish, Moroccan, Jewish, Native American, Swedish, and Norwegian. And perhaps it's because I grew up in Chula Vista, on the border of San Diego and Mexico, in a violent part of the country. My neighborhood was near the border, and there was a heavy gang culture. By the time I was in seventh grade, when we moved away, many of my friends were in a gang. By the time they were eighteen, nearly all my buddies had been to juvenile detention or had been to rehab or were dead from an overdose.

Growing up in a border town caused me to ask questions early in my life to which there are no good answers. I went surfing an hour into Mexico every weekend with my mom, and I saw the disparity in the two worlds. I asked lots of questions about why life on that side of the border was so different from our side.

My mom and I had long conversations about poverty. She was willing to listen to my frustration and to engage it. Even though there weren't great answers, we talked about why we allow the world to be like this. Even though she hadn't studied those things, she never shut down my questions.

Instead of sheltering him, Sean's mom exposed him to a broader and uncomfortable reality, and she encouraged him to think and care about it.

Sean also told me about something his mother did when he was in fifth grade that had an enormous impact on his life. Starting in fourth grade, he was "obsessed," as he put it, with the latest craze, the game of pogs, in which small flat cardboard discs, or pogs, are flipped with a heavier piece, a slammer. The player who flips all the pogs wins them all:

My parents never gave me any money, because they believed that if you wanted something, you earned it, so I started out with just one pog.

I did it constantly—during recess, after school—and I kept winning. It was like Texas Hold 'em—I got all the pogs! I loved it.

By the time we got to fifth grade, the teachers said it was too distracting, and we couldn't do pogs in school anymore. We ignored them, snuck them into school, and kept playing. One day the teachers came and confiscated all the pogs. I freaked out.

I came home and had the biggest tantrum ever. I was screaming at my mom, "It's so unfair! The injustice!" I was so mad.

And my mom, who wasn't really a protest kind of person, looked at me and asked, "Have you ever heard of a petition?"

And she taught me all about petitions, and how people collected signatures as a way of fighting for something they believed in. She gave me a history lesson, explained how petitions had been used to create change, taught me the context and the principles.

Instead of telling her son to get over it, or calling the principal to demand the return of his pogs, Sean's mom treated the situation as an opportunity to broaden her son's perspective. She helped him make a connection between his own frustration and injustice around the world. With that, Sean was off and running:

So I wrote a sign that said: WE WANT OUR POGS. And then I got every kid in fifth grade to sign the paper. And we

marched into the principal's office, and we got our pogs back.
We couldn't play at school, but we had won. It was then that
I first learned the power of the people, and that when we are
organized, authority can't win.

Sean told me that the experience changed his life and ultimately led to his being able to make a difference in the world.

Then when I was thirteen, my parents decided Chula Vista
was too violent, and they wanted to get my younger brother
Breton and me out of there. So they moved us to Austin,
Texas, which was a completely different world. The commu-
nity was wealthy, and the kids wore khaki pants and pink
polo shirts. I hated it. I had fit in in Chula Vista. I didn't fit
in there. I ran away all the time.

But I understand why they wanted to leave. The fear
that comes from violence envelops you like a cloak. In Austin,
I remember the first time I was out late at night when a car
drove by and I didn't have to jump behind a rock, because I
knew it wasn't a drive-by shooting. Living in a safe environ-
ment, without the fear, I could calm down and blossom.

Sean told me his parents didn't simply encourage him to
question rules and find a better way of doing things. They also
encouraged him to trust his own sense of right and wrong:

My dad taught me that no rule is real unless it demands the
allegiance of your conscience. You make up your own mind.
Even when I was in first grade, he allowed me to question
authority in every respect, even his. If I could construct an
argument that was better than his, if I could articulate it
calmly, saying, "I think you're wrong because...," he would
consider it and change his mind if I presented the better
argument.

This was so important to me. I felt respected. I felt that what I thought could shape reality. Of course, sometimes it also got me in trouble because my teachers didn't like being questioned.

That statement—"I felt that what I thought could shape reality"—captures the essence of the entrepreneurial mind-set. Entrepreneurs grow up believing not only that their ideas and beliefs and passions matter, but also that they can use them to change the world. And because Sean was encouraged to develop his own deeply felt sense of right and wrong, rather than simply obeying arbitrary rules handed down from an authority, he developed a powerful moral compass:

As I got older, the same things applied to drugs and alcohol and sex—the hard ones for teenagers. My dad sat me down and said, "I've done these things, and this is how it affected me, and this is how it affected my friends. You have to make up your mind about what's right." So I never felt the need to break rules. I made mostly good choices. And when I didn't, it wasn't because I was acting out of rebellion, as it was for so many of my friends.

That's the most important lesson my parents taught me. At some level, you know what's right and what's wrong, and you have to know how to listen to that voice and have the courage to follow it.

I have always loved the quote from Mahatma Gandhi: "Remember that all through history there have been tyrants and murderers, and for a time they seem invincible. But in the end they always fall. Always."

I went to the University of Texas and dropped out three credits short of graduating. I just couldn't take Biology 301, and I wanted to get started with the rest of my life.

In his twenties, Sean moved to Los Angeles and met TOMS founder Blake Mycoskie. In 2008, Sean went on the second TOMS shoe drop, which was in South Africa. It was then that he started backpacking around Africa, and he went to Congo, where he met the former child soldiers who inspired him to cofound Falling Whistles.

Falling Whistles became an influential nonprofit, but Sean was frustrated with the slow progress toward ending the bloodshed. People were still dying, an election had been challenged, and Sean didn't think the U.S. was doing enough to change things. He and his team spent months speaking with key parties in the region—organizations, policymakers, academics, corporations, and activists—and decided that the U.S. State Department needed to appoint a Special Envoy to signal the importance the U.S. placed on relations with Congo and on stopping the violence. Sean tried unsuccessfully for months to convince policymakers they should implement an existing law to appoint the Special Envoy, but he was getting nowhere. And then he thought back to when he was in fifth grade, and he decided he needed a petition.

Sean and his team launched the petition drive on a Monday, and within a week they had ten thousand signatures. In the end, the petition had twenty-four thousand signatures, including thirty-five Members of Congress, sixteen U.S. Senators, and representatives of eight U.S. and seventy-one Congolese aid organizations. Sean got his Special Envoy: former U.S. Senator Russ Feingold. Sean hopes that this diplomatic effort will change the relationship between the U.S. government and the Congolese people and help bring peace. He got the U.S. government to respond to his demand, and he did so with a petition—something his mom had taught him how to do when he was in fifth grade.

Parents often shelter their children from struggle and suffering out of fear of making them feel sad or scared. That's a natural impulse, but most of the mothers I talked to took a less fearful, more hopeful approach. By exposing children to real problems and showing them that they can affect those problems, they helped their kids learn to embrace the world rather than fear it. It's an affirmation of both reality and possibility. The lesson the child learns is: Yes, there is suffering in the world, and yes, there's plenty you can do about it.

In Sean's case, his parents talked with him honestly about their personal adversity and about the poverty he saw in the world. And by showing him how to take action to get his pogs back, they helped him learn to fight for justice—and gave him the tools he'd use to put his compassion into action.

Sean's mom couldn't have known that when he came home from school upset about pogs, her response would ultimately have an impact on world affairs. Instead of comforting him or dismissing him, she encouraged him to take action, and she changed the way he looked at the world. That's part of the responsibility and excitement of raising an entrepreneur—you never know which of your smallest actions literally may have global ramifications.

RULE 8

Be a Great Family

Most of the entrepreneurs I talked with were very close to their parents and siblings. Whether an entrepreneur grew up in a family that was big or small, rich or poor, traditional or unconventional, with one working parent or two, the effect seemed the same—an abiding sense of security and faith that a safety net would be there if it were ever needed.

Lots of close-knit families don't produce entrepreneurs, of course, but supportive close-knit families tend to be the ideal environment for incubating confident children; and confident children often grow up to be can-do, risk-taking entrepreneurs. What seems to have made the difference was the encouraging, trusting, supportive attitude of their parents.

I looked carefully at family structure to see if there is one type of family that produces these remarkable entrepreneurs; there isn't. Some are from the archetypal nuclear family—Mom, Dad, a couple of kids. Lots had divorced or single moms. Some had moms who stayed at home to raise the kids; some had moms who worked; and some had moms with intense careers who worked all the time. Some kids were the oldest of several siblings; some were only children; some were in the middle of three or four; some were the youngest of three or four or five or seven. Some were wealthy; some were middle class; some were barely scraping by. Some were in blended families with stepsiblings and half-siblings. Some grew up with adopted siblings.

Looking at all these families, I had to conclude that what matters most isn't how your family is made up, or whether your parents are married or even whether you have two parents. What matters most is your parents' attitude.

So you look at Greg Gunn or Blake Mycoskie or Eric Ryan, and you think, of course they turned out to be great entrepreneurs. They each came from what's commonly considered to be a perfect family: the parents are happily married, the kids who became entrepreneurs were the eldest, everyone loved each other. But for every Greg, Blake, or Eric, there are many incredible entrepreneurs who were raised in family situations that couldn't be more different. In fact, of the entrepreneurs in this book, those three were the exceptions, not the norm. Family structure didn't matter because each entrepreneur was raised in an atmosphere of love and support. They drew strength from their family, which they always knew stood behind them.

It's not just about having your family—whatever your family looks like—love you. It's about having them *believe* in you, encouraging you to follow your passion, trusting you to make the right choices, and not being driven by fear that you won't succeed.

From Great Families to Great Companies

If it's no accident that most of the entrepreneurs I talked with came from great families, it's also no surprise that those entrepreneurs have formed great companies that are like second families. These entrepreneurs trust and support their employees, honor their employees' differences, and create workplaces where their employees want to spend time. This is the new generation of business, where there isn't an autocratic, omniscient boss who arbitrarily orders people around. In these companies, as in the homes where these entrepreneurs grew up, people take care of each other.

Deena and Jess Robertson: Just Say Yes

We met Deena Robertson, who cofounded Modo Yoga with her sister Jess, when we explored adversity (rule 6). Their mom, JJ, is a legend to family and friends alike. When I asked JJ how she'd raised her daughters to be self-confident, successful entrepreneurs, she said, "I didn't do anything special. I raised my girls with the principles of listening to your kids, honoring your kids, and raising your kids with gratitude. Isn't that what all parents do?" I wanted to answer, "If they did, the world would be a better place."

This is what Deena told me about JJ:

> My mom always says kids are there to be your teachers. She'd say, "I never thought just because I'm the parent, I have all the answers." And her motto was "Life's more interesting if you say yes to everything."
>
> Everyone loves my family. My mom has an amazing ability to see everyone's core. She sees all their possibilities. She tells everyone they're awesome, and it makes them feel good.
>
> My mom has an endless supply of love. We never had to compete with each other for her affection, because we all knew how much she loved each of us. And she never put us in boxes—whatever we wanted to do, whatever we wanted to be, was fine with her. I think the reason I never fought with my sisters was because we never needed to vie for my mom's love and attention. We each knew we were her top priority. She loved being a mom.

Deena also told me that their family was constantly taking in strays—dogs as well as people. A couple of those people ended up staying for years.

"You have your given family and you have your chosen family," Deena said.

This attitude toward community, combined with the belief that there's always enough love to go around, is reflected in the Modo Yoga studios, where Deena and Jess want everyone to feel immediately at home.

JJ gave me several examples of how the family environment when her children were young is reflected in the Modo Yoga studios today:

Our motto was always "Silly is good." When I overhear a parent in the grocery store telling their child, "Don't be silly," I think, How sad! We made colorful, silly piñatas with papier-mâché. At their yoga studios, the sense of play and fun is continued. I think that sense of fun is one reason why they have such a loyal following.

An essential part of my girls' upbringing was play. We'd use toothpicks and chickpeas and we'd make Buckminster Fuller structures. It taught them about design. I smile when I think that Deena and Jess have designed five yoga studios and consulted on seventy others. When they were little, they designed and made all the furniture in their dollhouses—from cardboard, from dough. It stimulated more imagination than ripping plastic off of packaged toys.

We also did a lot of candle dripping. We made sculptures with different colored candles dripped into bowls of water. After an hour or so, they'd have fantastic sculptures. It taught them to take their time. If you don't rush it, the end result is stunningly beautiful. It taught the virtues of patience and dedication. Today, Deena and Jess grow their business organically.

I always honored how different each of my three daughters was. If we were making zucchini bread, I would set up three bowls so each one had her own station and could make her loaf differently. I observed and encouraged their differences. I think one reason Jess and Deena are so good at business together is that they know who they are and who the other is, and they respect the differences.

The individuality of the girls was always apparent. Jess always wanted to read. She was very academic and went to McGill. Deena didn't want to go to college. She was very hands-on, could fix anything. They're so different, and they respect each other's talents. And they bring harmony to each other. Jess's quiet scholastic interest and eco-awareness perfectly balance Deena's athleticism, enthusiasm, and involvement with teams of all kinds. I think this translates into the Modo recipe for success: Deena cheerleads the team, keeps everyone laughing and happy, and Jess grounds it with her wisdom and stillness.

The family also created important traditions, according to JJ:

Our family was very observant of Jewish holidays and traditions. During the eight-night celebration of Hanukkah, each person had a night when, instead of giving a present, they gave out wishes to the others in the family. They'd say, "I wish for you...," and it had to be something they'd thought about and knew would make the others happy.

JJ thinks this wonderful tradition shaped her daughters' attitude toward their business:

I think this is important for entrepreneurs—what will make people happy. Not just for them, but for their employees and their customers. At the yoga studios, before they put up the mirrors that cover the walls, they invite people to come and write on the wall what they want to happen. Everyone who comes into the studio who wrote on the wall knows it's there, with their hopes and dreams, right behind the mirrors. They call it a wall of intention. They believe that if you think it and you write it, it will happen. We used to do that at home.

My mom always said, "If you lead a good life, you'll find a parking spot." I believe that. We are filled with gratitude for everything we do. We are grateful for our gifts, our blessings, and our family.

My parents died in their fifties, before my kids were born. I'd bring them into my girls' lives by telling them "olden days" stories. Whenever we'd see the number 1003—for instance, if that was the time, 10:03—I'd tell them a story about my parents, because that was the address of the house I grew up in.

So how did JJ create a family life that encouraged all of her daughters to be entrepreneurial?

"Take time to listen to your kids," she told me. "Don't multi-task. Just listen. Let them show you the way. They know what they need. That's the bottom line."

Blake Mycoskie: Company as Family

When you hear what Blake Mycoskie has to say about running his company, TOMS, you can't help noticing the influence of his mom, Pam, who modeled grit and compassion for her kids and trusted them to act on their passions. Great families beget great leaders. The lessons he learned about being part of a great family translated into his being a great boss. Blake often says that one of his jobs as the leader of TOMS is to help others do their jobs better, and he does that by telling his top people to serve everyone in their groups. He calls this approach "servant leadership."

He sees mistakes as a net positive that will help the company learn and grow, and he says that one way he builds trust with his employees is by admitting his own mistakes and showing that mistakes can become opportunities. And Blake says he's made lots of mistakes at TOMS, but because he's willing to admit them, he demonstrates to his employees that he isn't going to cover up his errors or blame them on anyone else. As he says in his book, *Start Something That Matters* (2012), "If you extend more trust than you might normally be comfortable with—and more than most business books tell you to do—even though those mistakes will come with a price, over the long term you'll be paid back with interest."

It's inspiring to watch these entrepreneurs put into practice the guiding principles their families taught them by what they did every day, even more than by what they said.

The parents in this book all supported their children; the entrepreneurs support their employees. The parents honored their children's differences; the entrepreneurs honor their employees' differences. The parents trusted their children; the entrepreneurs trust their employees. The parents created a fun, loving home for their children; the entrepreneurs create a business environment where their employees want to spend time. Even though the families were different, each of these successful entrepreneurs came from a great family, regardless of how it's defined, and they've built great—though very different—companies and organizations.

INCUBATING ENTREPRENEURSHIP

As I spoke with entrepreneurs and their moms, I was struck by how often a family's values and practices—around food and nourishment, say, or principles of inclusiveness and self-reliance, or the importance of learning—ended up influencing the specific work the entrepreneurs went on to do in the business they created and the causes they spearheaded.

Ellen Gustafson: There When It Counted

We heard Ellen's story in the chapter on adversity (rule 6)—how she was teased mercilessly when she was young, but developed the confidence to try her hand at acting and go on to cofound FEED Projects and other food programs. She talked with me about the importance of growing up in a close-knit family, and told me how features of her family life—meals, political discussions, world travel—helped inform the important work she does as an adult.

When Ellen was in high school, her dad became an entrepreneur. He had some successes and some failures, she said. "This showed me that it was possible to be an entrepreneur—that if you had a strong family unit to support you, people would be there for you even if things didn't work out."

Before I started interviewing entrepreneurs and their moms for this book, I tried to imagine what the rules would be, and I thought one would be "Eat a Family Dinner Together Every Night." I was wrong. It did happen with some of the families, however, and Ellen's was one. She told me:

> We always had a home-cooked meal. We had a garden, and we shopped at a local farmers' market. My mom said that was because it was cheaper, but it certainly helped me in my current career.

Dinners with her parents—one liberal and the other conservative—were also occasions for raging political debates and taught her that there are two sides to issues. She read *Time* magazine cover to cover every week to keep up.

Ellen and her parents also traveled extensively together across the U.S. and through the Middle East, and they spent a month in Russia:

*It was just the three of us. It made us so close as a family.
And it also gave me the confidence to travel on my own later.
We didn't have the kind of money to go on glamorous vacations, but my parents took every opportunity to show me the
world.*

The family also hosted two foreign exchange students, the
first from France and the second from Spain, and Ellen is still
close to both: "My parents exposed me to so many different
people, cultures, ideas. I wouldn't be doing what I am today if
they hadn't."

Like many other entrepreneurs, Ellen had a mom who always
worked. The most important reason she became an entrepreneur,
Ellen said, was that her parents not only told her she was a
capable person but also let her *be* a capable person:

*My parents expected me to do well, but perhaps because my
mom always worked, they weren't up my butt about doing
homework. They just expected me to do it. My mom really
understood that. She did well with the balance of helping me
and letting me do it. And when it counted, she was always
there, even though most of the time I had to do things on my
own—for example, I walked to dance class after school, but
she was always there when class ended, or when I really
needed her.*

Alexis Jones: Rich in Love

After playing sports, working as a model, and giving acting a
try, Alexis Jones founded I AM THAT GIRL, an online empowerment community for girls (rule 1). Alexis told me, "My mom is
the most incredible person I've ever known—the greatest gift
from God I could have been given."

When I read that statement to Alexis's mom, Claudia Mann, she said, "Alexis gives me too much credit." Claudia told me that, although Alexis lived primarily with her, their large extended family—father, stepmother, grandparents, four older brothers, half brothers, and stepsisters—"all contributed to the fine woman she has become."

Claudia herself grew up in Oregon, the daughter of a logger, in a family without high school graduates. She had a stepbrother who was favored over her, and she eloped when she was sixteen. When she had a family of her own, including stepchildren, she made sure there was no favoritism: "From day one, it was a package deal—you take one kid, you take all of them. I work in family law, and I hammer my clients—it's not about the ego, it's about the kids."

Living in Austin, Texas, Claudia worked nights as a bartender. During the day, she taught auto repair through University of Texas extension classes—one of the rare women to do that, showing Alexis that gender didn't matter in careers. Her kids watched her struggle to improve her skills by earning a college degree as a full-time mom. "I was forty-three when I went back to college to get my BA," she said. "It was always my goal to have my kids finish college when they were young, so they'd have choices I didn't have."

Alexis is the youngest of five kids, eighteen years younger than the oldest and four years younger than the next youngest. She and her brothers played sports competitively, and each of them was supported by the entire family. "I always told them school was first," Claudia said, but she was still willing to go the extra mile, literally, to attend their games. One week she put a thousand miles on her car driving to games in San Antonio, Houston, and Dallas, even though she was working at two jobs. Claudia passed on to her daughter that will to keep showing up:

I taught Alexis to be independent, and not to rely on anyone but herself. My mom had told me that you can do anything you want, you just have to work hard. So I'd tell my kids that lots of people are applying for the same job. It's the person who's going to work the hardest, work the longest, be the most dependable, who's going to get it.

Claudia said, "Nobody gave Alexis anything. She works twelve-hour days, six days a week. I told the kids, "You can have anything you want. You just have to figure out a way to do it."

Alexis wanted to go to grad school at USC, and she'd gotten accepted, but we had no money. Her friend said, "You can live in our garage in Beverly Hills if you pay the $135 monthly storage fee to move out the stuff that's in there." So I paid that, and Alexis paid for school with scholarships and student loans. You find a way.

I'm sure Alexis was the only USC grad student living in a garage. And she did two years of grad school in one year to make it more affordable. She worked her butt off. I told my kids, "You're only limited by your imagination."

I AM THAT GIRL encourages girls to support one another and discover their true capabilities, and so Alexis, in effect, is doing for girls around the world what her family did for her. Here's what Alexis told me:

My story goes back to my mother, who had the audacity to raise a daughter to believe she could do anything. My mom worked two jobs and went to night school. She wanted all the kids to feel equally loved. Even though there were half-brothers and stepsisters, my mom always said, "Family is family." My mom set this expectation for the household: We love each other unconditionally, these are your people, we always have each other's back.

I was so rich in unconditional love and support, I felt like I'd won the lottery. My mom always told us, "If you have love, it doesn't matter if you're not pretty or if you're not wealthy." We never considered that things could be impossible. When I told my mom I wanted to champion girls and women, my mom said, "Why not you? Our generation has Oprah. Your generation has you!" It was so wonderful to grow up with this.

Matt Mullenweg: Dropout to Superstar

Matt Mullenweg cofounded WordPress, the most widely used online publishing platform, after founding Automattic, which powers WordPress; its sites reach half a billion people every month. He's been on the cover of the *San Francisco Chronicle* business section, was named one of *Inc.* magazine's "30 Under 30" in 2008, and was the youngest of *Business Week's* "25 Most Influential People on the Web" in 2009. His angel investment firm, Audrey Capital, has backed thirty start-ups. Matt is also a photographer as well as a sax player. He grew up in Houston with a sister, ten years older, who's a computer engineer. Here's what Matt's mom, Kathe, told me about her son:

The first thing I said when he was born was, "He's going to do amazing things." I think every child has infinite potential if you find what they're passionate about. If you tell a child twenty times a day from the time they're born that they're going to be fantastic, they'll be ready for kindergarten.

We made a decision when we had children that I'd stay home. I tried to foster their sense of curiosity and wonder. I believe that leads to educating yourself your entire life.

Matt's passions evolved over time, Kathe said. He also learned to compete in something other than sports:

Matt's love in the beginning was music. He just loved the saxophone. I wanted him to play violin, but he put his foot down and said, "I want to play saxophone!" That was in second grade.

So we sent him to a magnet school that emphasized performing arts. He did competitions on the sax from grammar school through his graduation from the High School for the Performing and Visual Arts.

I was considered a strict parent. There were no TV or video games during the week.

Matt spent a lot of time on the computer from third grade on. He was shy when he was young, but I would tell him, "Talk to people. Listen—everybody has a story."

He loved baseball and played Little League. We had lots of pets. We had a huge sandbox with big PVC pipes. The kids would build things: they'd make teepees; they made a weather station. Both of them were loving, happy children, and we were all very close.

The family's life centered on the joy of learning. Matt's mom encouraged him to choose and pursue his own interests:

Our family was all about reading. Every couple of weeks, the kids could choose a new book. At Christmas, they could choose a book, a game, and a toy. They spent the summers in the library program. I also had Matt read the private school reading list because I thought, Why should he have gaps, even though he's in public school?

Matt became an entrepreneur at a young age. He started his first business when he was in kindergarten. He had a big cardboard box with Windex and a spray bottle of water, and he wrote on the side, in big letters, MATT'S CLEANING COMPANY. CASH IS KING. He wanted to earn enough money to buy a Walkman.

He started his next business when he was in third grade, helping his grandma's friends with their computers. He made business cards with his name that said AND A LITTLE CHILD SHALL LEAD THEM. He loved the idea of getting paid, but he always forgot to cash the checks he got.

Matt spent a lot of time on computers, and sometimes he'd break one and had to figure out how to fix it before his dad got home. By the time he was eleven, Matt was spending Saturdays with the Houston Area League of PC Users, helping elderly people fix their computers for free. Then he started a PalmPilot users group in middle school. When Matt was in high school, he was asked to teach computers at the local community college.

Matt was also fascinated by economics. He entered the High School Fed Challenge, and his team went to Washington, D.C., and came in second. It was the first time his school had ever won an academic award, because it was a performing arts school.

Kathe encouraged Matt to be independent, even when it was painful for her:

I felt that because he was almost like an only child, he needed to spend time with other kids, so I sent him away to summer camp, starting in second grade. It was the hardest thing I ever did. The first time, he went to the Texas Catholic Boys Camp for a week. He loved it and went every summer all through middle school. And the whole time Matt was in school, he was very involved with his music and computers. I learned a lot about jazz, which he was passionate about.

He went to the University of Houston, but while he was in college he kept getting job offers. And he was working on WordPress. Matt agonized about whether he should finish,

*but finally decided school was pointless, and there just weren't
enough hours in the day for everything he wanted to do.*

For a family that valued education so highly, it must have
been tough for Kathe to accept that Matt wanted to drop out of
college. But like every great entrepreneur's family, she supported
him in his decision:

> *He got an offer to work at CNET part time while he was
> working part time on WordPress, so he quit school. And after
> a year, he left CNET to work full time on WordPress.*
>
> *I wasn't thrilled that he dropped out. But I drove him to
> San Francisco anyhow, so he could start his new job, and
> helped him move into an apartment there.*
>
> *I've always been there for him—I've seen that as my job.
> I've always enjoyed hanging out with him. I love the quote I
> have on my fridge that paraphrases Winston Churchill:
> "Never, never, never give up."*
>
> *And I always tell him, "I can't wait to see what you do
> next."*

Entrepreneurs Raising Entrepreneurs

Some of the entrepreneurs I talked with are now raising children
of their own, and I was especially interested in hearing what they
had to say about raising potential entrepreneurs themselves.
After all, they're the ones with firsthand experience of what it
takes to become an entrepreneur. I wanted to hear about the
families they're building and the lessons they're passing along.
One thing these parents know from their own childhood experience is that they can nurture any entrepreneurial spark their
children may have, but they can't turn their children into entrepreneurs if the spark isn't there. Regardless of whether their

children grow up to be entrepreneurs, though, they want their kids to have the same drive, passion, and work ethic they themselves had growing up. To be entrepreneurial. To do something they love. To grow up happy and fulfilled.

The entrepreneurs raising their own kids expressed concern about how successful parents can replicate the best parts of their upbringing with their own children when their kids are growing up in very different circumstances. In his book *David and Goliath* (2013), Malcolm Gladwell talks about the challenge for affluent parents to raise kids who aren't spoiled. He says parents want to set limits, but at some point, "No we can't" becomes "No we won't," which is harder for parents to say. He quotes psychologist James Grubman: "I have to teach them: 'Yes, I can buy that for you. But I choose not to. It's not consistent with our values.' But then that, of course, requires that you have a set of values, and know how to articulate them, and know how to make them plausible to your child..." (51).

In other words, it's not about pretending you don't have money or other advantages. It's about refusing to let those advantages distort the values that are important to you: values your parents taught you and values you're determined to pass on to your children.

Robert Stephens: Withholding Our Agenda

Robert Stephens, the founder of Geek Squad whom we met in the chapter on pursuing a passion (rule 1), is married and has two teenage sons. He's given a lot of thought to raising his children and applying the best lessons he learned from his own experience growing up.

Robert knows that if he doesn't give his sons something, it's because he won't, not because he can't. He wants them to grow up with the same grit and determination he did. He told me he makes his sons bike to school every day, even in bad weather, even though the family has more than one car, and despite their loud complaints, because he wants them to have to work hard to succeed.

He is also taking what he considers the best part of his upbringing—his parents' support of who he was—and using that as a model for raising his children. What he told me was echoed by one entrepreneur after another:

I think, looking back, that one of the most important things a parent can do is not influence, but recognize in their children the things that emerge, and then just support them. Every kid is giving you clues about who they are and what they love and, if you pay attention, you'll find it. When you do, be supportive by providing freedom, encouragement, and praise. Being critical never helps. Give a lot of praise.

My brand around the house when I was growing up was as the fix-it guy. It fostered my direction. You're letting the child lead. You're saying, "I know you can do it. What do you need from me to help?"

If parents look closely, they'll start recognizing the pattern, just like mine did. Then we have to withhold our agenda and give our children the freedom to thrive.

Caren Merrick: Resilience Is Everything

Caren Merrick, along with her husband, Phillip, cofounded software giant webMethods. "You never know what's going to happen," she says. "We've created an environment in our family that says you can try anything, you can do anything, you can make anything of yourself if you're willing to take risks and work hard. So I tell my sons, 'Be open to opportunities, and follow your passions.'"

That's just one way Caren is passing on the lessons she learned. Another way is by having her kids do chores to earn spending money. When Caren was growing up as the third of four kids, her two older siblings had already started a business. "They were huge role models," she told me. "Our parents gave us a lot of responsibility. We had a lot of chores and were always expected to earn our own money."

I ran into Caren at a conference on inspiring children's charitable giving. A young boy had just spoken eloquently about contributing money saved from his chores and gifts to Nothing But Nets, the anti-malaria program started by Elizabeth Gore at the U.N. Foundation (whom we met in rule 4), and he turned out to be Caren's son Jackson, then eleven years old. He said, "I was at a basketball tournament and I saw a sign that said 'Nothing But Nets' and I thought, 'That's a cool sign!' So I looked into it, and I realized they were saving kids' lives by keeping them from getting malaria. I thought, 'That would be a cool thing to do with my money that I have left over from my chores and presents—to save kids' lives!'"

Caren and I talked later about what lessons she was trying to teach her children. She told me that she wants her kids to get used to trying lots of different things, and she wants them to get used to failure, too. She thinks a child's ability to handle failure is not only the key to that child's becoming an entrepreneur, but also the key to the child's parents' learning how to handle their child's failures. With that in mind, Caren supports her sons' interest in sports. Both boys have played soccer and basketball since they were five, and she loves the resilience it has taught them.

"The law of averages is that most people aren't going to succeed in most of the things they try," Caren says, "so resilience is the key."

She particularly likes the attitude of her sons' football coach: "We lost, we learn from it, we figure out what we're going to do, and we go back in."

"I'm so happy he's my sons' coach," Caren told me. "He's taught them that losing a game isn't a terrible thing if they keep working and learning and moving toward their goal."

Susan Wojcicki: Part of the Team

We heard from YouTube CEO Susan Wojcicki's mom Esther in the chapter on instilling confidence (rule 2). Esther told me that Susan, who is married and has five children, has talked extensively on work-life balance, saying she always tries to be home to eat dinner with her family. Esther, who always worked full time while raising her three daughters, told me that despite Susan's high-powered job, she is raising her kids the same way Esther raised her girls:

> My grandkids have an allowance, and they have to help out with the family. They're not waited on hand and foot. So often today, in middle- and upper-middle-class families, parents are servants. They live as their children's coordinators. I think kids have to be part of the team. Give kids the responsibility. My grandkids have to help around the house with chores that are tied to an allowance, just like my three girls did growing up.

Arturo Nunez: "I Don't Do That?"

Arturo Nunez, Apple's head of marketing for Latin America, previously was Global VP of basketball marketing at Nike. He's a great, outgoing storyteller; names like "LeBron," "Kobe," and "Magic" roll off his tongue. He gave a wonderful TEDx Women talk about changing the paradigm for manhood from someone tough to someone caring (Nunez 2014).

Arturo grew up poor in Harlem, the son of immigrants from Venezuela and Cuba. When he worked at Nike HQ, he lived with his family in Portland, Oregon. We spoke about how to raise children so they grow up with the same grit you did, even if it's under more comfortable circumstances. He told me a great story. When he was young, he loved basketball and played whenever and wherever he could. He was home one day and wanted to shoot a few baskets with his young son. He looked outside and there were leaves on their basketball court, so Arturo said to his son, "Hey, go sweep off the court and we can shoot some hoops." And his son said, not with arrogance but merely explaining the world as he knew it, "I don't do that. I'll tell Mom to call Alberto."

You have to picture Arturo telling this story, his voice rising: "I said to my son, 'I don't do that'? Are you kidding me? 'I don't DO that'? I DON'T DO THAT!!!! You get your butt outside and clean off those leaves so we can play basketball!'"

After we stopped laughing, we talked about the different challenges successful parents have raising their kids to be fighters, to have the same drive, discipline, and work ethic as children who grow up without a lot of advantages. He talked about how he wants to imbue his kids with the same character he learned growing up in Harlem. How he wants them to fight for what they're passionate about, to develop the foundation that leads to building success on their own.

Michael Wilbon: Up to Par

Later, I retold Arturo's story to ESPN sports commentator and cohost of *Pardon the Interruption* Michael Wilbon. He told me another funny story that also demonstrates how hard it can be for parents to raise their children the same way they were raised, when they're living in vastly different circumstances.

His son loves to play golf and had developed a great swing. Michael brought him to a tournament and his son was hitting golf balls. After a while, his son made some bad swings, threw down his clubs in disgust, and started to walk away. His mom said, "Hey, pick up your clubs!" The five-year-old replied, "Gee, where's a caddy when you need one?"

We laughed so hard. Michael, of course, wants to make sure his son does not grow up feeling entitled, and says he'll make sure his son is a caddy himself all through school. And not only because he believes that's the best way to learn golf—but, more importantly, to be sure he learns the right work ethic.

Karolina Kurkova:
You Are Your Children's Example

Karolina Kurkova, the supermodel we met in the chapter on instilling confidence (rule 5), says that now that she has children of her own, she thinks all the time about the lessons her parents passed on to her. One of the most important things to remember, she told me, is that you are your children's example—they learn less from what you say than from what you do:

> *Today I want to expose my son Tobin to lots of different things and let him find his way. I do that by truly listening to him. What are his strengths? What are his weaknesses? If you watch closely, you can see what he likes, what he's good at.*
>
> *We expose him to everything, and then, as a parent, I pay attention to what he likes, what his skills are. But when he gets frustrated, I don't let him quit easily. I try to get him to take a step back and pause, and I explain what the point is. Then I try to decide, is it too hard? Or is it just not for him?*

> *I give him freedom to explore, but I also have an expectation that he'll stick with something for a while and not quit because he's frustrated. It's a fine line.*

Karolina told me that she and her husband, Archie Drury, take Tobin with them as much as they can, and that he travels everywhere with them. She's trying to raise him the way she was raised:

> *There have to be rules. We're not permissive, and I don't want a spoiled kid. He needs to survive in the real world. But we're also teaching him how to be independent. We want him to be kind and compassionate as well as responsible.*

Karolina told me how important it is to her and Archie that Tobin not take things for granted:

> *I want him to understand what is important about work and how you get a reward for your effort. He helps us cook, and he does chores to earn money for a toy. He's learned that he worked for it, so he can buy it. It gives him pride.*

And then Karolina summed up a key lesson, one echoed by other parents I talked with:

> *I want to do the best I can to support him and love him. I want to understand my son so I can be the best parent I can be, and so he can be confident and thrive.*

Robert, Caren, Susan, Arturo, Michael, and Karolina are striving to raise their kids the same way they were raised. But the vast majority of the many entrepreneurs I've spoken to, both those in this book and many others, didn't have parents who were successful entrepreneurs. What they did all have, regardless of their family's income, were parents who believed in them and supported their passions. And none of them were coddled; all of them had parents who helped their kids learn to work hard to achieve success.

A supportive family won't turn every child into an entrepreneur. But if your child has that spark to begin with, there's no greater way to nurture it than by creating an environment of love, learning, and support. Whether your children grow up to pass those values along to the organizations and businesses they create, to their own children, or both, the impact will spread far beyond your home.

Show Them There's Something Bigger

As we've seen, entrepreneurs aren't simply born with extraordinary courage and commitment. It's instilled in them by the way they're raised. For some entrepreneurs, support from family members is enough. But many also benefit from believing in something bigger than themselves.

The extent to which this was true surprised me at first, but during my interviews I came to understand it. Entrepreneurs choose a difficult path. Inevitably, they face moments of crisis, when everything seems aligned against them—when the world is telling them they're crazy, that their ventures won't work, and that they should make a safer choice. It's at moments like these that they may need a motivation bigger than themselves.

And so I discovered that many entrepreneurs are brought up to believe that there is a larger purpose to which they are called than their own happiness or material success. I found this to be true not only for those entrepreneurs who run nonprofits, profits for purpose, and activist organizations, but also for those who have founded for-profit businesses. For some, the belief in something bigger came through religion. Others are fueled by a more general sense of morality or ethics.

The ten rules discussed in this book aren't always easy to implement. For many of the moms we've met, a strong sense of faith was a factor underlying all the others, especially when times were difficult. That faith powered everything they did—supporting their children's passions, instilling confidence in them, helping them overcome adversity, providing a loving family life. Most of all, though, it helped them imbue their children with a sense of purpose. For many who grew up to be entrepreneurs, the sense of belonging to something bigger than themselves is fundamental and has shaped their lives and contributed to their unshakable belief that they are in the world to make a positive difference.

FAITH AND VALUES

WordPress founder Matt Mullenweg's mom, Kathe, told me that she always stressed values, not as abstract concepts, but as guiding principles for taking action:

> Our motto was "If you can make something better, what are you waiting for?" I got some of that from church, but I personalized it. I wanted my children to have the ability to put themselves in other people's shoes. We placed a lot of emphasis on the Golden Rule. I used to tell Matt, "If you don't stand up for something, you'll fall for anything." I remember hearing that when Matt was in third grade, an obnoxious little girl in the class was being picked on. I heard later—and it made me so proud—that Matt said, "That's enough! Just stop." And the children stopped teasing her. He didn't like her either, but he said it just wasn't right.
>
> We always had a family project for charity. Our kids had some friends who had so much money, so I'd take my children to the poor part of town to do service work, and I'd say, "You're so lucky." Matt does a lot for charity today. He's very involved with ten causes that are meaningful to him.

218

UnderArmour founder Kevin Plank's mom, Jayne, told me that religion played a big part in the way she raised her boys. "All five of my sons are not only good people, good fathers, good husbands, and good sons," she said. "They all also love their God, their families, and their country."

Adam and Scooter Braun's mother, Susan, talked about the importance of maintaining religious traditions for her children:

Both our parents came from semi-Orthodox backgrounds, although they themselves weren't Orthodox. We sent our kids to Hebrew school and summer camp. They'd light candles Friday nights to celebrate Shabbat, even when basketball players from their teams were at our home for dinner. The other kids knew about it and knew what their religion meant to them.

Blake and Paige Mycoskie's mom, Pam, told me how faith shaped her family's values and actions:

We are all committed Christians. We always taught the children to put other people first, to treat others better than themselves. We tried to teach them to serve others, to be grateful for what you have, and that it's always better to give than to receive. We wanted the children to realize how blessed we are. When we prayed together, we would say, "God pours into our lives, and we pour out to others." I think this is part of why Blake wants to give. We believe we have to do something to make a difference.

charity: water founder Scott Harrison's mom, Joan, described how her son's belief gave him the courage and confidence he needed to launch his ambitious mission and see it through:

When Scott wanted to start charity: water, he had no money to his name and no place to live. He was, in fact, in debt. Yet he was driven by a passion to help the African people and a confidence that God had laid out a plan for the nonprofit that would become charity: water. He decided that 100 percent of all donations would go directly toward providing clean water, that every well would be tracked through GPS, and that he would regularly take donors to Africa to inspire them with their work.

Film director Jon Chu's mom, Ruth, told me how faith had strengthened her family members' bonds with one another and instilled a strong moral compass in her son:

Jon has God in his life, which makes a big difference to me. Whenever I'm scared, I pray for him. For a while, I had turned away from God because of my handicapped child, Howard. I said, "If You want to punish me, punish me, not my child," and my friend said, "He didn't punish your child. He sent your child to your family because He knew you'd love him."

I was afraid to send Howard to Boy Scout camp alone, so Jon went with him to his special Boy Scout camp for years, to be with him. For years. Instead of regular Boy Scout camp. He'd never tell you that story, but it shows that's the kind of boy he is.

Invisible Children cofounder Jason Russell's mom, Sheryl, told me how faith helped her support her son's passions so he could fulfill his potential:

We had a faith-based approach to parenting, and we believed God had a plan for them. Each child has a passion and, as a parent, it's important to know your child's bent and to encourage them in it. There's an old proverb, "Train up a child in the way he should go, and when he is old, he will not depart from it." I have always interpreted that to mean training them in their bent, to nurture their natural God-given abilities. Each of our four children had different gifts, and we encouraged all of them to develop those gifts, to use the talent they were given, and grow it through time. And they have each used their gifts in different ways.

webMethods cofounder Caren Merrick told me how spirituality shapes her own parenting:

I think about faith all the time in raising my children, from a perspective of What's their purpose, Where did they come from, and Why are they here? That informs our lives as people of faith. I want them to know that part of why they're here is to make a contribution, especially to those less fortunate. Service has always been an important part of our lives. This year, instead of a vacation, we went to serve alongside friends of ours in Madagascar. We served others there for ten days, and I hope it made as big an impact on our sons as it did on us.

LIFE Camp founder Erica Ford said her belief is what enables her success:

The discipline, the faith, of what I believe in helps me get where I am today. It gives me dedication and commitment. This is not a job. This is my life. My undying love keeps me committed to my people until my glory day takes me away.

FINDING THEIR OWN COMPASS

For many of the entrepreneurs I talked with, developing faith wasn't a matter of embracing the religious traditions of their parents. Some were encouraged to explore spiritual alternatives.

221

Others were taught moral or ethical principles, rather than religious beliefs. Often, however, childhood exposure to the idea of a larger purpose helped shape who they went on to become, though perhaps not in ways their parents expected.

Sean Carasso: Many Realities Are Possible

The playground petitioner who grew up to cofound Falling Whistles (rule 6) told me that his parents had raised him in several religions. Their own background included different traditions, and they wanted him to know the best in each, so Sean was able to see what it meant to be a Christian, a Jew, and a Buddhist.

Sean's father, whose grandmother had survived the Holocaust, resisted the concept of one true religion. He wanted his sons to know what matters—being moral and honorable, knowing what's right and what's wrong, and having the courage to follow the voice of conscience inside you. When I asked Sean to describe how religion had played a role at home when he was growing up, he told me a story:

> Skiing was my family's favorite thing to do together. Even when the family couldn't get along, we could always ski together. So my folks would save every penny and nickel, and we would do whatever we had to do to get the money to ski. And when my dad would finally get to the top of the mountain, with us boys next to him and my mom right there, all geared up and ready to go, he would raise his poles to the heavens and scream, from a deep place within, "Banzai!" Down the hill we would charge, full speed ahead, come what may.
>
> And I think both my parents took that approach to life. They certainly took it with religion. They were perpetual explorers—seekers on a journey of self-discovery. We went

everywhere, tried everything. Siddha yoga houses and Jewish temples. Catholic churches and Buddhist temples. The house of Hare Krishna and the Church of Self-Realization. Conscious Harmony and Southern Evangelical. And we explored deeply. Banzai! All in.

That was when I began to see that there were many realities, and that my perspective creates my reality, and vice versa. This has allowed me to create a belief system rooted in what I consider basic truths stripped of unnecessary excess. Interdependence. Cause and effect. The inherent value of life.

I think this exploration has had a fairly dramatic effect on my life, and I continuously evaluate and reevaluate. My only certainty is that there are few certainties. This has allowed me to question my circumstances and, in so doing, wonder how they could be better. This is what makes me love being an entrepreneur. And I owe this almost entirely to my folks.

Quddus: Choosing His Own Way

Quddus, whose given name is Benjamin Quddus Philippe, has been called "sort of the Ryan Seacrest of the hip-hop generation" (Wyatt 2008). By the time he was eighteen, he had gone from DJ-ing at high school parties, to hosting a radio show during his one semester in college, and then on to becoming a host on MuchMusic, Canada's answer to MTV. Two years later, when Carson Daly left the hit MTV show *Total Request Live*, Quddus moved to New York and replaced him. He has also directed music videos, and he started his own production company to create online content through a website and video series called *The Q Side*. He's now consulting, developing a *60 Minutes*–type show called *The Connected* to give younger people a new reporting gateway to what's happening in the world, and hosting events such as the Grammys red carpet live stream.

Quddus grew up in Toronto with an older brother, Nate, a basketball coach at American University. His dad is a dentist from Haiti, and his mom, Jacoba Devos, is a Canadian educator. Although Quddus always got along well with her, for many years there was a lot of friction in his relationship with his dad:

Whatever I could dream up, my mom encouraged me to do and supported me. My dad was on the other end of the spectrum. He had been raised by my grandpa, an orphan who'd been raised by Catholic monks. The church was his life, and he was fanatical about getting me to church.

When I was seventeen, I decided that I had a different idea of what I wanted for a relationship with God. I told my dad I didn't want to go to church with him anymore, and it created a storm.

Both my parents had told my brother and me that we needed to have a positive impact on the world, but my dad believed it had to be in the context of the church. I decided I was going to prove to my dad that I didn't need to go to church to be a good man. I was determined to prove I could be impactful without going to church. It wasn't easy to challenge his passion.

It really lit a fire in me to prove something to my dad—which, looking back, is probably not the best way to go through life. But I was so driven to prove to him that I could have an impact out of the church that I took on like a mission to change the way he judged me. I said, "I'm going to be the one to prove that you don't need to go to church to have a platform to influence the world in a positive way."

My mom was completely different from my dad. She encouraged me to think independently. She'd say, "Whatever you want to do, honey." Her family was liberal, progressive, not religious. She was Baha'i, a very tolerant religion, and she taught me that values weren't based in a religion.

When I was born, my dad chose my first name, Benjamin, from the Bible, and my Mom gave me my middle name, Quddus, who was a martyr in the Baha'i faith. So when I was seventeen and challenged my dad and left the Catholic Church, I began to go by my middle name. I felt that name represented my mom and a new way.

The process of defining his own relationship to faith might not have pleased his father, but for Quddus, it was a necessity. He said it's what drove his entrepreneurial spirit:

When I decided to make a stand, it changed me and redefined my relationship with my dad. It gave me courage. And I think that's what made me an entrepreneur. That fearlessness, the idea that I wouldn't go along with expectations—that's where my drive came from, where being an entrepreneur was born.

My brother went along with my dad. He went on a standard path, went all through university, got a job he was supposed to get. I went on my own way. I was more brazen.

My relationship with my dad has healed. He used to call me every Sunday to ask if I'd been to church. Eventually he stopped asking and accepted me when he saw I was making the world better in my own way and was contributing to society. I don't need to prove anything to him anymore.

Quddus needed to prove to his parents that he could reject his father's view of how to make a positive difference in the world, yet still live up to their expectation that he would make an impact:

I spend a lot of time with nonprofits like Generosity Water and A Place Called Home in South L.A. My biggest passion now is incorporating emotional intelligence as a curriculum in school. We have enough case studies—it's time to incorporate an additional curriculum in charter schools and then into public schools. I always say, "If it's gonna be, it's up to me."

INSPIRATION IN ACTION

Some entrepreneurs told me that what shaped them the most was the way their moms combined teaching them a faith with serving as living examples of that faith. That combination has guided the choices they've made and helped them stay grounded and focused during turbulent times.

Emmanuelle Chriqui:
So Much Grace and Beauty

Emmanuelle Chriqui has had starring roles in HBO's *Entourage, You Don't Mess with the Zohan,* and other TV shows and movies.

Like the musicians we've met, actors and other performers embody the entrepreneurial spirit in that they make something out of nothing; they're entrepreneurs of the imagination. Taking on each new role is like starting a new business, with all the planning and dreaming when something is created from scratch. And that's not even to mention the work of running the team that works to advance an actor's career: who finds the best scripts; chooses the right projects with other actors, writers, and a director you believe in; supports you during filming; and generates publicity. Apart from her acting work, Emmanuelle has been involved with a number of charities, including the Somaly Mam Foundation to end sex slavery, St. Jude Children's Research Hospital, and Colon Cancer Canada, as well as with causes like peace in Congo.

Emmanuelle, now in her thirties, was born in Montreal and raised in a small town outside Toronto. Her parents were Moroccan Jewish immigrants. She has an older brother, Serge, a photographer, and an older sister, Laurence, whose company sells personalized baby gifts. She told me that two things have carried her through her life—her religion, and the voice in her ear of her mom, Liliane, who died when she was sixteen:

We were the only Jewish family in the community. I had friends of every denomination and color. On Friday nights, if my friends wanted to see me, they would come to our home for Shabbat dinner. It was okay with my family for my friends to join us, but it was never pushed aside, it was always very important to my family that I be there. We had arguments about my not wanting to do it every Friday night, but now that my parents aren't here, I understand it really shaped who I am. It gave me a moral compass. In a flighty business, where things tend to be ungrounded, I come from a place where I'm grounded.

Entrepreneurs of all kinds live with much bigger ups and downs than people who take more conventional paths. Drawing on a bedrock of belief can help keep them from losing their way. Emmanuelle gets that stability not only from the traditions her family observed together, but also from the loving, generous spirit of her mother:

When I was seven, I was asked to be in a play at a local community theater—my friend's dad ran it—and that was it. I played a baby ghost. I loved it. After that, I was hooked. I was one of those kids—if there was music, I would start dancing, and a circle would form. I always loved to perform, and my parents always supported me.

I was lucky to go to a wonderful high school for the performing arts near where we lived. I majored in theater and performed a lot. My mom was really sick by then and was in and out of hospitals.

We were rehearsing commedia dell'arte. One day, the director said, "Come to the green room, I have a surprise for you." They had brought my mom to see a show. Even in her weakest moments, she was there for me.

I only had her for sixteen years, but she shaped who I am today. How I act when I'm out in public—my flair, my style—I learned everything from my mom. She always had an amazing sense of style. She was beautiful. She had wanted to act when she was young, but her parents didn't want her to. When she recognized that passion in me, she wanted me to pursue it, to have a chance to do what she couldn't.

In the time I had her in my life, my mom had such an impact! She was fiery, passionate, creative. Both my parents were lovers of the arts. They were always going to the opera or the theater, had classical music blaring at home—they were baking from scratch, growing a garden. Everything was done with so much grace and beauty.

Emmanuelle told me the inspiration she got, and still gets, from her mom was combined with the freedom and support we've heard so much about from so many different entrepreneurs:

Most of my successful friends—not just successful in their careers, but fantastic people who have great lives—have solid relationships with their families. They have parents who were courageous enough to allow their kids to be who they are, not who they want them to be. They didn't jam something down their throats because that's what society expects.

I was just a little Jewish girl from a small town, with really big dreams. We knew nobody in the business. We had *no connections. I believe my mom has carried me all this way. She said, "You will become an actress for both of us." It's carried me through the difficult times. It's that voice that keeps me going.*

Mike de la Rocha: A Model of Love

Mike de la Rocha, the founder of Revolve Impact, uses his skills as a musician and public speaker to effect social change, specifically juvenile justice policy. As a legislative deputy, he also implemented innovative youth development programs in Los Angeles, building coalitions for prison reform. In 2012, he created the Living Rooms Across America Tour, in which he sings and speaks to inspire people to get engaged in the civic process.

Mike has an older brother Albert, a university administrator, similar to his dad, a professor. His parents were on the more involved end of the parenting continuum when he was growing up. Here's what his mom, Gloria, told me:

I always wanted my sons to have the Lord in their life. Mike has very good values. I told him to show love and be love and be there when needed. We taught the boys that nobody is better than anyone else, and no matter how much or how little other people have, you always have to be there for them. I wanted my sons to consider others' needs, to be willing to give of themselves. We're there to help each other. We give from the heart. Mike knows that without love, there's nothing.

When I talked with Mike, he told me about his mom:

I am who I am because of her. My spiritual belief is that babies choose their parents. I tell my six-month-old, "Thank you for choosing me to be your dad."

I wasn't supposed to happen. When I came into this world, I was very premature. There were many complications, and they didn't think they could save both me and my mom. It was almost a miracle, but we both survived, and from then on, my mom and I had a very close bond.

Because of her own difficult background, my mom really valued education. She worked two jobs to get me a good education. My dad believed in public schools, but she wanted to send us to Catholic school because she wanted us to have more individual attention. So she worked in a day care center after her regular job as a Head Start teacher to get the money to pay our tuition. Plus, my parents gave me a lot of attention at home, making us know they viewed education as a priority, as a way to achieve our dreams. My mom only has a high school diploma, and she worked so hard to give us the opportunities she didn't have.

It obviously paid off; Mike graduated with honors from UCLA and went on to get a master's.

Like most of the other entrepreneurs I talked with, Mike made it clear that for his family, faith wasn't just a matter of attending a religious school or following certain traditions. His mom made the concepts come to life:

For my mom, love was a guiding principle. My mom embodies the principle—she spent her life helping low-income children. She embodies the values of passion and love, and she lives every single day serving communities that are often underserved, not given enough resources.

She worked so hard and continued to persevere and tells every child she teaches that they can succeed despite their obstacles. She tells them that they have value—they have a gift they can share with the world. She gave me a foundation. I always knew I could fail, and she would be there to hold me up.

Our greatest entrepreneurs are our mothers. My mom turned her entire energy and focus to raising us. She sacrificed for us—which I want to acknowledge and appreciate—but her dream was to raise us. Her lessons of love inspired me to do the work I do today, to make a difference in my community.

Maimah Karmo: Faith and Fearlessness

In 2006, when she was thirty-two years old, Maimah Karmo was diagnosed with aggressive breast cancer. While undergoing her second round of chemotherapy, she made a promise to God to give Him her life in service. The next morning, the idea for Tigerlily Foundation was born. She was still sick, she said, but "I felt stronger than ever, bolder than ever."

Maimah's family is from Liberia, and now they all live in the U.S.—her parents Maie and Armah, and her three younger brothers: Armah, now at the NIH; Walter, at Verizon; and Kanda, in healthcare. I've known Maimah for several years as the passionate founder of a successful nonprofit, but I never knew that her entire family barely escaped death when she was a child.

When Maimah was young and still in Liberia, she had several close encounters with death:

So many things have happened to me that I'm not supposed to be alive.

I escaped three separate wars.

I was held at gunpoint.

I was hit by lightning—I had picked up the phone in a lightning storm and was struck and died. I knew it wasn't time, and I came back. My eardrum was burst, and I had to have surgery. I was wearing a crucifix, and it burned a mark on my chest.

They'd take little children to be child soldiers, or worse. I was still in high school. One day when we heard sirens, my father said, "You have to leave the country tomorrow."

I took one suitcase and put The Diary of Anne Frank *in it and got on a flight and came to the U.S. I was fifteen, all alone.*

Maimah's story is a lesson in the power of faith in the face of circumstances that were not just challenging, but horrific:

Seven years earlier, when the first war started, my father got word they wanted people who owned businesses to come to a meeting. He knew it would be an ambush.

My dad took his watch off that he always wore. We were all scared. It was a tribal war.

My mom was crying, begging him not to go. He told us to leave our home.

We lay on the floor of a car and drove to an aunt's house and hid there.

My mom decided she had to go and get her husband. She said, "I'm going to get your dad. I'll be back later."

Our relatives begged her not to go. They said, "You'll be killed."

She said, "I'm going."

All the cabs were afraid to take her. Eventually she was able to bribe someone to take her as far as the outside gate.

She walked in and sat down and waited for hours. They finally came in and said, "What are you doing here? You don't belong here."

She said, "My husband is here falsely. He hasn't done anything."

My father was a kind man. Whenever poor people came to his factory, he would give them rice. It turned out that years earlier, my dad had given the rebel leader some food when he needed it. He was now the rebel general, and he agreed to let my dad go.

My dad had been beaten. He was naked in a small cell. The general told his people to give my dad some clothes and to drive him and my mom out of the complex.

The next day, they took the other thirteen men he'd been with to the beach and lined them up and shot them. If my dad had been with them, he would have been killed, too. I was eight years old.

The courage of Maimah's mother had a permanent impact on her daughter, who would never underestimate the power of belief:

People ask me, "Why is your faith so strong?" I say it's because of the example of my parents.

When I was eight, they risked everything. My dad risked everything for his family, and then my mom risked everything for him and for us and for something that was bigger than herself. It taught me to be fearless. It taught me to see what's in front of me, and to hold that vision. It taught me about faith.

Whenever I doubt, I see my mother's look of faith that God would protect her. I became a fearless little girl that day, and since then, I've known that whatever happens in my life, something bigger than me is in control. I know that something powerful is carrying me all the time.

You're here for something bigger than you can even imagine. I saw faith walk in action to conquer fear. I knew that if she could do that, what could I not do in America, where everything is possible?

When Maimah got sick, that knowledge was transformative:

*I thought of that when I got cancer. So many people are afraid
of cancer, as I was and still am at times. But the thing that I
fear most is not living, and merely existing, which is a sure
and slow death.*

*The morning I decided to start Tigerlily Foundation, my
life changed. I made a vow to live as loudly as possible, to
jump into things that made me afraid, to risk everything, to
feel, to live, and to love—most of all, to be fully present in life
and give of myself so that others may have the incredible joy
I feel every day.*

*When I got sick, I had a three-year-old daughter. I had
no money. I had no experience in running a nonprofit. I was
a young single Black woman with no experience who
somehow believed she could start a foundation.*

Since starting Tigerlily Foundation, Maimah has raised more
than a million dollars and helped more than five thousand
women between the ages of fifteen and forty who were diagnosed
with breast cancer. She has been featured in *Essence* magazine,
has appeared on *Good Morning America*, and in 2012 she published *Fearless: Awakening to My Life's Purpose Through Breast
Cancer*, a book that almost immediately became a best-seller in
its category on Amazon. Today, Maimah and her daughter,
Noelle, are thriving.

Whatever religion is part of your family—or even if you don't
believe in an organized religion at all—it's important to raise
children to have a strong character, to be moral, to be honorable,
to have a set of values, to care about their community, and to
recognize that today, their community may be the world. As

these entrepreneurs have shown, it was important for them growing up to believe that there is something bigger than them, that there is a higher purpose than making money.

Not only the artists, activists, and nonprofit founders, but also the for-profit company founders profiled in this book are deeply involved in charities and causes they believe in. I didn't talk to one person when I was doing interviews for this book who made important choices based primarily on how much money they would make. They all care deeply about making the world a better place and giving back. And that desire was often bolstered by a moral perspective instilled in them in childhood.

RULE 10

Lead by Following

A lot of future entrepreneurs need time to discover their paths. Many experience periods when it's unclear where they're going. In this situation, some parents may see their kids as getting lost. But the parents of kids who grow up to become entrepreneurs are more likely to see their kids as exploring.

Here's the tough part for a lot of parents: if you want to incubate an entrepreneur, you need to lead by following, regardless of where your child wants to go. It's one of the hardest things for most parents to do: knowing what your kids' strengths are; understanding what path would be good for them; and judging when—and how—to support that path. Many of the moms I talked with did this naturally. All of them did it eventually.

Kenneth Ginsburg, coauthor of *Building Resilience in Children and Teens*, offers this advice:

> Getting out of the way is a tough challenge. We want to help, fix, and guide kids. But we have to remind ourselves that when we just let them figure things out for themselves, we communicate this powerful message: "I think you are competent and wise." (2014, 37)

In other words, see what *they* want, what *their* passion is, what *they* are good at, what makes *them* happy. Allow their gift to reveal itself. Then support it. Tell them how proud you are of them for succeeding in their chosen path. And then tell them again and again, until you're sure they believe it.

Doing that may not be easy. But there are ways to help your children as they discover their gift. It doesn't necessarily mean they will become entrepreneurs. But they will almost certainly be happier, and that's a good thing, regardless of their career path.

In her 2015 book, *Clay Water Brick*, Kiva cofounder Jessica Jackley echoes this insight when she says that even if you don't become an entrepreneur, you "can choose to think in a more hopeful, optimistic, entrepreneurial way, and...this mindset paired with consistent entrepreneurial action is vital to building a better life" (xxv). Such an approach to life is "...not just for those who want to start an organization of their own from scratch.... It is for anyone who wants to be inspired to make progress toward their dreams despite the challenges standing in their way...anyone who wants to spend each day tapped into the kind of energy, creativity, and passion that the best entrepreneurs in the world embody...anyone who wants to live and work in a more opportunity-finding, solution-building way."

If your kids seem to have an aptitude for something, let them take lessons or classes or join a club. If your child wants to fix things, or build things, or sew things, or sell things, or play on their computer, or play chess, or write for the school paper, or sing, or dance, or act, let them. Don't choose for them. Don't push them into *your* passions. Watch them. See what they're good at, what they love, and then support it. And if they want to switch and try something else, let them. And if they happen to learn differently from other kids, that's okay too.

If they want to stand in the back of the class, or take time off from their regular classes, or get their homework done in school so they can spend more time playing sports or acting or singing after school, let them. If they want to go to a different school that lets them pursue their passion more intensely, or study in a different environment, even overseas, let them.

Many of the parents I know resist the idea of following their children's lead because they think it means encouraging their kids in pursuits that aren't serious. Especially if their children are already showing signs of not being hard workers at school, parents may tend to focus on what society thinks are good qualities, rather than on what motivates their kids. They ask, "Why doesn't he have more discipline?" when the better question is often, "How can I help him find something that inspires him to work hard?"

Do What You Love, Love What You Do

All of the entrepreneurs told me that because they loved what they were doing, and were encouraged to pursue it, they developed a strong work ethic. Many followed their passion directly into a career; others became passionate about something different. But they all learned to work hard, which has made them successful today.

When I talked with Dot2Dot.com founder Michael Skolnik, he spoke for a lot of entrepreneurs as he talked about his work ethic:

> *I became a film director for twelve years. I was lucky to win several awards. I don't know how talented I am, or how smart I am, or how good a film director I am, but I have an unbeatable work ethic. I will work longer. I will get there earlier. I will stay later. I will out-hustle you. My grandfather always quoted Confucius: "If you love what you do, you'll never work a day in your life." That really stuck with me.*

Shareablee founder Tania Yuki was equally emphatic about the importance of doing what she loves:

I can't imagine hating my job. I think all entrepreneurs feel like I do. If I didn't love my company more than anything, I wouldn't do it. I'd do something else. I talk to younger people all the time who ask me what they should do to get to where they want to go. I tell them, "It has to be organic. You have to do what will be fun, what will stretch you and excite you. You can't know going in what the end result will be."

Let Them Find Their Way

More than most people, entrepreneurs need space and freedom to find their own way—and, paradoxically, that makes emotional support from their parents even more important. When they're not getting the immediate rewards and positive feedback that conventional jobs bring, their parents' belief in them becomes more valuable.

Many of the moms I talked with described a balance between providing support and encouraging independence. Even the parents who were closely involved with their children's activities weren't afraid to let their kids go when the time came.

Brooks Bell: Always Another Chance

Brooks Bell, who founded Brooks Bell Interactive, a leading U.S. data testing firm, was raised in Anchorage, Alaska, with a sister and a brother, both younger. Her parents got divorced, Brooks told me, and her mom, Rebecca Poling, had a constant message for her: "Your self-worth is what you achieve. You've been born into privilege. You have to give back. Do something great." Her mom's words created a "burden of high expectations," Brooks said, but her mom also gave her the gift of independence:

My mom did something right with us. We were each always very different, but she encouraged all of us, and today we're all successful in wildly different ways.

My two younger siblings wanted more structured lives: my sister's getting a Dartmouth MBA and working for a start-up; my brother's a lawyer. My mom was busy running her orthodontist practice. So she empowered us to run our own lives, which helped us all. She told me, "You are responsible for yourself. You own your life, your experiences, your decisions."

In high school, I thought I wanted to be a graphic designer. My mom let me pursue that. I got a job after class in an advertising agency. It was a terrible experience. I hated having a boss. I wanted to have freedom and be in control of my existence.

It was one of four internships I had in high school. I also worked at a local news graphic arts department, a video company, and another ad agency. An advisor at school helped me. I found the companies, and she helped me structure the internships. She was a great mentor. My mom let me make my choices.

In high school, I was also in a church group through my dad's church, which my mom didn't approve of. I wanted to go with the church to a retreat in Seattle and asked her to pay for it. Even though she didn't like the idea, she let me go. She thought I'd learn from it. I did. I eventually grew out of it.

My mom respected me as an adult at an earlier stage than my friends' parents. She thought that I should put myself in as many learning situations as I could, and that I would find my own path.

Her mom did some of the hardest things for a parent to do: She let her daughter make decisions, own them, realize her mistakes, and learn from them. And she let her daughter go far away to college, to the school she had chosen, Duke, in North Carolina:

> In college, I thought I wanted to be an entrepreneur, but I had no idea what I wanted to do. After my freshman year, I wanted to stay in Durham for the summer. I saw a sign that said DON'T GET A SUMMER JOB—START A SUMMER BUSINESS. So I told my mom that's what I was going to do.
>
> My mom was disappointed that I wouldn't be coming home for the summer. But she had always told me to make my own decisions, so I knew she had to let me stay. She knew if I came home, I'd be miserable. And her whole thing was "This is your life." She didn't want to force me to do something I didn't want to do. I was beginning my independent life, and she wanted me to be responsible. She felt I had to figure it out.
>
> That sign fit right into where my mind was. I started a Tuition Painters franchise. I drove a paintmobile. It was a disaster. I lost money on every single job I did. I finished $2,000 in debt from the project and waited on tables to pay it off. I thought, I hope being an entrepreneur isn't always like this!
>
> But my mom was pleased. She could see I was learning a lot—about myself, about business, and about the world.

In her junior year at Duke, Brooks turned her final project for her graphic design class—a website—into a Christmas present for her mom:

> It turned out to be the seed of my company. She loved it—she was so impressed, it blew her away. She said, "You should incorporate. You should do this for a living. There's no down-side—it will be a great learning experience, and you're

amazing at it." So I incorporated NovelProjects, a website development firm, with my boyfriend. The business became a success. Within a year we had $300,000 in revenue. So we brought on two more developers—it was just me and three guys. Eventually we sold it. I had already started my second company. And I married my boyfriend.

Brooks explained how her mom's supportive approach, especially when it came to learning from mistakes, has influenced her professionally:

I always act with a lot of integrity. If people know you truly want the right things for them, then even if you make a mistake, they know your heart is in the right place, and you'll always get more opportunities.

Growing up, I established a habit of saying yes to stuff. Opportunities would come to me—I think I gave out positive energy—and then I'd have a little success, like designing that website for my mom. And that would lead to a little more confidence to work my way up. An opportunity would come, and I would try it, and in that way I worked my way up the confidence ladder.

I always had confidence that I'd make the right decision—if not this time, the next time. I learned that it's never over. I learned to trust that I'd always have another opportunity. It gave me the resilience I needed. Every time I fell down, I'd tell myself, You'll have another chance. It got me through. It still gets me through. It puts things in perspective. I learn something from every opportunity.

Caren Merrick: Open to Opportunity

webMethods cofounder Caren Merrick's parents also saw their daughter move far away—to Australia—with her husband,

Phillip. They'd been married only a year, and wanted to be near Phillip's dying mother. By then, Caren had already learned the value of finding her own way. When she was growing up, her passions kept evolving, and her family supported whatever she did:

My passion when I was young was drawing cartoons. Every week my elementary school had a contest for Junior Art Champion. I earned money entering art contests. I entered a lot and I won a lot, two dollars each time I won. I loved it.

Later, I put myself through college by working at the UCLA Placement Center. I had wanted to make the world a better place, but looking at the available jobs and opportunities led to my interest in marketing.

On my first date with Phillip, I told him, "I'm going to start a company." My grandfather, brother, and sister all have small businesses, and I saw how hard they worked. I wasn't sure I was ready for that. But then I realized that it was the only way I could do what I loved, and that I'd rather work hard at something I loved than not work very hard at something I wasn't passionate about.

The first company I started—in 1994, Creative Marketing Alliance—was at the beginning of the Internet. I hired a group of contractors to create online marketing for these new companies. AOL was my second customer.

Some might consider that good luck or good timing, but it was possible only because Caren's parents had encouraged her to try new things and work hard at them. If she'd learned instead to play it safe, the moment could have passed her by. Her sense of exploration fueled her career as an entrepreneur.

"It's important to be open to opportunities," Caren told me, "and not have a fixed idea of where things will lead." It was just that attitude that "opened all kinds of doors," she said, when she and Phillip moved to Australia:

I got a marketing job. And Phillip got an engineering job with Open Software Associates. The Internet exploded while we were there. It was 1996, and we started thinking how to make the Internet a platform for integration. Phillip's company didn't want to do it, so we moved back to the U.S. and started webMethods.

In 2007, they sold WebMethods to Software AG for half a billion dollars and now do angel investing through Bibury Partners, their next company. Caren also developed the Pocket Mentor mobile app; Phillip is CEO of Message Systems. They both sit on several corporate boards and are very involved in philanthropic giving.

Amanda Judge: "I Did It!"

Amanda Judge is the founder and CEO of the Faire Collection, which employs 225 local artisans in South America to make jewelry that she sells at stores like Anthropologie. It's a multimillion-dollar company that's making a difference in the world. The company's motto, "Wear the change you want to see," illustrates Amanda's commitment to honoring fair-trade principles and providing economic uplift in developing countries.

Amanda told me that when she was growing up, her parents saw her passion and supported her:

My uncle ran a hardware store, my mom worked from home, and my dad started a business, so I grew up in an environment where people worked for themselves. We were a blue-collar family, and the motto was definitely "Do it yourself."

I've heard my mom, Carol Pollen, say hundreds of times that my first sentence was "I did it." My mom always said that reflected my personality. I loved doing things myself, and I loved that my mom was proud of me for doing things myself.

When I was a child, I asked my parents if I could have an allowance, and they said no. So I said I was going to shovel my neighbor's driveway. They said that was fine. I always earned my own money.

When I was twelve, I wanted to take a class to get a certificate to babysit. My mom said, "If you can organize it, you can do it." So I took the class and got the certificate and started babysitting.

There was never any extra money to go around. If I wanted an ice cream cone, I needed to find the money to buy it. My mom always supported us as we figured out ways to make money. Later, I had to figure out how to get money to go on vacation, and then I had to figure out how to get money to go to college.

I have one brother, who's one and a half years younger and in a PhD program. He's very school smart, whereas I'm common sense and practical smart. Our mom was very loving and gave us both a lot of confidence. I think confidence is the only trait my brother and I have in common. She also allowed me to have these crazy ideas, but she always wanted me to figure out what I wanted to do and how I was going to do it.

We also had a very egalitarian household—we could definitely express our minds. Our parents always talked to us as though we were adults and treated our ideas with respect.

Amanda went to public schools. She told me she had little idea of what career prospects might be open to her:

I read The Economist—I was interested in what was going on in different places—but it never occurred to me that I could actually do something in the world.

I majored in finance in college because I knew that way I could make money. Then I worked for an accountant for two and a half years.

I woke up one day and realized I was either too young or too old to be doing this for the rest of my life. So I went abroad and found a family that wanted to learn English, and I lived in a little farming village in northern Italy. It helped me break out of my shell. For the first time, I realized I didn't have to have a traditional, routine career.

So I started volunteering. I knew I had to do something bigger than me. I learned Spanish and enrolled in grad school at Tufts, in poverty-reduction strategies. Then I went to Ecuador and came home with a bunch of jewelry I wanted to sell.

I started the Andean Collection while finishing grad school. I worked eighteen hours a day and moved to New York. We expanded into three new countries and changed the name to the Faire Collection. Now I have fifteen full-time employees. My mom was right—I did it!

Amanda is doing something that's completely different from what anyone else in her family has done. But her parents let her explore, and she knew she had their support as she figured out what she wanted to do with her life. Now she's not only doing something she loves, she's making a difference in the world.

GIVE UNCONDITIONAL SUPPORT

Following kids' lead is easy when they're taking the world by storm or making decisions that parents agree with. The true test for parents is whether they can remain supportive even when their children seem lost or haven't yet figured out how to make a career out of doing what they love, or when they take a turn that makes their parents nervous. Following children's lead doesn't mean loving—or pretending to love—every choice they make. It means supporting and encouraging them even when parents wish they were doing something else.

Jesse Barber: Recipe for Success

Chefs are some of the country's most recognizable new entrepreneurs. Jesse Barber is the chef-owner of Dudley Market, a farm-to-table restaurant in the Venice neighborhood of Los Angeles that has been getting a huge amount of buzz since it opened. He was previously chef at Barnyard, a few blocks away, which got rave reviews from the LA *Times* and food blogs. His wife, Celia, is the general manager.

Jesse grew up in Eugene, Oregon; his younger brother works at Intelligentsia Coffee, and his younger sister is a recent college grad. His parents, Larry and Christine, are both psychiatrists; his dad is also a pastor.

He told me that his path to becoming a successful restaurateur was not straight, easy, or obvious, but his parents supported whatever he chose:

I barely graduated from high school. I think I took chemistry three times and still barely passed, although I probably only went to a total of three classes.

My parents were always supportive. I played baseball in middle school. I was on a really good team, and I was never that into it. But my mom was at every game, videotaping me, rooting, and hollering. No matter what I did or how good or bad I was, she was always there.

Later, I did cross-country and basketball. I really cared about those, so I worked harder and was pretty good. My dad helped coach the basketball team when I was in high school because I wanted to play, and he wanted to spend extra time with me. He's really good, and we still play. He can still dunk on me.

I went to community college to study psychology. I hated college. I dropped out. I just walked out one day. I had a friend who was going to culinary school. I thought, Wow! You can do this instead of college! So one day I just enrolled in culinary school.

My parents weren't thrilled, but they wanted me to have some direction in my life. So they said, "It's good you found something you like."

I've often made impulsive decisions. If I decided I wanted to do something, I'd just do it. Sometimes it works out, and sometimes it doesn't. I think that when I was growing up, my parents were always slightly appalled by me. I never did what I was supposed to do. But they had pushed us to think for ourselves. I think it sort of backfired on them.

I loved culinary school. I was on the honor roll, and I spoke at graduation. My parents were happy that I was finally doing something I liked. Whatever I wanted to do, they were always 100 percent supportive, even when it wasn't their choice.

But Jesse told me that his parents always combined support with honesty:

I never have to wonder what they're thinking. They'll let me know, whether I want to hear it or not. I know what they thought of Barnyard, because in the first eight months after I opened the restaurant with my menu, they flew in five times to eat there, to let me know how proud they are.

I don't know what I would do without them. They've always been there for me.

Nicole Patrice De Member:
"Mom Taught Me to Move On"

Nicole Patrice De Member is a serial entrepreneur who cofounded High Orbit, a data platform. Previously, she played a key role in hip-hop and electronic dance music by founding the influential Effigy Studios, which she sold to Eminem; Raves.com, an interactive site for the music community; and Groovetickets .com, one of the first online ticketing companies. She's since changed fields, and ran special projects at Founder's Fund, a San Francisco–based venture capital fund, before starting her new company.

Nicole grew up in Michigan and Arizona. Her dad, a mechanic, works for the U.S. Department of Labor's safety administration, and her mom is an engineer at Honeywell. Nicole has a younger brother, David, who's also an entrepreneur; an older stepsister who's a nurse; a stepbrother who's a stylist; and two younger half-brothers who are still in school.

As with Jesse, school wasn't Nicole's passion, but—again, like Jesse—her parents always supported her choices:

> I was kicked out of college twice and lost interest. My mom was very supportive that I didn't get a degree. In fact, she supported everything I ever came up with. No matter how wild the idea, instead of shutting it down, she'd help us explore how to make it happen.
>
> In sixth grade, I made candy by boiling sugar in water and dye. Then I'd put it in a cupcake holder, let it harden, and put it in a baggie. It looked like a hockey puck. I sold them for one dollar. Mom was really encouraging and helped me get the supplies.
>
> In shop class in junior high, I made wooden items like napkin rings and cassette tape holders, and Mom let me sell them at her office. I made several hundred dollars. The school had wanted us to have a mini-business, but I'm the only one who actually created one. I took so many orders, I had some of my classmates working for me!

I felt so lucky having a brother so close to me. We'd always help each other. I feel so bad for entrepreneurs going through it alone.

And Mom was always really encouraging of everything David and I did. Having that kind of support and understanding from my mom and my brother meant everything to me. Not to have your family support you—I can't even imagine.

Nicole told me that her mom encouraged her to explore, keep on looking until she found what she was meant to do, and then look some more:

Some things worked, some things didn't, but Mom was always willing to let me throw ideas at the walls, and when it didn't work out, we'd just switch walls. It's like whiteboarding—you just try a different approach. I learned to keep playing through. Mom taught me never to dwell on a past problem, just to move on.

Help Them Find Their Strengths

As we've seen, some kids have a passion from a young age. Others try different things until something clicks. As the phrase "lead by following" implies, some parents get out of the way and let their kids do what makes them happy, but others aren't passively stepping aside and waiting for their children to do amazing things. Many of the parents I talked with did a lot to help their kids identify what it was they loved to do.

Ellen Gustafson: Encouraged to Trust Herself

As you'll recall about FEED Projects cofounder Ellen Gustafson, she was teased when she was young (rule 6), but she still developed the self-confidence to give an acting career a serious try. This led to her confidence to do public speaking about the causes she's involved in. Her mom, Maura, told me:

> *Ellen was always a voracious reader. That was her passion outside of school. We thought she'd gone to bed, and we'd find her with a flashlight under the blankets, reading.*
>
> *And she was always a performer. From the time she was little, she'd be putting on costumes, singing, dancing. She also played sports, but that wasn't her strong suit.*
>
> *In high school, she had to choose between basketball and being in the school play—her school wouldn't let her do both. Lots of kids were getting kudos playing sports. We didn't think that was her future, but she had to decide.*

It can be extremely tempting to make choices for your kids. After all, you're the adult, you know your children better than anyone else does, and you don't want them to suffer. But Ellen's mother resisted that temptation:

> *We encouraged her to be independent, and to think for herself. I'd tell her, "Trust, but verify. Check it out. Be sure it's true. Don't drink the Kool-Aid. Just because everyone else is doing it, that doesn't mean you have to."*
>
> *Your most important job as a parent is to help your children figure out what their true strengths are. As a parent, you can see what their strengths are, but you have to let them figure it out. I think the best way to do that is by asking them questions. You want them to grow up to be cautious, but not fearful. You want them to have confidence in themselves.*
>
> *So I said, "You have to make the choice. Which do you see yourself doing in your life—playing basketball or acting? You choose which would be more helpful to you in the future."*
>
> *She chose acting. She even went to L.A. to try to make it.*

She ended up deciding not to pursue acting. I think that, ultimately, she found it boring, and she didn't really like just reading someone else's words. I think she knew she wanted to make a difference in the world.

But I think acting helped her find her comfort level in front of a crowd. She does a lot of public speaking now, and she's a natural on the stage—really connects with her audience.

Part of following kids' lead is paying attention to where they're going. If you're not engaged with what your children are doing— what they're good at, what makes them come alive—then you'll have a hard time supporting those activities. Here's how Maura explains it:

If you don't help your kids figure out their strengths, you're abdicating your role as a parent. I taught social studies in high school. Parents would come in and say, "I don't know what their strengths are," and I'd think, My God, you don't know their skills by this point in their lives? I think it's one of the most important things a parent can do—help your kids figure out their strengths.

Adam and Scooter Braun:
They're Who They Need to Be

We've talked about the Braun brothers and their inspiring mom, Susan (rule 2). For her, the "lead by following" principle goes beyond letting kids do what they enjoy. She told me that it's also about letting them be who they are:

None of us knew what we were doing, but we just followed them. The smartest thing we did was not squash a passion. All kids have a passion, but parents often negate it. I was charmed by my kids and didn't feel a need to protect them. I realized early on that my kids had very large personalities, and I always tried hard to understand my kids and appreciate them as individuals.

Unlike some parents, who are invested in successful outcomes that will reflect well on them, Susan believed differently. This is the Kahlil Gibran poem she keeps in her kitchen:

Your children are not your children.
They are the sons and daughters of Life's longing for itself.
They come through you but not from you,
And though they are with you yet they belong not to you.
You may give them your love but not your thoughts,
For they have their own thoughts...
You may strive to be like them, but seek not to make them like you.

Susan told me that for her this poem means that her kids aren't a reflection of her. They're who they need to be. It was her job, she said, to be a stable force in their lives and not to try to live their lives for them. She wanted them to know their strengths and understand their inner essence and project it out.

Eric Ryan: The Joy of Parenting

We met Method cofounder Eric Ryan in the chapter on winning and losing (rule 2). His mom, Pam, always let him figure out what he wanted to do, always supported him, and always enjoyed that process:

We have a saying that we made one mistake with Eric—we should have let him drive home from the hospital because he has been such a positive, forceful energy in our lives, and in his brothers' lives. He's introduced us to things we never thought we'd be doing, things we've had so much fun doing.

254

Then Pam said words that were echoed by so many other moms I talked to—a key to raising a successful entrepreneur:

My husband Tom and I had a list of things we wanted them to know how to do—ski, ice skate—but then they chose what they were interested in. We always believed in our kids. We always told them, "There is nothing you can't do." So we helped our children pursue their interests.

Like many other moms I interviewed, Pam had fun raising her kids. Maybe because kids doing what they love tend to be happy kids. She told me:

We had fun doing it. We didn't think what we were doing was special, because we thoroughly enjoyed it. We also loved their friends. We always had kids spend a lot of time at our home who were involved in sailing. One year, we had four kids come for the summer. I was fortunate to be a stay-at-home mom. I would say I was home patrolling the troops. I loved that I could be there for them, and for their friends. But I wasn't afraid to be a tough mom, too. I had rules.

Eric always worked different jobs. Even when he went off to college and was on the sailing team, he had a job hauling I-14s, a sailboat he raced, around the East Coast. At school, when he loved a subject, and had a passion for it, the sky was the limit. But when he wasn't interested, it was tough—it was like pulling teeth. He always had a tremendous amount of confidence, but was never arrogant or entitled.

According to Pam, Eric got practice persuading his future customers by having to convince his parents when he wanted something:

So often, the oldest one has to be the pioneer. Eric paved the way for his brothers. There were times when he'd really have to persuade us to let him do some of the things he wanted to do. I remember once he wrote a proposal to convince us to buy him a little sailboat. He was so persistent and determined to keep going until he had proved his point. He wouldn't stop until he'd convinced us that his idea was a good one.

When he'd present an idea to us, we made him work hard to convince us, though we always let him do it in the end. We told him recently, "Sometimes we think we owe you an apology." He said, "No, it was good you were so tough. The first time I had to present at a meeting, it really helped me that I'd had to present to you and Dad all those times. I just pretended I was presenting to you."

Pam enthusiastically supported everything Eric did, from sailing to selling soaps.

The first time I saw one of his soaps in a store, I was so excited! Then I saw that one bottle was broken, so I bought it.

Eric said, "Mom, why'd you buy a broken one?"

I answered, "Honey, I didn't want someone else to buy it and think you sold broken products."

He laughed and told me, "Mom, they'd have replaced it!"

Eric continues to amaze us. He has led us on an incredible journey. I wouldn't have missed this ride for all the tea in China. And I look forward to all the adventures to come.

It's not always easy to trust in outcomes we can't yet see—especially when it comes to our children, whom we cherish so much. Eric, like most of the entrepreneurs in this book, chose a career his parents might not have picked out for him. Pam, like all the other moms, talked to her kids about—and demonstrated—the importance of playing to their strengths, pursuing their dreams, and following their heart. And every budding entrepreneur, like Eric, had their family's support the entire time, through every twist and turn and bump in the road.

Pam ended our chat with words that summarize the current that runs through every one of the ten rules I discovered while writing this book. She told me: "My favorite saying is 'Always believe in your child. Trust them. Be there for them.'"

Conclusion

Believe in Your Child

When I chose the entrepreneurs to interview for this book, one of my goals was to achieve a broad sample, both in terms of inputs—gender, race, religion, ethnicity, sexual orientation, family income, parents' education, their own education, where they'd grown up—and outcomes: I wanted them to have started big companies, small companies, nonprofits, or profits-for-purpose, or to be artists, or activists. Given all these differences, I wondered if I'd find any common threads, let alone universal themes.

To my amazement and delight, every single one came from a family that conveyed one fundamental message: we support you; we believe in you; follow your passion. Sometimes following through on that message required a big gulp, or even a leap of faith. But every parent said it. And meant it.

Maybe you're thinking: that's not so unusual—all parents believe in their children. But that's not true. All parents love their children. That's not the same thing as truly believing in them—as truly trusting them.

As parents, we want what is best for our children. Or, at least, what we *think* is best for them. And what we almost always want for them is, in a word, *success*. That's partly because we tend to see professional and, often, material success as offering them protection from some of the world's harsher realities. But wanting success for our children, even when our desire for their success comes from love and our concern for their welfare, is not the same thing as truly believing in them.

Believing in our children involves having wholehearted trust and faith in them—even when their road is rough, or their choices are...shall we say, unexpected. It means understanding that they're not going to be immediately successful at everything they try—and that ultimately this is, in fact, a very good thing, because without some struggle, there is no growth. It means supporting kids as they find and follow their passions, celebrating their triumphs with them, but also being there for them as they pick themselves up after setbacks. It means lovingly standing by and trusting them to handle adversity instead of jumping in to handle it for them. It's how we teach our kids that failure is nothing to fear, that they have what it takes to recover and grow from it. That they can trust themselves. That's a great message for any child, but it's indispensable for a child who's a budding entrepreneur. Fearless kids who are doing what they love most—following their hearts, rather than trying to please their parents or anyone else—are poised to have great adventures. They're also getting the best kind of training for making the world a better place.

Consider these statements many loving parents make to their children:

- "Don't spend so much time playing on the computer. Join some activities so you have a more well-rounded college application."

- "I guess you can minor in music, but you have to major in something useful."

- "You can major in that, but you need a teaching certificate so you have something to fall back on."

- "You can work full time on your little company after you graduate from college. First things first."

All of these parents mean well—they intend to support and protect their child, and steer her toward success. But what else do statements like these tell that child? It's something like this: "We don't think you will succeed if you follow the path you want. We don't think you're good enough to be successful if you take such an unconventional route. We're afraid you will fail."

None of the parents I spoke to for this book communicated such a fearful message to their children. Instead, they all said: "Go for it! We know you'll succeed." And all of these entrepreneurs did.

Were all of them successful at everything they tried? Certainly not.

Did they all hit bumps in the road? Of course.

Will all their ventures succeed? No.

Will some of them abandon their venture and join someone else's, starting a project within a bigger company, becoming entrepreneurial rather than an entrepreneur? Probably.

Does any of that matter? Not at all.

Because their families will support them as they start on their next great adventure. And because these entrepreneurs will be doing what they love, rather than what they think will please their parents or anyone else. Becoming an entrepreneur is not for everyone. But if it's for your child, what a wonderful journey it can be.

WHAT DOESN'T MATTER

As fascinated as I was to find the many common traits among the diverse entrepreneurs, I was just as interested to find that certain factors I assumed would matter a lot don't seem to make a difference. For example, I thought I might find that a high percentage of the entrepreneurs would share a particular place in the birth order, such as first born; or have highly educated parents, or entrepreneurial parents; or come from small families; or come from financially secure families; or have attended highly rated high schools or prestigious colleges. I was wrong. Factors like birth order, family size, family income, and education—of both the parents and the entrepreneurs themselves—did not seem predictive of the entrepreneurs' success, in either their careers or their characters.

Birth order didn't matter at all. Interestingly, however, many entrepreneurs I interviewed seemed to think that their particular situations—*whatever they were*—were advantageous. For example, many thought that wherever they were in the birth order was an advantage; several told me that, because they were the middle or youngest child, they were given more freedom than their siblings. Many felt that the size of their own family, from one to seven, was an advantage. That says a lot about the kind of attitude these kids grew up with: they all believed their family circumstances worked perfectly for them.

Family composition also varied widely, and didn't seem to matter. Although many were raised in traditional two-parent homes, some were raised by single moms, others had blended families with stepparents and stepsiblings and half-siblings, and one had adopted siblings. Family composition didn't appear to matter, since the parents treated all of their children the same.

Family income was all over the map, with several low-income and working class families and the full range of middle class incomes, too, from lower to upper. Interestingly, though, I noted that even in the wealthier families, the kids did not grow up feeling entitled—in fact, most of these families' kids always had a job growing up, because they were required to earn their spending money.

And being poor didn't seem to affect the kids from those families, because their families showed them they could always find a way to do what they wanted—attend college, travel abroad, give to those less fortunate—so they were empowered to go for their dreams.

In fact, what all of the families had in common was that they didn't emphasize money as the yardstick for success.

Schooling also didn't matter. There was an enormous range in the entrepreneurs' academic performance. Some were great students from kindergarten on. One-third graduated in the top of their class from top universities; one-quarter of them got advanced degrees. But about 20 percent left college without graduating to get on with the next phase of their life. And others struggled in school until they found a subject that ignited their imaginations. Still others simply struggled in school, period.

Nor was their parents' level of education a predictive factor. Some parents hadn't graduated from high school, while others had advanced degrees. There didn't seem to be a correlation between how educated the parents were and how much education their children got. For instance, two of the entrepreneurs had parents without college degrees, yet both were academic stars through college and beyond. Regardless of their own education, most of the parents stressed the importance of education. And, just as key, regardless of how educated they were, if their children wanted to drop out of college, the parents supported their decision.

I thought entrepreneurs might have been obvious leaders from the start—the kind who take charge on the playground. Indeed, some seemed to have been born leaders—but plenty of others didn't blossom until much later. They all got there eventually.

What surprised me the most was that not all the parents were closely involved in their children's lives. A lot of moms were very present in their kids' daily lives, both working moms and stay-at-home moms. And there were plenty of others who were much more hands-off, setting firm ground rules and then trusting their kids to make good choices. In fact, how many rules the parents had—how strict they were—didn't seem to matter. And, interestingly, many of the kids who grew up in homes with the most rules also were given the most freedom.

For me, letting go in a thoughtful way was the hardest part of raising children. If I had to do it all over again, I would give my children even more freedom at a younger age.

In fact, if I had one piece of advice for parents, it would be to let go a little bit more. To let your daughter know what you expect and then trust her to do it. Not to fix it for your son when he screws up, but to let him fix it on his own. And if life is uncomfortable for a little while, that's got to be okay. Of course, sometimes you really do have to step in. But check the impulse to do so, and, whenever possible, let children meet their challenges themselves.

WHAT MATTERS

You never know which of the ten rules will make the biggest difference for your child. But several themes stood out in the stories of most of the entrepreneurs I profiled:

Passion (Rule 1): Almost every entrepreneur was passionate about something outside of school. For many of them, their passion was sports, and that intensity and drive translated into entrepreneurial success later on. Others started with a passion while they were still in school that became their passion in life, such as music, film, or computers. Others had passions that evolved over time, but they learned grit, focus, determination, and the desire to win by pursuing something they loved.

I think this is the key takeaway for parents. If the passion isn't obvious, help your child explore different areas to figure out what they love and what they're good at, and then nurture that. If they love something, they will work at it tenaciously, they will develop grit, and they will achieve success. Every one of the entrepreneurs I interviewed told me they had a strong work ethic. Every one told me they worked harder and longer than anyone else. And every one told me it was because they love what they do.

Don't force your daughter to spend all her time studying subjects she hates. Don't let your son think you don't respect him because he doesn't have straight A's. A child who excels in one area may have a better chance of achieving extraordinary things—and living a rich, satisfying life—than a child who is pretty good in every area. You want your child to develop grit, and the only way to do that, other than forcing them, Tiger Mom–style, is for them to *want* to work hard because they love it and they want to master it—whatever "it" may be.

Competition (Rule 2): The more I talked to entrepreneurs, the more I began to see their dogged pursuit of excellence in sports and other competitive pursuits as a key ingredient in their later success. For about half the entrepreneurs in this book, learning to compete was key to their learning about the trade-off between hard work and results, how to prepare for a challenge, how to take risks, the value of failure, how to regroup after failing, and how to win with humility.

It also led to their desire to excel in their professional lives. They learned not to be afraid to fail, which led to their willingness to take risks, which is key to starting an organization from scratch.

Mentors (Rule 4): Quite a few future entrepreneurs had one or more mentors who were influential in their life. These could be family members other than their parents, teachers, coaches, or people in the profession they eventually went into: simply a trustworthy adult who recognized their talent and encouraged them.

Adversity (Rule 6): Many of the entrepreneurs grew up in idyllic environments. But many others faced difficulties, including physical disabilities, learning issues, being bullied, experiencing a divorce, or losing a parent. All overcame their troubles, grew, and thrived. In families where there was no real adversity, the parents or grandparents often had experienced adversity growing up, and the stories they shared helped their children understand resilience and learn how to cope.

Compassion (Rule 7): Many of the entrepreneurs were brought up with a focus on helping others. Many were raised with the strong belief that they had to give back and, in fact, most of the entrepreneurs in this book do give back today, either through their nonprofit or profit-for-purpose organizations, through the mission and

practices of their for-profit businesses, or in volunteer work, often combined with generous financial contributions, for causes they believe in.

Something Bigger (Rule 9): I also found that regardless of what religion they were raised in, or how formal their religious upbringing, most of the entrepreneurs believed in *something*; their beliefs fed their commitment to service, and their sense that they have a duty to contribute to the world. This ethic is as true for those who create products as for those who spearhead causes.

WHAT MATTERS MOST

I can't claim that every thriving, engaged, motivated entrepreneur in the world was raised by parents who followed the same rules. But all of the extraordinary entrepreneurs I talked to did share the same core experience growing up: all of them felt truly supported.

Every mom I talked to adored her kids; every entrepreneur I talked to adored his or her mom. The moms said things like, "It was a privilege to raise them." The entrepreneurs said things like, "My family was always there for me." Or, "I always knew if I needed my family, they were there, which gave me the strength to take risks." Even in families where parents worked all the time, or became ill, the children knew they were there when it counted.

Without my asking, most of the entrepreneurs told me how important their family was to them. Many also told me that they've incorporated the values their families imparted into their companies or organizations—things like trust, not overreacting to mistakes, empowering employees to make decisions, and telling coworkers not to be afraid to fail.

Every one of the families in this book did a fantastic job raising confident, caring, successful people. And every one of the entrepreneurs knew that they could always fall back on their family. In some cases, that meant the family provided practical or financial support. In every case, it meant the family provided emotional support. It meant that no matter what, the entrepreneurs knew their family believed in them. That's what gave them the confidence to take risks.

So many parents today hear the word "support" and immediately worry about providing too much support, or providing it for too long. We've all heard stories about the twenty-five-year-old who still lives at home. The focus is usually on finding a way to get that young person to develop a sense of responsibility. But that may not be the real problem. Perhaps what he lacks is passion. He hasn't yet found what he loves to do—or quite possibly, he *has* found it, but he's been led to believe that pursuing it with all of his heart is too risky.

The parents in this book let their children find their passion and then nurtured and supported it however they could. They all let their children decide what *they* loved and what *they* wanted to do. The parents didn't say, "You're going to be a doctor like your dad, aren't you?" They said, "You want to do what? Really? Oh… great!"

All of the entrepreneurs in this book are extremely confident. Some may think, "Sure, success will do that." But I believe that their confidence led to their success, rather than the other way around. It isn't the kind of confidence that's built on a false sense of self-esteem that came from being praised regardless of whether they succeeded. It's a deep-rooted confidence that comes from realizing they have mastered something, that stems from having worked really hard and gotten really good. And it was a precursor of their success as entrepreneurs. They knew they could do it, so they did.

Sometimes parents try to help their children by interceding on their behalf: calling a teacher to get a grade changed or arguing with a coach to give a child more playing time or a better position. They mean well. But the unintended effect is a child who isn't growing up believing that *she* can master something, that *she* can succeed, and that it is *her* effort that has made the difference. And that if she fails, she can work harder and smarter and try again, because maybe she'll succeed the next time. And if she doesn't, her family will continue to cheer her on and be proud of her successes, whenever they come, in whatever she pursues.

BELIEVE IN YOUR CHILD

I loved discovering the ten rules that emerged over the course of my interviews. I believe that each of them will help you nurture your child's confidence and independence. But there's another rule so important, so pervasive, that I couldn't break it out into its own chapter. It's an inseparable part of every story, every innovative idea, every big dream, every courageous failure, and every success in this book.

Every one of the entrepreneurs in this book said something like this: "My mom believed in me, so I believed in me." And every mom said something like, "We always trusted him and believed in him." Parent after parent; one entrepreneur after another. Every single one.

The parents in this book gave their children the following messages:

- We love you.

- We trust you.

- We believe in you.

- We support you in whatever you want to do.

- We love that you've found your passion; we encourage you to pursue it.

- We know you'll do great things.

- We'll always be here for you.

- Don't worry if you make mistakes; you'll learn from them. And anyhow, they're just bumps on the road to your success.

- We're excited to follow you on your journey.

- We can't wait to see everything you're going to accomplish.

My hope is that more parents will say these things—and mean them—when they talk to their children. This kind of wholehearted trust in a child's capacity is the secret to raising an entrepreneur—the ten rules boiled down to a few simple sentences.

BEYOND ENTREPRENEURSHIP

When I started to write this book, I thought it would only be useful for parents of kids who want to be entrepreneurs. I didn't think its lessons would apply to parents whose kids are pursuing a more conventional path.

On reflection, though, I think I was wrong about that.

It began to dawn on me, after I'd talked to dozens of entrepreneurs and had begun to see the patterns that coalesced into the ten rules, how beneficial those rules can be for anyone. No matter what their career path, no matter whether they're starting at the bottom in an established profession or organization or creating their own new thing, helping your children believe in themselves will serve them.

Even if your child doesn't want to be an entrepreneur, encouraging them to *become more entrepreneurial* by promoting certain attitudes can only be a good thing. All children thrive if they learn:

- To believe in themselves

- To pursue their true passions

- To find new ways to solve old problems

- To see opportunity where others see the status quo

- To be willing to take on a challenge without proper credentials

- To work with single-minded determination to achieve a goal

- To take on risk if the project is worth trying

- To learn that building something wonderful is its own reward, regardless of how much money you make

- To view failure as feedback and setbacks as learning experiences

- To dream big dreams

Say your daughter becomes a manager at a large firm. She'll know how to treat subordinates so they feel valued and trusted. Or say your son becomes a school principal. He'll be equipped to run it like an enterprise that he's poured his life into. Or say that both of your kids enter the nonprofit world. They'll be able to bounce back from inevitable setbacks and find new ways of seeing problems.

Not everyone wants to be an entrepreneur. And not everyone has the makeup to be an entrepreneur—not everyone thrives on risk, loves to create something from scratch, can tolerate living with uncertainty, or wants to put in crazy-long hours. It's important to reiterate that parents can't turn their children into entrepreneurs if their children don't have the urge—just like parents can't turn their children into doctors or orchestra conductors.

Whether your child has an entrepreneurial bent or not, whether she knows exactly what she wants to do in life at age twelve or hasn't a clue at twenty, the principle is always the same: wherever her passion, fascination, ability, and drive lead, support her pursuit.

Perhaps you're a doctor and your daughter always wanted to be a doctor, and she does really well in all her science classes. Or perhaps you're a lawyer and your son loves to visit your office and hear about your work, and he's really good at debating and reading and writing long, analytical pieces. Or maybe you own a business where your child has worked every summer—and she can't wait to start full time when school's over. Some kids, entrepreneurially minded or otherwise, know what they want from an early age and go after it with all they've got. Fantastic!

But perhaps your son loves school but can't figure out what he wants to do with his life because none of the careers he's heard about excite him. Or your daughter is really smart, but is not particularly motivated by schoolwork. Or your kids love what they're doing outside of the classroom—playing sports, writing music, making art, acting, filming, running for school office, playing chess, selling golf balls, traveling, singing, dancing, playing with their computer, volunteering at nonprofits, starting a little company, fixing broken things, making things in shop class, organizing protests—more than school itself. It just may be that their passion—their true calling in life—is somewhere down one of the roads they're beginning to walk. And maybe if you let go of whatever anxieties you have about their future, and encourage them to pursue their passion with all they've got, something great will happen. Something great for them and, possibly, something great for the world.

No matter what your child is going to do, knowing that someone believes in them—and believes they can do anything they set their mind to—will help them.

So, parents, think about how the ten rules apply to your family. Encourage your kids to follow their dreams, because whatever they want to do with their lives, your trust and support will help them get there. Kids, thank your parents for believing in you. And give your mom a big hug while you're at it.

Stumbling Into
(Some of) the Rules

This book is not about my husband and me, and it's not about our kids, so I didn't want to include much about our family. But in the course of writing it, I had plenty of opportunity to look back and think about what our family was like, and what we did and didn't do, compared to the families I learned about through all my interviews.

No one is more amazed than Mark and I that we raised two entrepreneurial kids. Our sons certainly didn't get the entrepreneurial bug from us. I started in the federal government's anti-poverty program, got an MBA, moved to D.C., worked for a while on Capitol Hill, and then worked in government doing economic policy and international development for the next twenty years.

Mark and I met when we both worked on Capitol Hill. He got a law degree, practiced law, and then worked for airlines and tech companies. It wasn't until our older son was in college that Mark started a company, Bisnow Media, which is now the largest commercial real estate publisher and events producer in the U.S.

Our older son, Elliott, was Mark's first employee. After a few years, Elliott left to found the national conference series for young entrepreneurs and other creatives called Summit Series (which

Joel Holland referred to earlier in this book). Established to incubate cutting-edge ideas, start-up companies, and nonprofits, it was called "the hipper Davos" by *Forbes*. Elliott has raised millions of dollars for charities, was named to *Inc.*'s "30 Under 30" list when he was twenty-four, and has been profiled in many publications. In 2013, he and his Summit team raised funds to buy Powder Mountain, a 10,000-acre ski resort one hour from Salt Lake City, to create the world's first permanent community of entrepreneurs. We attend his conferences and spend as much time at the mountain as we can. It's through Summit that I've gotten to know many of the entrepreneurs profiled in this book— and, through them, their moms.

Our younger son, Austin, is a very different kind of entrepreneur: songwriter and lead singer of a band he started, Magic Giant. In a notoriously difficult field, he's been privileged to have an opportunity to work with many great artists, and a song he cowrote, produced, and played piano on, "Listen," was sung by John Legend as the title song on superstar DJ David Guetta's album. Magic Giant has been gaining fans, touring, and playing festivals. We fly in for as many of his shows as we can. Austin works eighteen-hour days, seven days a week, and loves what he does.

When our boys were growing up, we didn't know a lot of entrepreneurs. We didn't talk about start-ups around the dinner table; we talked about politics. In fact, looking back, I now think it's odd that Mark and I each changed jobs several times in the 1980s and '90s and neither of us ever once thought about starting our own business. Never. When Elliott applied to college, his essay wasn't "I am an entrepreneur." It was "I am a tennis player."

It's only after the fact, as I look back, that I realize how many things we accidently did that helped them become entrepreneurs. So here's how we did, according to the rules:

Both of our kids had a passion outside of school (rule 1). For Elliott, it was tennis, and we were always supportive, and proud of how hard he worked at it. We were the opposite of tennis parents; he had to push us for everything. We let him take lessons—although he did have to make a strong case to us for private lessons, because they were expensive. I realize now that was good: he had to convince us he needed those lessons, and he couldn't just take them for granted. Our family went to all his tennis tournaments—first all around the area, then the region, then the country. We cheered when he won points; we were supportive when he lost (which, during the first few years, was almost always); and we believed, with him, that he could be the next Andre Agassi. He got up to thirty-fifth in the country in the juniors and played on the varsity team at the University of Wisconsin. Then he moved on.

For Austin, it was always music, although he stumbled into songwriting. He had signed up for basketball camp when he was thirteen, and broke his ankle on the first day. I desperately looked for a program that had an opening and found only one: a camp that taught MIDI, writing music on a computer. It clicked. He's been writing music ever since. Because he loved to perform, we let him take voice lessons and piano lessons and drum lessons and guitar lessons and dance lessons when he asked for them. We went to the school musicals and the band concerts and chorus concerts. We let him go to a summer songwriting program at Berklee College of Music and, as his high school graduation present, paid for him to have sixteen of his songs recorded and produced on a CD. He majored in music composition at the University of Colorado and has worked nonstop at it ever since.

Tennis and music were their passions, not ours. We didn't play tennis or know anything about music. Our sons chose what *they* wanted, and we supported them, encouraged them, and believed in them. So overall I think we did a good job with this rule, and in doing so, also made the grade with rule 5—instilling confidence—and rule 10, leading by following. When we supported the development of the mastery of their passionate pursuits outside school, we supported the growth of their self-confidence. As we saw where their interests lay, we supported their priorities with our time, money, and organizational abilities, as well as our pride in their accomplishments. We didn't have any motive other than loving to see them working hard at something that made them happy.

Did we let them compete and learn to lose as well as win (rule 2)? I'd say so. For Elliott, losing was a big part of pursuing his passion: because he started playing competitively so late, he lost most of his tennis matches for years. Austin entered singing, acting, and dancing competitions, and he also played competitive sports through college, probably losing more than he won. Like many of the families profiled in this book, we found that sports was a great route to learn about competing, the trade-off between hard work and results, grit, resilience, and determination. Although, again, that's not why we did it. We didn't have a grand plan. We simply had two very active boys who loved athletic activity.

Neither of the boys were academic stars in high school, but they shined brightly in the things that mattered to them. And we couldn't have been prouder of their achievements in those areas; we demonstrated our joy in their progress over and over; although we were more academic, we tried very hard not to worry about straight A's (rule 3).

Looking back, one of the best things I did was something I *didn't* do. When Elliott dropped out of college halfway through his junior year to help his dad expand his new company, I was appalled. My dad had been a professor, and it never occurred to me that I might have a kid who didn't graduate from college. Elliott told me he would take off just one semester. Then he asked for one more. I now think it was one of the smartest things he did: to get on with his life rather than spend time studying subjects he wasn't interested in. Today, I'm so pleased that I didn't insist on his graduating. I wasn't happy at the time, but I swallowed hard and trusted him to make his own choice.

Both our kids had incredible mentors (rule 4), to whom we owe a great deal. I didn't find them; our kids did. Elliott had two extraordinary tennis coaches during his middle and high school years, who instilled a strong work ethic and stressed honor and integrity on and off the court: Martin Blackman and Vesa Ponkka. Austin had several mentors in high school who taught him about perseverance and character: high school band director Earl Jackson; football special teams coach Drew Johnson; athletic director Neil Phillips; track coach Tre Johnson; his favorite teacher, Rick Kirschner; and his college football coach, Dan Hawkins. And the fact that they believed in him more than compensated for the fact that some of his other teachers didn't.

We were blessed to have these extraordinary men take part in our boys' lives, because they taught values that guide them today. Martin, for example, told Elliott when he was in eighth grade that if he wanted to be a champion on the court, he had to be a champion off the court. And when Austin was in college and had just turned twenty-one and someone wanted him to buy him alcohol, he said, "My coach says, 'Nothing good can come from going to a liquor store.'" If those words of advice had come from a parent, would they have had the same impact? Thank you, Coach Hawk!

While we're on the subject, I'd like to add that parents need mentors, too. In addition to having had extraordinary parents myself, I realize looking back that I had a parenting mentor, Landon Lower School headmaster Marcos Williams.

I remember one example in particular. Elliott was in third grade and had spent a lot of time on his homework the night before. When I went into his room in the morning after he'd gone to school, I saw it on his desk. I got in the car and drove to school and stopped in the office to see if they could get it to him. Marcos came out to talk to me, and said something like this:

> Margot, he will or he won't get into Harvard. But it will have nothing to do with the grades he gets when he's in third grade. On the other hand, what lesson have you taught him if you bail him out? You will have taught him that if he doesn't do something, you will do it for him. Isn't that worse than whatever bad grade he receives in third grade for turning his project in one day late? Don't you want him to learn that he has to face the consequences for his actions and become responsible?

So I took the homework back home.

I needed to hear what Marcos had to say that day and, looking back, I think he pointed out a weak point in my parenting: that my desire to "make it better" could be stronger than my ability to stand back and let my kids take their lumps.

I stood up for my sons a lot—possibly too much. Sometimes I let them fight their own battles, but other times, when I thought someone in charge had treated them unfairly, I got involved. In hindsight, it may have been the biggest mistake I made: being too helpful, too concerned, too involved. But at least my sons knew I had their back.

Some of the families in this book have taught me quite a bit about other facets of parenting that weren't such a factor for us. Our family was very fortunate not to experience any significant adversity (rule 6) while the boys were growing up. No one has control over adversity striking their family or their child—illness, death, and misfortune can come without warning. Many of the parents, and their children, I talked with for this book met it with such strength and grace that they emerged resilient and more courageous than ever. I can only hope we would have handled adversity as well.

I would also say that a lot of families I interviewed were much more deliberate at nurturing compassion (rule 7) than we were: they made it a central theme of their lives. Actions matter: families profiled here did big things like adopting needy kids, as well as significant work regularly doing service for others, such as volunteering in shelters. These families made a priority of showing their kids that there's something bigger than they are (rule 9) and that being part of it adds meaning and purpose to life.

I do think that we were a great family (rule 8). There are as many different ways *to be* a great family as there *are* great families. As for us, we always ate dinner together. Someone asked me once what time we ate, and I said, "When the last person walks in the door." We all went to Austin's concerts and plays and football games; we spent every vacation for three years going to Elliott's tennis tournaments.

And we traveled extensively together. I wanted the kids to get to know different places and I hoped it would make them aware that there were other cultures and other ways of doing things. It turned out that it had a more important and unexpected dimension: it strengthened us a family, because we were alone together, creating shared experiences. I can't recommend family travel enough. I cherish the memories of the four of us together, creating a bond I hope will last forever.

If you have kids who dream of changing the world, I'm excited for you. You're in for a challenging, thrilling, and rewarding ride—one that may take you places you can't even imagine. I hope that wherever their journey ends, they'll know you were with them the whole way. I can't wait to hear what they accomplish.

References

BOOKS

Dweck, C. 2008. *Mindset: the New Psychology of Success.* New York: Ballantine Books.

Gibran, K. 1923. *The Prophet.* New York: Alfred A. Knopf.

Ginsburg, K., and M. Jablow. 2015. *Building Resilience in Children and Teens,* 3rd ed. Elk Grove Village, IL: American Academy of Pediatrics.

Gladwell, M. 2008. *Outliers.* New York: Little, Brown and Company.

Gladwell, M. 2013. *David and Goliath.* New York: Little, Brown and Company.

Jackley, J. 2015. *Clay Water Brick: Finding Inspiration from the Entrepreneurs Who Do the Most with the Least.* New York: Random House.

Karmo, M. 2012. *Fearless: Awakening to My Life's Purpose Through Breast Cancer.* Dallas: Brown Books Publishing Group.

Mycoskie, B. 2012. *Start Something That Matters.* New York: Random House.

Rosenthal, N. 2013. *The Gift of Adversity: The Unexpected Benefits of Life's Difficulties, Setbacks, and Imperfections.* New York: Penguin.

Roth-Douquet, K., and F. Schaeffer. 2006. *AWOL: The Unexcused Absence of America's Upper Classes from Military Service—and How It Hurts Our Country.* New York: HarperCollins.

Roth-Douquet, K., and F. Schaeffer. 2008. *How Free People Move Mountains: A Male Christian Conservative and a Female Jewish Liberal on a Quest for Common Purpose and Meaning.* New York: HarperCollins.

Saylor, M. 2012. *The Mobile Wave: How Mobile Intelligence Will Change Everything.* New York: Vanguard Press.

Sternberg, R. 1997. *Successful Intelligence: How Practical and Creative Intelligence Determine Success in Life.* New York: Plume.

Tough, P. 2012. *How Children Succeed.* New York: Houghton Mifflin Harcourt.

Wojcicki, E. 2015. *Moonshots in Education: Launching Blended Learning in the Classroom.* San Francisco: Pacific Research Institute.

ARTICLES AND VIDEOS

Bercovici, J. 2015. "The DNA Whisperer." *Inc.*, October. http://www.inc.com/magazine/201510/jeff-bercovici/the-dna-whisperer.html

Bounds, G., K. Spors, and R. Flandez. 2007. "The Secrets of Serial Success." *Wall Street Journal*, August 20. www.wsj.com/articles/SB118712720309797680.

Cunningham, L. 2015. "Duke Business School Dean Talks About the Secret to Inspiring the Next Tim Cook." *WP On*

Leadership (blog), www.washingtonpost.com/business/on
-leadership/.

Duckworth, A. 2013. "The Key to Success? Grit." *TED Talks Education,* www.TED.com/talks/.

Fast Company: The Most Daring CEO. November 2013, single-subject issue.

Goldman, M. 2013. "Blue Man to Blue School: Encouraging Innovation." *Arcade* 31:2, May 7. arcadenw.org/article/blue
-man-to-blue-school.

Graft, L. 2012. "Howard Schultz, Founder of Starbucks—The Walk" (video). https://vimeo.com/57622029#.

Guth, R. 2009. "Raising Bill Gates." *Wall Street Journal,* April 29. www.wsj.com/articles/SB124061372413054653.

Lanning, R. 2013. "In Defense of the Nap Year." *Brain, Child,* June 3. http://www.brainchildmag.com/2013/06/in-defense-of
-the-nap-year/.

Lassiter, J., W. A. Sahlman, and J. Biotti. 1998, revised 2. *Nantucket Nectars.* Harvard Business School Case 898–171. Boston: Harvard Business School.

Miller, C. 2015. "Mounting Evidence of Advantages for Children of Working Mothers." *New York Times,* May 15. http://www
.nytimes.com/2015/05/17/upshot/mounting-evidence-of-some
-advantages-for-children-of-working-mothers.html?_r=0
&abt=0002&abg=0

Mulligan, M. 2014. "The Three Most Important Questions You Can Ask Your Teenager." *Huffington Post Education* (blog), www.huffingtonpost.com/education.

Nunez, A. 2014. "A Brave New Paradigm of Manhood." TedX Austin Women, https://www.youtube.com/watch?v=hQsmw
ivCId8.

Prewitt, A. 2013. "Alex Len Has Journeyed Far to Chase His NBA Dreams." *Washington Post,* June 24. https://www.wash ingtonpost.com/sports/wizards/alex-len-has-journeyed-far-to -chase-his-nba-dreams/2013/06/24/38d8cb1e-d8fc-11e2-a9f2 -42ee3912ae0e_story.html.

Strauss, V. 2013. "John Lennon's 'Bad Boy' Behavior: School Detention Records Up for Sale." *Washington Post,* November 11. https://www.washingtonpost.com/news/answer-sheet/wp /2013/11/11/john-lennons-bad-boy-behavior-school-deten tion-records-up-for-sale/.

Springwise. 2006. "Top 10 Financial Service Ideas in 2006." www.springwise.com/top_10_financial_service_ideas.

Wyatt, E. 2008. "Latest Reality TV: Dancing (Along) with the Stars of Nickelodeon." *New York Times,* April 5.

Acknowledgments

It's been a long road, and I want to thank the many people who inspired me to persevere. The first would be my wonderful husband Mark, who always said, "Take your time, do it right." And our incredible sons, Elliott and Austin, who first encouraged me to write a book when I expressed surprise that, when asked, every entrepreneur told me, "I turned out this way because my mom believed in me." They introduced me to many of their friends who, along with their moms, agreed to be interviewed.

Thanks to Adam Braun, who introduced me to his agent, who introduced me to mine, Ryan Harbage, who believed in the book from the start. To Susan Leon, who did the first edit, and to David Hayward, who did the next edit. To Shauna Shapiro for introducing me to Tesilya Hanauer at New Harbinger, who immediately understood what the book was about. To all the wonderful folks at New Harbinger who put so much effort into this book. To James Marshall Reilly for showing me how to write a book proposal. And especially to the sixty-plus entrepreneurs and their moms who shared their experiences so that others may learn how to raise an entrepreneur. I couldn't have done it without every single person, and so, to all of them, I am grateful.

 **Margot Machol Bisnow** is a writer, wife, and mom from Washington, DC. She spent twenty years in government, including as an FTC Commissioner and Chief of Staff of the President's Council of Economic Advisers, and eight years writing a popular daily online social newsletter. Her son Austin has written successful pop songs and started the popular band Magic Giant. Her son Elliott founded Summit Series, a noted international conference series for millennial entrepreneurs, and led the purchase and development of Powder Mountain ski resort in Utah as a permanent home for their community. Her husband, Mark Bisnow, founded a national newsletter company, Bisnow Media, which was acquired in 2016. Their dog is the only one in the family who gets enough sleep.

Elliott Bisnow founded Summit Series, which has hosted thousands of young entrepreneurs at frequent events, and whose philosophy is that good business should be good for the world; *Forbes* called it "The Davos of Generation Y." Summit is an investor in Uber, Warby Parker, and change.org, and has spearheaded philanthropic efforts that include building a seventy-one-square-mile marine-protected area in the Bahamas. Elliott cofounded Bisnow Media, which was acquired in 2016, and served on the United Nations Foundation Global Entrepreneurs Council.

Austin Bisnow is the lead singer of Magic Giant, the Los Angeles-based folk revival band known for anthem-like sing-alongs and euphoric live experiences, whose single "Set On Fire" charted #4 on Spotify's US Viral 50. He is also an accomplished songwriter and producer who has worked with artists, including John Legend, will.i.am, David Guetta, and Steve Aoki. Austin and his brother Elliott teamed with Grammy-winning producer Benny Blanco to cofound the Get Well Soon Tour, a nonprofit that raises the spirits of hospitalized children across America.

MORE BOOKS *from*
NEW HARBINGER PUBLICATIONS

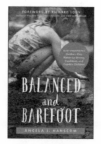